REVIEWS

'This interactive workbook is fantastic! Camilla connects so skilfully with the reader through her numerous relatable examples and spaces for the reader to consider their own thoughts and reactions, ensuring supported change from the heart of the problem and the heart of us as parents trying to do our best. I can't recommend this workbook enough.'
Rebecca Groome, Children's Psychotherapist, Free Your Mind Therapies

'An excellent evidence-based, practical workbook. Camilla, thank you for sharing your insight and child-parent collaborative approach that supports and enhances our experience of being mindful and happy parents growing and nurturing confident and secure children. It's a must-have for all parents!'
Dr. Vanessa Owen, Consultant Clinical Psychologist

'The best parenting book out there! I always come back to it when faced with any challenges! Now I realise where I was going wrong all these years and why! This book has been a life changer for my family. Having read this book, I realised it's not my children's fault; it's how we reacted to them. Such a fantastic way to understand why us parents and our children behave in certain ways.'
Sylvia Latif, Parent

'This workbook just makes sense! Full of practical advice that works.'
Sophie Vincent, Parent and Primary School Teacher

'If only I read this book years before when my boys were younger. The strategies described in this book would have prevented many arguments from escalating. Nothing really prepares you for being a parent. You constantly analyse when things go wrong, and you blame yourself. This book allows you to understand what's really going on and how you're not at fault. It allows you to see your child's behaviour from a different perspective. It's so powerful. I'm a teacher, and I have applied Camilla's strategies set out in this workbook at work. It just makes sense. This is an invaluable book. A must read.
Claire Cossins, Parent and Teacher

'Parenting is one of the most important jobs we do, and yet we receive no training for it. Finally, here is the parenting manual you have always longed for. It provides a formula for parenting which is so simple yet so transformative and delivers it through a series of practical steps and advice. It will teach you how to be your child's coach, empower your child and build their self-esteem. Every parent and teacher should read this. Just brilliant.'
Katie Wright, Parent

'As a dad to two boys, I had my moments of losing my cool and raising my voice. I knew I didn't want our days filled with arguments and shouting but didn't know how to change things. This workbook changed everything. Camilla's insights made me see how my behaviour impacted my boys, giving me a fresh perspective on parenting. Since reading the book, home life is happier, and my boys are listening to me more. My goal is to raise confident kids with strong self-esteem, and this book provides the practical tools I needed. It's not only improved my parenting but also strengthened our bond. Every parent can benefit from reading it.'
Matt Leaver, Parent

'I highly recommend Camilla's workbook to anyone who is looking to change their relationship with their child to one of openness and mutual respect, who wants to help their child develop important skills that will allow them to know who they are and what are the right things for them, and who is tired of struggling to help their child learn and grow. As an added benefit, I have found that using the tools has definitely made me not only a better parent but also a better partner and a better person in general. I am also able to act as a role model for my children to demonstrate what healthy boundaries and looking after yourself look like. It's easy to tell children what to do, but children learn much more from what they see us doing.'
Emma Zaozerskaia, Parent

'A really simple, yet revolutionary approach that turns what you think you know about Parenting on its head. Yet it makes total sense and even better, it works! Camilla is an excellent, patient teacher, and I recommend her workbook to anyone struggling with parenting issues or even just ways to build better connection with your family.'
Victoria McLafferty, Parent

'This book teaches you to regain control over family life while also leading your child to their own brilliance. Simple principles, clearly explained – everyone should read this!'
Susie Jones, Parent

'Keeping Your Cool Parenting is definitely a book designed with "MORE" in mind - more understanding, connection, certainty and joy. Camilla shows us that another way is possible if we approach parenting consciously and equip ourselves with the right tools. This is a book of lived wisdom and practical steps towards the more contented family life we aspire to create.'
Shelley Ensor, Parent and Little Signers Club

SIMPLE PRINCIPLES CLEARLY EXPLAINED

KEEPING YOUR COOL PARENTING

How to Bring out the Best in Yourself and Your Child

From Toddlers to Teens

An interactive workbook based on Language of Listening®

Camilla Miller

Edited by Sandra R. Blackard

All author and client stories included in this workbook are based on actual events. Some names and details have been changed to protect the identity of individuals or for teaching purposes. Clients' stories, examples and quotations are shared by permission.

© 2024 CAMILLA MILLER. ALL RIGHTS RESERVED.

This workbook contains content licensed by Blackard Enterprises, LLC, to Camilla Miller for commercial use. Licensed content includes the registered trademarks Language of Listening and SAY WHAT YOU SEE and material copyrighted by Language of Listening.

The author is a parent coach, not a medical or mental health professional. This workbook is intended for adult use and meant to be thought provoking. It is not intended or implied to be a substitute for advice, diagnosis, guidance, or treatment by a licensed medical or mental health professional.

If you have concerns about the wellbeing of your child, yourself or others, you should consult a licensed medical or mental health professional. Neither the author nor the author's sources shall be held liable or responsible for any loss or damage in connection with the use of the information or suggestions contained in this workbook. You are responsible for your own choices, actions and results.

ISBN: 978-1-3999-6750-1

ACKNOWLEDGEMENTS

I am delighted to introduce my workbook, which has been a labour of love and a reflection of my journey so far as a parent coach. I could not have done this without the incredible support of those who have been a part of my life.

Special thanks to my wonderful mum, **Susan**, for your endless love, support and encouragement.

To my husband, **Nicholas Miller** – the love of my life and the wonderful father of our children. You've been my support and champion through life and this incredible book-writing journey. Your patience, your countless cups of coffee deliveries and your readiness to assist me with all things tech-related have been truly priceless. Here's to a future filled with even more incredible adventures together.

To my two children, **Jack and Libby**. You make my heart burst with love. I'm so proud of the individuals you are. As you continue to grow and navigate the world, know that my love and support will always be with you. Libby, you're my inspiration for this workbook and the reason I became a parent coach. (And, of course, she insisted on making sure you all know that she's the driving force behind it all!)

To my mentor, **Sandra R. Blackard**, author of the Language of Listening® coaching model I teach. Writing a workbook is no easy feat, and without the incredible coaching tools of Language of Listening, it would not have been possible. Your editing and insights have taken my work to the next level. I cannot thank you enough for all that you have done. I'm truly fortunate to have you in my life.

To my oldest and BFF, **Sophie Vincent**. Your friendship means the world to me. Our daily check-ins and your encouragement has kept me going, even on the days I wanted to pack it in.

To **Sylvia Latif**. Thank you for being the first reader of my workbook. Your feedback and insights have helped to shape my work and made it even better. Thank you for being such an incredible cheerleader and for all the support and encouragement you have provided. You are a true gift.

To **Victoria McLafferty.** Your eye for detail and support in making this workbook user-friendly and effective have been invaluable. Thank you for being an integral part of bringing this project to fruition.

To my dear friend, **Sarosh Zaiwalla**. My heartfelt thanks for our treasured friendship, countless cups of tea and seaside strolls.

To all my clients who have given me permission to include your stories in my workbook. Thank you for your trust and contributions. To all those who have supported me along the way and encouraged me to write this book, thank you from the bottom of my heart. This workbook is a testament to the power of love, support and motivation. I hope it serves as a valuable resource for parents everywhere.

WELCOME

There's no question that you want the best for your child. You love your child and want to see them grow up to be the best version of themselves, to go out into the world believing in themselves and knowing how to get what they want out of life. And at the same time, you want to enjoy your family and manage the day-to-day without the usual meltdowns, shouting and conflicts.

Parenting can often feel like it's *Groundhog Day* filled with power struggles, frustrations and kids taking over family life. What if it didn't have to be like that?

I used to struggle with my daughter's out of control behaviour. Looking back, I wish someone had taken me aside and said: *'There is another way.'* I could have saved years of heartache and stress.

This workbook is 'another way'.

My parenting experiences with my daughter motivated me to become a parenting coach. After years of studying and training in different parenting models, I found Language of Listening® to be the most effective. Following over two years of intensive study with it's creator, Sandy Blackard, I achieved master coach status. Today, I support numerous families in applying these methods to transform their family life.

This workbook brings my distinctive Language of Listening-based teaching approach to you. As you read, you'll uncover all of Language of Listening's key elements complemented by other tools and personal insights I thought you would find useful.

The new tools and way of parenting you're about to discover are here to help you achieve significant changes in your parenting. Think of it as your parenting guidebook to building the family life you want.

This workbook will help you reflect on why you and your child do what you do, strip away generational beliefs about parenting often imposed upon you by family, society and your culture, and give you new eyes to view your child and your parenting goals. It will show you what it looks like when these actionable steps are implemented into family life.

Thousands of parents just like you have used the tools I teach to draw on the power of a strongly connected relationship, healthy boundaries and a child's innate drive to succeed and cooperate.

I absolutely believe in the magic of the Language of Listening coaching model I'm going to be sharing with you. Over the years, I've seen the profound effect it's had on my clients and their children as well as experiencing it myself.

The coaching model is simple. It's not always easy, mind you, but when you're feeling very triggered or have run out of patience, it's simple enough that you can use it in the moment and get the results you're after. It will give you simple yet powerful tools and strategies to change the way you parent.

> ## IMAGINE:
> ✗ No more shouting out of pure frustration
> ✗ No more bribing or threatening just to get your kids to do as you ask
> ✗ No more power struggles or stress

Let's go on a journey of discovery and parenting awareness.

When you do the work and implement the tools and skills you'll learn in this workbook, you will transform your parenting, alter the outcome of tricky situations, and literally change the course of your parenting journey.

This workbook is a mixture of theory, exercises and practical how to's. It's structured in a way to best support you, help you reflect on your own childhood, understand how you and your child 'work', and give you actionable steps and skills to transform your parenting. The tricky part is making a commitment to take action and put your new skills into practice. (The great thing with parenting is that you'll always have opportunities to practise!)

You'll get the most out of this when you work your way through the workbook in order, take your time to do the exercises, reflect on the questions and write notes. If you find yourself dipping in and out of the sections, make sure that you find the time to come back and do all the exercises and implement all the steps.

That way, by the time you've finished the workbook, you'll have the foundation for your new parenting journey.

THE 3 SECTIONS

Building Awareness

The first section sets the stage for long-lasting change. It will forever change the way you look at parenting. The truth is we can't change what we don't know. If we don't understand the impact of the way we currently interact with our child, we can't make positive changes. Awareness is the first step to change. You'll become aware of how your thoughts, emotions and behaviours are all interlinked and how they affect your parenting. You'll learn powerful communication tools that will build deep connection and prime your child to want to listen to you and your guidance.

Making Sense of Behaviours

The second section is about understanding why your behaviour and your child's make perfect sense even if you don't like those behaviours. You'll get tools to achieve more willing cooperation, see a reduction in arguments, and be able to support your child to find their own solutions while holding firm with your boundaries.

Empowering Your Child

The third section will show you how to respond in a way that brings out the best in your child. You will get tools to help your child see their capabilities and use their self-control and self-motivation to manage their own future behaviour. Plus, you'll learn how to put your new tools together to handle tricky situations with confidence, empower your child, and empower yourself to build the family life you truly want.

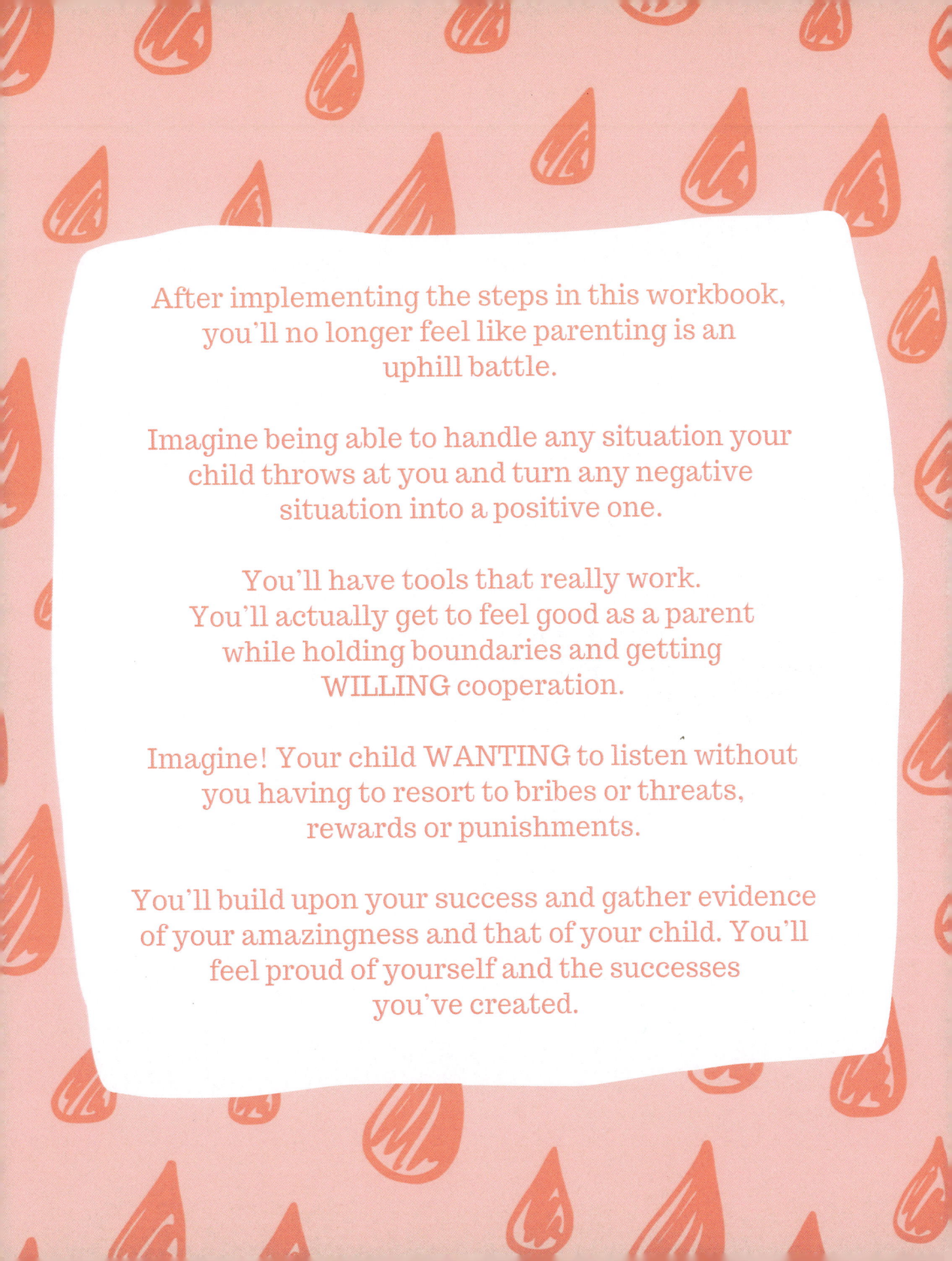

After implementing the steps in this workbook, you'll no longer feel like parenting is an uphill battle.

Imagine being able to handle any situation your child throws at you and turn any negative situation into a positive one.

You'll have tools that really work. You'll actually get to feel good as a parent while holding boundaries and getting WILLING cooperation.

Imagine! Your child WANTING to listen without you having to resort to bribes or threats, rewards or punishments.

You'll build upon your success and gather evidence of your amazingness and that of your child. You'll feel proud of yourself and the successes you've created.

THE CONTENTS

Building Awareness

Content

Let's start at the beginning 1

The Language of Listening® way 7

Language of Listening coaching model 15

Parenting styles 18

Rethinking parenting strategies 24

Rethinking bad behaviour 38

Behaviour iceberg 40

The control cycle 42

A true reflection of your parenting skills 46

Step into your child's world 48

The way you speak matters – the 4 NO's 55

From judgements to observations 72

Don't believe everything you think 79

The first step in your coaching model – SAY WHAT YOU SEE® 93

How beliefs are formed 112

Self-compassion 124

Authentic self-esteem 134

Responses that poke the bear 138

When validation and connection are not enough 142

What to do when your child says 'No!' 144

Making Sense of Behaviours

Content

The second step in your coaching model – CAN DOs 149

What is a NEED? 159

Actions children take to meet NEEDs 161

Diving deeper into boundaries 172

Wants – our true motivation in life 176

A simple and effective way to gain willing cooperation 178

Don't look for blame; look for solutions 187

The difference between boundaries and rules 192

From wants to possibilities chart 196

Why we slip up when holding boundaries 199

Super-star starters 205

How to stop most of your family arguments 206

What stops you holding healthy boundaries 212

How to hold a boundary while coaching your upset child 215

People pleasing 218

Emotions and behaviour 225

Range of feelings list 228

How our feelings help us meet our NEEDS 236

Spotting needs in tricky situations 242

Recognising emotions in your body 246

A daily practice 250

Empowering Your Child

Content

The third step in your coaching model – STRENGTHs 253

List of STRENGTHs 256

The importance of the STRENGTH Tool 261

Say What You See and add a STRENGTH 265

STRENGTHs and praise are not the same 270

STRENGTH of the week 273

Hidden STRENGTHs 274

Seeing the best intentions 278

5 ways to acknowledge hidden STRENGTHs 280

The Running Leap 282

Using STRENGTHs to help change behaviour 288

Small steps in the right direction 285

Spotting self-control 286

Success Training 292

Recap – putting the 3 steps together 300

Getting your family on board 302

Preparing your child for the real world 307

Success tracker 310

About the author 315

LET'S START
AT THE BEGINNING

without judgements, blame, shame or should haves.

Just, *'I now want something different for my family.'*

LET'S START AT THE VERY BEGINNING

You picked up this workbook for a reason. What are the top three changes you would like to see in yourself and your family?

What are the energy levels of harmony and joy in your family today?
Use a scale of 1-10 with 10 being harmonious/happy and 1 being chaotic/stressful.

What are you struggling with right now?
What's happening? With whom, when, how often?

How do you think these struggles are affecting your overall well-being as a parent?

What is your relationship with your child(ren) like now?

What would happen if things continued as they are?
What are your worries?

In what ways would you like your home life to be different?

What is working for you at the moment?

What parts of your day do you enjoy?

What's important to you about making changes in your parenting?
What are your core desires or values?

Whatever your family goals, your core desires connect you to your motivation.

Once you're connected to your true desires, your motivation and energy is there.

But often, what is lacking is the ability to see what action to take because you may not be aware of another way to parent that could get you to where you want to go. You've simply run out of options and skills using what you already know.

If you haven't yet got what you want, rather than thinking you've failed, remember that parenting is a beautiful and messy journey. When something isn't working, new tools like those you will find in this workbook can give you a new way.

As you begin to use your new tools, you'll become aware of small moments of change and start to see what you and your child are doing right. Your successes and your child's will provide proof that your core desires are possible. And that proof will motivate you to use your tools even more – no more feeling stuck in your parenting!

Sound too good to be true? Try it for yourself!

Let's get going...

I'm going to show you a new way to parent.

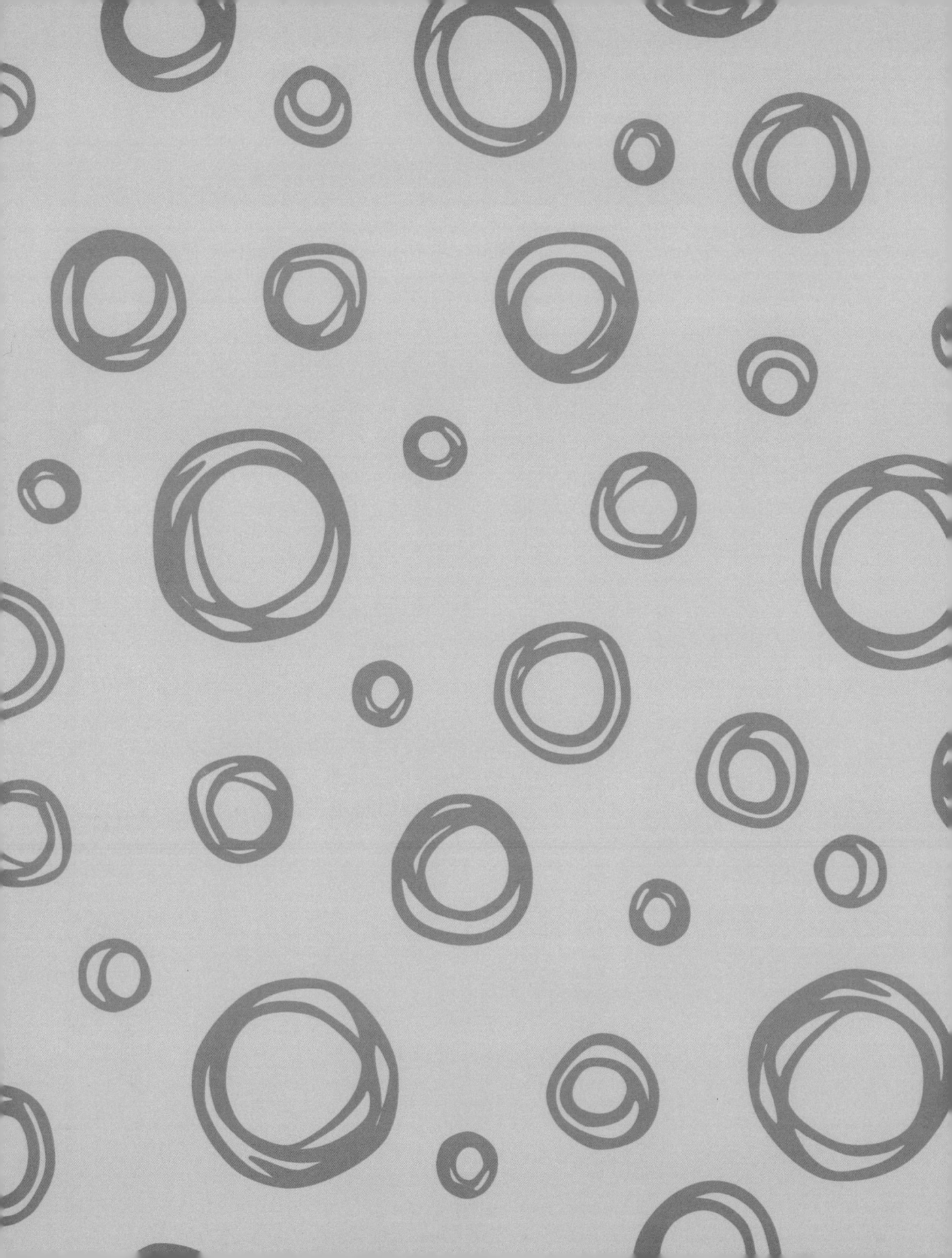

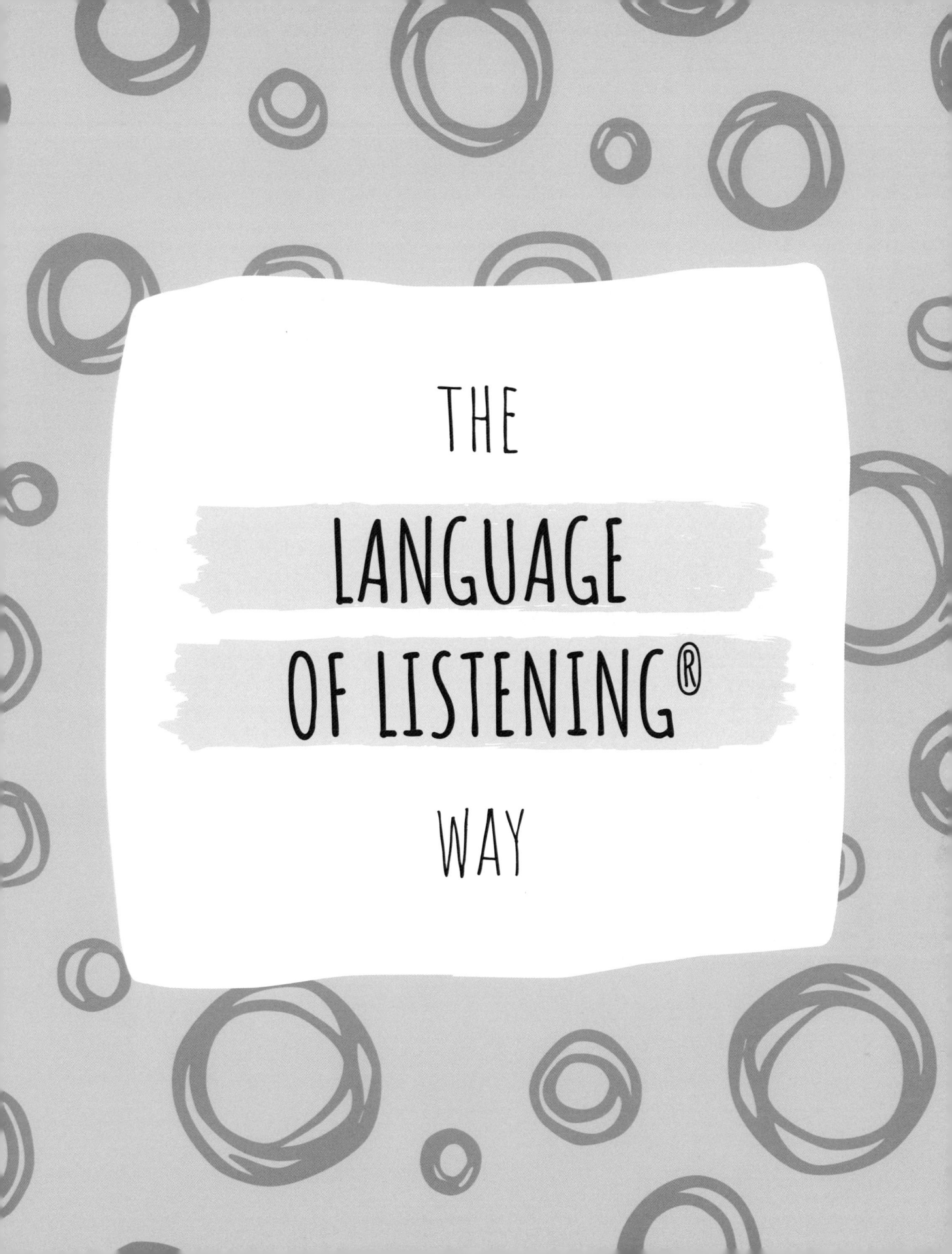

THE LANGUAGE OF LISTENING® WAY

WHY LANGUAGE OF LISTENING?

Through many years of studying and training, I've found that applying certain tools and techniques is crucial in helping families parent happily. As I mentioned on the Welcome page, one of my trainings is called Language of Listening. It's at the core of my teachings and serves as the foundation of this workbook.

Founded by Sandy Blackard, Language of Listening is a groundbreaking understanding of human behaviour. Sandy has distilled and integrated principles and techniques from positive psychology, transformational coaching, and child-centered play therapy into a user-friendly, 3-step coaching model. Her profound insights into how humans work not only enhance parenting but also make it more enjoyable. Working *with* human nature is one of the main reasons my clients and families adopting the Language of Listening approach experience significant positive changes in a short time. Families often express, *'It just makes sense!'*

Language of Listening gives you the simple tools to become your child's life coach.

It's all about being on your child's side – rooting for them, bringing out their best and helping them grow into the best version of themselves. You'll learn how to be the one in charge, hold healthy boundaries and gain willing cooperation. Your child will learn to control their own behaviour and develop positive self-esteem, self-belief and confidence in their abilities.

Language of Listening's coaching tools:

1. **A rock-solid, 3-step coaching model.**
   After all, who has time for complicated methods?!

2. **Four key premises.**
   These will change your beliefs about yourself, your parenting skills and your child.

This simple yet powerful framework takes you to the core of personal growth.

Personal growth is an ongoing process promoting our:

Self-belief – confidence in our own abilities and judgement.

Skill set – our skills, learnt or gained through experience.

Knowledge – our insights, awareness and understanding gained through experience.

Behaviour – our actions, mannerisms, habits and reactions.

Strengths – our character traits, abilities, capacities for self-control and connection with others.

These are all essential for living a happy life. They are the basis of success in every single area of our lives. I don't know any parent who doesn't want their child to have a healthy belief in themselves and feel like they can succeed in life. Your child's awareness of their greatness connects them to their natural desire to succeed in life and helps them reach their full potential.

With Language of Listening, YOU are coaching and supporting your child in THEIR personal growth. It's through personal growth that your child is able to show up in the world as the most extraordinary version of themselves.

The 3 steps in the Language of Listening coaching model work together as your parenting tool kit.

This workbook gives you a detailed breakdown of each step. It includes the theory behind why the steps work, examples of how to use them, and exercises to complete so you can comfortably implement the steps in your family life.

Becoming fluent in using these steps is like learning a new language. And just like starting anything new, it can feel overwhelming. But here's the good news: you'll not only get better with practice but it will also become easier. And the easier it becomes, the more you can use the tools naturally and without conscious effort.

ns of # 3 Language of Listening Steps

SAY WHAT YOU SEE® (SWYS)

You literally **SAY WHAT YOU SEE** your child doing, saying, feeling or thinking. It's the step of connection, validation and empathy and the first thing you do when interacting with your child.

CAN DO

When you see something you DON'T LIKE, you offer an alternative within your boundary – literally, what your child **CAN DO** that's still within your boundary. It helps you gain willing cooperation and helps your child gain problem-solving skills.

STRENGTH

When you see something you DO LIKE, you point out a **STRENGTH**. Think of it as praise in a new way – a way that actually works to help your child see their inner greatness and gain confidence in their abilities.

Let's look at an example.

Your child is busy playing, and you want them to stop and go for a bath. You start off asking nicely, but they don't listen to you. **So, there's the problem – conflicting wants.** Your child wants to keep playing, and you want them to go for a bath.

This is a great opportunity to use the SAY WHAT YOU SEE step. This step is so important because when your child feels understood first, they are primed to want to listen to you. And your child *wanting* to listen to you is the key for you to get the willing cooperation you're after.

Children have an innate drive to feel heard. In fact, the first premise of Language of Listening tells us that:

Children must continue to communicate until they are heard.

That means your child will keep on trying to tell you their message until they are sure you have heard them.

And what do we usually do? We keep talking!

We might think, *'I'm the adult. They need to listen to me first!'* But this typically backfires because your child will keep on defending their wants and escalating their behaviour. Before you know it, you're stuck in a power struggle.

When you listen to your child first and let them know that you see things from their perspective, it frees them up to listen and problem-solve.

SAYing WHAT YOU SEE could sound like this:

SWYS: *'Oh! Looks like you're not done playing yet. It's hard to stop and come for a bath.'*

Because you've stepped into your child's world, you SEE that they just want to keep on playing. It's not that they're not listening.

When you connect and understand your child's point of view first, you begin to interpret situations in new ways. SAY WHAT YOU SEE allows you to respond with curiosity instead of judgement. It changes how you interact with your child because it changes how you SEE their behaviour.

Then you can use the CAN DO step:

CAN DO: *'Hmm, there must be something you **CAN DO** to have fun AND come for a bath.'*

This all-purpose **CAN DO** turns the problem-solving over to your child (children as young as three can find solutions). Because your child doesn't feel told off or blamed, they're primed to want to cooperate.

They can reply, *'Can I just finish building this tower? I've nearly got to the top. It's the highest one I've ever built!'*

YOUR boundary hasn't changed; it's still bath-time. You can grant permission for them to finish if it's just a few blocks or make sure they get to come back and finish at a time that works for you both.

With **CAN DOs**, instead of trying to stop your child playing, you're on their side, looking at the problem together and finding a way where you can BOTH get what you want. Win-Win.

(At this point, it's important to note that if your child doesn't willingly cooperate, it doesn't mean it hasn't gone to plan. It simply means your child needs heaps more practice to handle disappointment and frustration and to connect with their self-control. You'll find tools for that later in the workbook.)

Back to the bath time example... You know how differently that situation could have gone if you went over and started saying:

'Stop playing! You're not listening. You're being disrespectful and rude. If you don't stop right now, I'm going to take your toys away. You won't get a sticker on your chart...' and all the typical things you're told to say and do to get your kids to listen and behave.

There would have been a big power struggle, resentment and arguments. It would feel like you against them. And that fuels more not listening and other forms of resistance because, like us, children are not really inclined to listen to people who don't understand them or who take their stuff away.

Instead... with **CAN DOs**, you gain willing cooperation that leads you straight to the next step.

You get to point out your child's STRENGTHs.

STRENGTH: *'You wanted to finish what you started. You found a way to stop playing and had a bath. That took self-control to stop what you were doing. You found a way to work together. You're a problem-solver.'*

Pointing out STRENGTHs is so important because your child's behaviour is guided by their awareness of their STRENGTHs. So, when they become aware of the ones you just pointed out, they will be able to use them at their next bath time and in other situations too.

Then, instead of managing, teaching or controlling your child's behaviour (which is actually pretty exhausting and ineffective but what many of us typically think our job as a parent is), you become a life coach for your child.

Language of Listening is ALL about bringing out the best in your child.

Using this coaching model, you help your child develop a positive self-belief, bring out their greatness and give them skills to manage their own behaviour. So much easier and more effective.

You can't control another human – that's an illusion! But you can guide and influence them. After all, you are your child's life coach. You are someone who looks to empower your child and support them to live a fulfilled life.

Every time you use this coaching model with your child, you will improve your relationship, build trust, gain willing cooperation, bring out more of your child's STRENGTHs, and connect them with their inner guidance.

I'm so excited for you to see how much simpler and more enjoyable this way can be.

Think of the heart model as your quick-reference, 'how-to' guide.
Everything will become a lot clearer as you work your way though the workbook.

Language of Listening®
COACHING MODEL

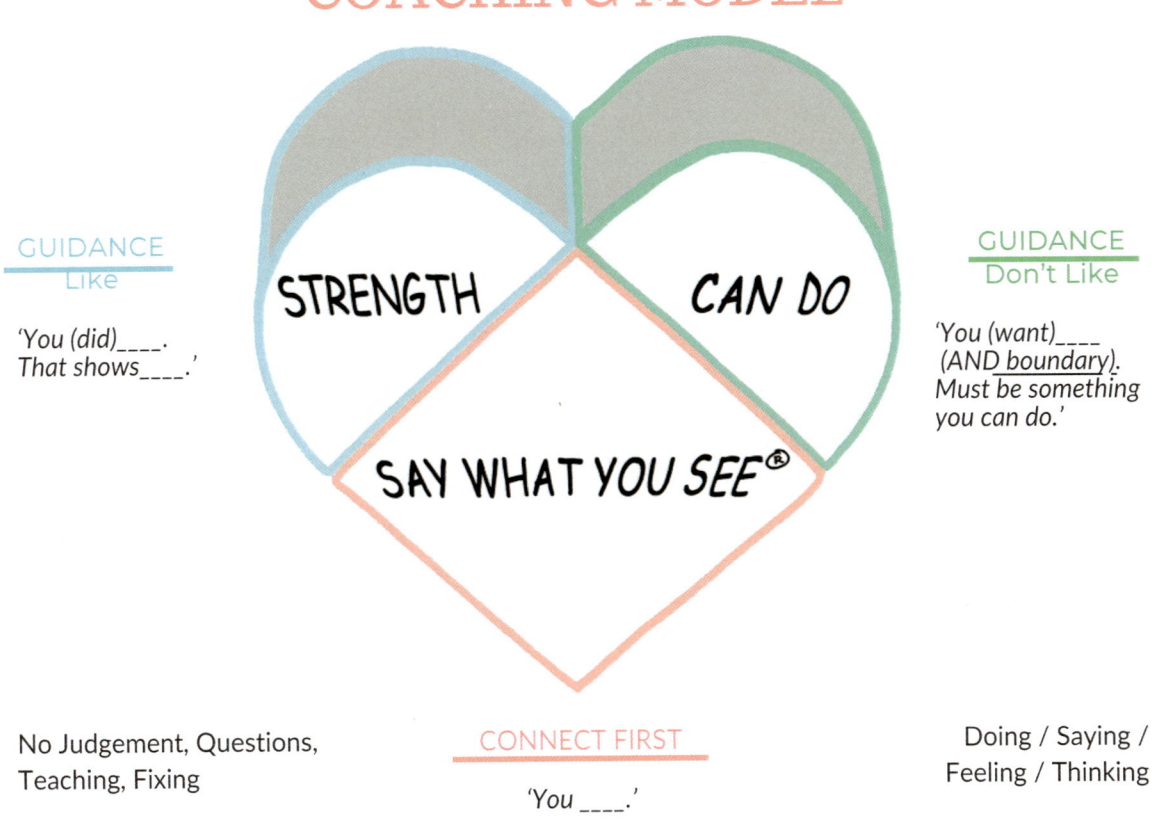

GUIDANCE
Like

'You (did)____.
That shows____.'

STRENGTH

CAN DO

SAY WHAT YOU SEE®

GUIDANCE
Don't Like

'You (want)____
(AND <u>boundary</u>).
Must be something
you can do.'

No Judgement, Questions,
Teaching, Fixing

CONNECT FIRST

'You ____.'

Doing / Saying /
Feeling / Thinking

PREMISES

1. **SWYS:** Everything children do and say is a communication.

   Children must continue to communicate until they are heard.

2. **STRENGTH:** All children have every possible inner strength.

   Children act according to who they believe they are.

3. **CAN DO:** All behaviours are driven by 3 healthy needs: **experience, connection, power.**

   Whatever children are doing is already meeting their needs.

4. **Overall:** All growth is through acceptance.

   Children set exactly the right level of challenge for growth.

© 2024 Language of Listening®. Reprinted by Camilla Miller with permission.

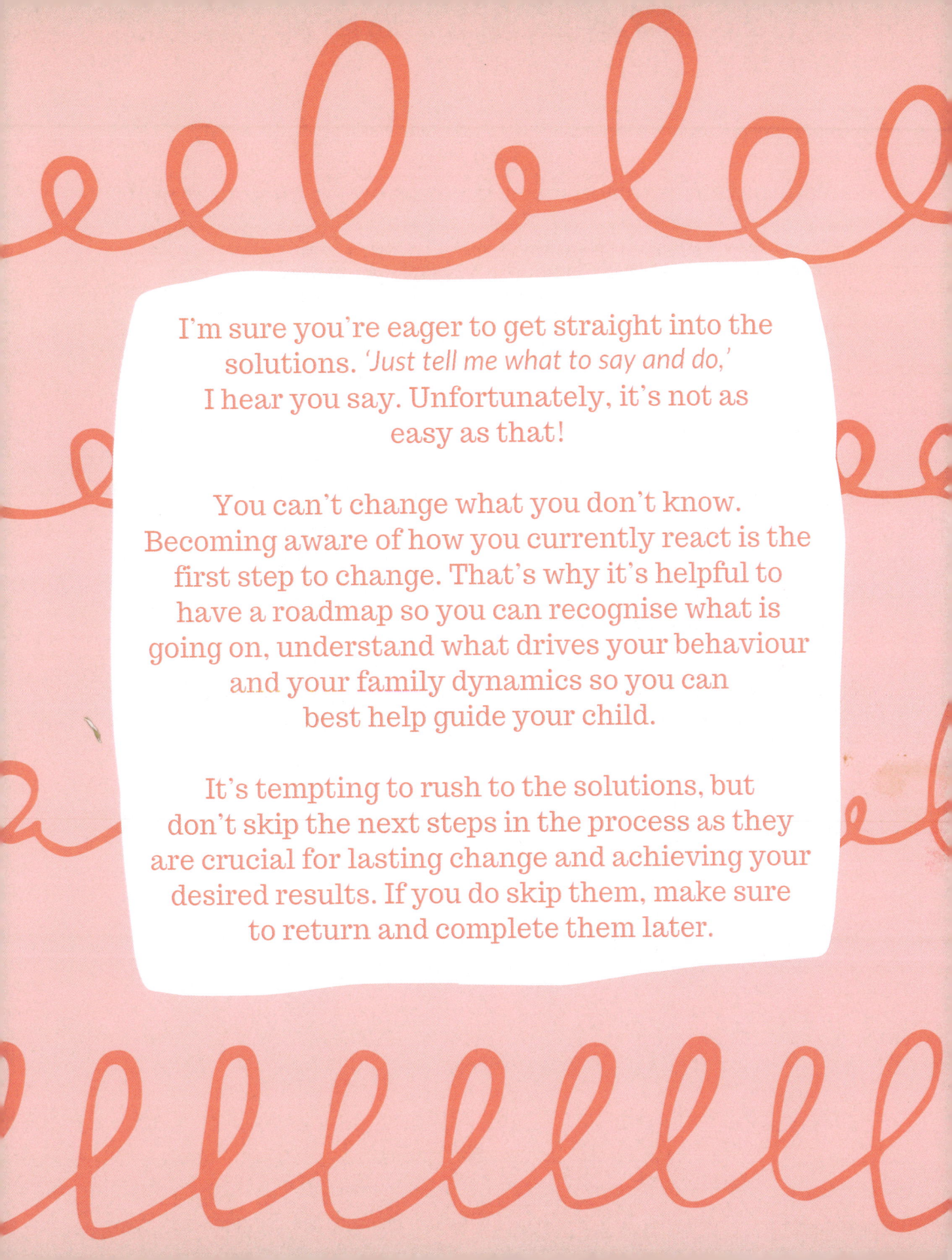

I'm sure you're eager to get straight into the solutions. *'Just tell me what to say and do,'* I hear you say. Unfortunately, it's not as easy as that!

You can't change what you don't know. Becoming aware of how you currently react is the first step to change. That's why it's helpful to have a roadmap so you can recognise what is going on, understand what drives your behaviour and your family dynamics so you can best help guide your child.

It's tempting to rush to the solutions, but don't skip the next steps in the process as they are crucial for lasting change and achieving your desired results. If you do skip them, make sure to return and complete them later.

Why your child reacts like they do to your parenting style

Your parenting style has a massive effect on your family.

Although every single one of us has a different approach to how we go about interacting and guiding our children, research has grouped these approaches into four distinct styles.

- **Authoritarian** (strict)
- **Authoritative** (more aligned with the coaching model discussed in this workbook)
- **Permissive**
- **Uninvolved**

Each one of these styles is a unique approach to how parents raise their children.

I'm going to discuss why the strict and permissive styles aren't our best options when raising our children. (I reckon most uninvolved parents won't be picking up this workbook in the first place.)

And I will teach you a different way, one based on the principles of positive psychology, transformational coaching and child-centered play therapy. It aligns most closely with authoritative parenting, although it has distinct differences.

I will show you how to successfully interact with and guide your child with some easy to use and remember techniques that will make a remarkable difference in a short space of time.

Use this space to record your thoughts and describe how you see your own parenting style at this moment. Look through the parenting style charts on the next few pages and list any styles that resonate with you.

There may be some days you resonate with more than another.

STRICT PARENT

Many strict parents judge the effectiveness of their parenting by their children's behaviour. They don't want misbehaving children and often believe the lack of punishments and consequences are the cause of out-of-control children.

Ironically, studies have shown children raised in strict households have more behavioural problems, not less. There's more anger, retaliation and aggression. Children raised this way tend to have lower self-esteem, self-control issues and mental health problems. They're more inclined to be unhappy, show more depressive symptoms and rebel in the teenage years.

MISTAKEN BELIEFS

Children need to be controlled, given consequences, punished or rewarded or they won't learn how to behave

Parenting is a battle to be won – you must not back down

If children don't behave, they need to be taught a lesson

Giving children what they want means they learn to keep pushing boundaries

If children misbehave or make a mistake, it's the parent's fault; it means the parent can't cope

YOU FIND YOURSELF THINKING

I want well behaved children

I'm not going to let them walk all over me

I'm in charge, I'm the adult – they do as I say

They need to learn to respect authority

Who do they think they are?

I'm not giving in

I don't want my child to end up in jail

POSSIBLE FUTURE RESULTS

Child becomes more defiant, resentful, aggressive or retreats into themselves

Lower self-esteem and self-worth

Unwanted behaviour stops in the short-term, but parent-child relationship erodes

Ineffective coping mechanisms for parent and child

Ineffective relationship skills for parent and child

Communication shuts down

Lack of empathy and understanding

The home becomes a battleground.

TYPICAL TOOLS AND STRATEGIES

Threats, punishment and rewards are used to control the child's behaviour

Not allowing children to voice their opinions or question parent's decisions or authority

Demanding that children blindly follow parent's expectations

Ignoring or stone-walling child

Shouting and fighting

PERMISSIVE PARENT

On the surface, the permissive parent can be warm and responsive – great qualities to have. However, the permissive parent usually has minimal or no expectations. They seem more like a friend than a parent, or they may not pay attention to what their child is doing.

On the surface, the child may look like they are happy and thriving, but without boundaries and expectations, children don't feel safe or taken care of. Children can become entitled or demanding as they've never been taught important life skills such as self-regulation, how to handle disappointment and frustration, how to find solutions, how to respect other people's boundaries or how to resolve conflict. Without these skills, they are not able to thrive emotionally and physically as an adult.

MISTAKEN BELIEFS

The parent's role is to make the child happy

The parent gives up on themselves to be loved by the child

A child can't handle feeling sad or disappointed; if they feel those, it means the parent has done something wrong

If a child doesn't like a boundary, the parent has to negotiate, convince or over-explain

A child needs protection from feeling big emotions

Holding boundaries is mean, controlling or selfish

YOU FIND YOURSELF THINKING

I really want x, but I'm worried about my child's reaction

No one helps me – I've got to do everything myself

I do so much for you, why can't you do anything for me?

My child can't handle big emotions – I need to fix things for them

I do everything for you, and you're still not happy

Whatever I do doesn't matter

POSSIBLE FUTURE RESULTS

Children become demanding, dependent on parent to fill their needs, appear entitled

Children don't learn self-regulation skills, conflict resolution or regard for others' wants and needs

Family enmeshment – everyone holds the others responsible for their emotions and/or meeting their needs

Healthy boundaries aren't modelled – parent becomes frazzled, resentful, burnt out

Collaborative problem-solving shuts down

Lower self-esteem and self-worth

Lack of empathy

TYPICAL TOOLS AND STRATEGIES

Pleading, negotiating, convincing and over-explaining to get the child to agree with your boundaries

Giving in to the child's demands

Giving up on your own expectations and boundaries

Ruled by emotions and holding unrealistic expectations of your ability to meet your child's every need

YO-YO PARENTING

What is Yo-Yo Parenting?

Yo-Yo parenting easily happens when we believe there are only two options: strict or permissive. Neither work in the way we hope they will or get the results we're after, so we find ourselves on a never-ending back-and-forth path of frustration.

You're strict one minute, coming up with rewards and punishments to control your child's behaviour...which leads to shouting, power struggles and stress...you feel guilty about shouting too much, and your child still isn't listening...so you become permissive...your child rules the roost...you can't stand it, your patience is waning...you yo-yo back to strict, blow your top... And so the cycle continues.

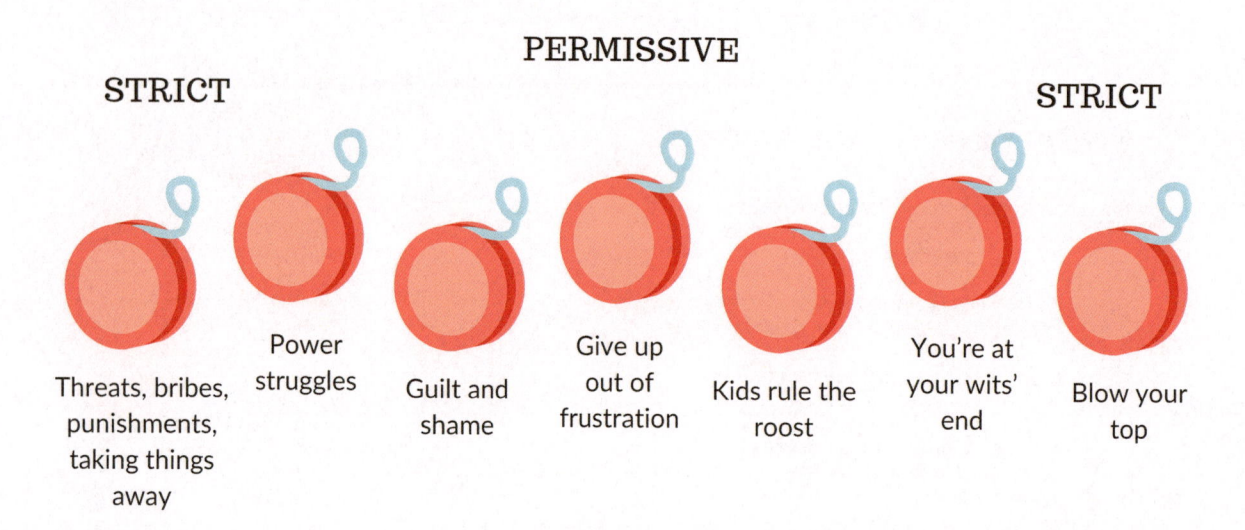

STRICT — **PERMISSIVE** — **STRICT**

Threats, bribes, punishments, taking things away | Power struggles | Guilt and shame | Give up out of frustration | Kids rule the roost | You're at your wits' end | Blow your top

What's your tendency? Are you currently more strict or permissive?

LANGUAGE OF LISTENING PARENT

Language of Listening is nowhere on the permissive or strict cycle. It's a different model entirely.

It's all about becoming a life coach for your child. Life coaches guide and influence their child by modelling behaviour with respect and love. They see that their child is inherently great and understand that their role is to see that greatness in their child and reflect it back to them.

By becoming a life coach, they naturally bring out their child's inner strengths, teach life skills, build deeply connected relationships, and coach their child to manage their own behaviour. Children grow up with a healthy sense of self, strong self-esteem and self-worth.

CORE BELIEFS

Children who feel valued, understood and respected will return our respect by listening to us and following our lead

Children don't need rewards or punishments to change their behaviour; they already want to behave and will when they are shown how to get what they need and want within the parent's boundaries

A strong, loving relationship results when the parent remains in charge by listening, connecting, empathising and setting clear boundaries and rules

You are your child's life coach – guiding, supporting and bringing out the best in them

YOU FIND YOURSELF THINKING

My child's intentions are always good

My child can think and want what they want (that doesn't mean I have to give it to them)

With coaching support, my child will gain the skills and self-control to manage their own behaviour

My wants and boundaries are as important as my child's

We look for solutions to problems together

When I see the best in my child, they learn to see the best in themselves

I'm on the same team as my child

POSSIBLE FUTURE RESULTS

Home is peaceful, fun and harmonious

Children grow up to trust themselves, know who they are and what they want out of life

Children have positive self-esteem and self-worth

Children know how to meet their needs in healthy ways, are emotionally literate, can solve their own problems, and know how to hold healthy boundaries in relationships

Open communication – children listen to the parent because they care what parent thinks and know parent is on their team

TYPICAL TOOLS AND STRATEGIES

Parent as child's life coach helps child find acceptable alternatives and self-correct

Parent and child work together as a team

Parent supports child to find their own solutions

Parent focuses on the driving force behind the behaviour and becomes curious about what's going on for their child

Parent brings out the child's inner greatness so child can see it and naturally change their own behaviour to reflect it

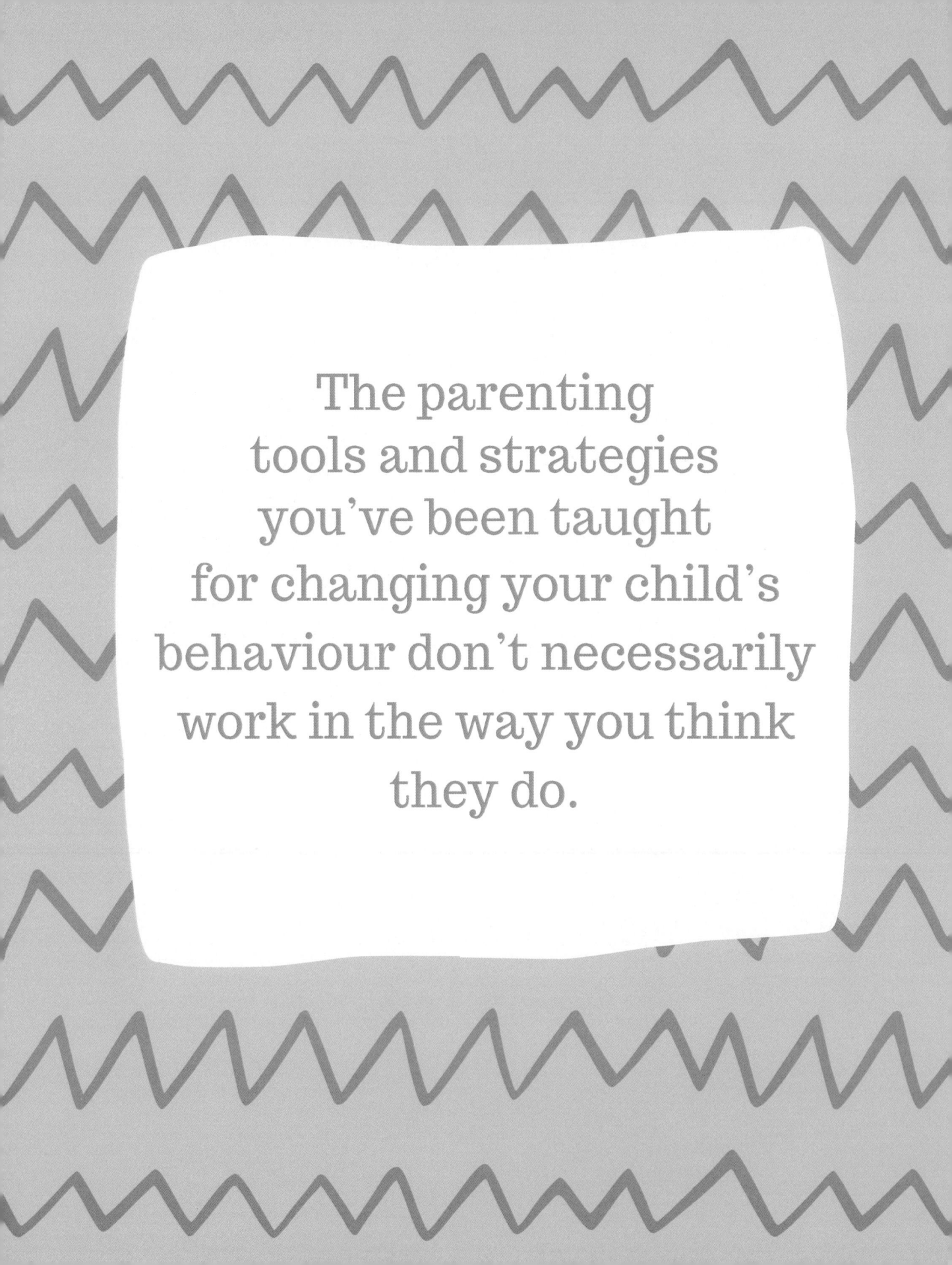

The parenting tools and strategies you've been taught for changing your child's behaviour don't necessarily work in the way you think they do.

Rewards, threats and punishments do not help your child learn self-control or manage their own behaviour.

The use of rewards, threats or punishments to control behaviour – rewarding them to behave a certain way, threatening them with consequences, punishing them by taking away favourite toys, stopping them from doing things they love or telling them off – is based on the idea that this will motivate children to change their behaviour.

But your child doesn't need motivation.

Your child needs to feel successful in their ability to calm themselves down, control their own behaviour and see possibilities for meeting their needs in healthy ways.

And NO amount of rewards, threats or punishments is going to give them the tools they need to manage their own behaviour. It will simply add to their frustration, making everything worse.

A child's behaviour doesn't happen in a vacuum. Their behaviour is a direct link to their environment, a reaction to our behaviour and the people around them. They don't answer back, whack their sister, refuse to go to bed or whine and tantrum for no reason.

When you look a bit deeper, you can see that they are probably experiencing big emotions, feeling tired or hungry, learning a new skill, feeling disconnected, frustrated, misunderstood...or a hundred and one other things.

This doesn't mean you let unwanted behaviour slide. It means you spend your energy on coaching your child to bring out their self-control, which in turn, allows them to put an end to angry outbursts and reactive behaviour that even they don't enjoy.

7 REASONS WHY REWARDS DON'T WORK IN THE WAY WE THINK THEY DO

On the surface, using rewards to change a child's behaviour seems like a good idea. Rewards may even 'work' for a short time, but they soon lose their effectiveness. Often, we think it's because we're not consistent enough, we're not doing 'it' correctly, or our child is defiant or rude. But it's none of that. Most of us are unaware of the many downsides of using rewards.

Even when rewards seem to be 'working', we need to ask ourselves: *'What are they really teaching our children, and are the short-term benefits worth the cost?'*

1 Rewards are based on wrong assumptions.

Rewards, like punishments and consequences, presume that misbehaviour occurs because of a lack of motivation to behave appropriately. But, for example, even if I were offered £1,000, I still couldn't play a guitar because I have no prior experience or musical ability. A reward would be ineffective if I am simply unable to perform the task required of me. It's the same for children. If they're not capable of completing a task, rewards are not effective because motivation is not the problem.

2 Rewards can feel like punishments.

Patrick was an energetic boy who struggled with managing his impulses and emotions. In contrast, his sister was calm and easy-going. To address Patrick's behaviour, his parents devised a reward system for both children with the promise of a prize if they could go a whole week without 'misbehaving'.

No matter how hard Patrick tried, he was unable to gain his reward or meet his parents' expectations. Patrick felt like he was failing. Meanwhile, his sister received her prize easily.

As time went on, Patrick grew increasingly envious and resentful of his sister, leading to animosity between them. Repeated failure and disappointment began to chip away at Patrick's motivation and self-esteem, causing him to doubt his own abilities. He began to lash out at his sister as a way of coping with his distress. To him, the reward system felt like punishment and an attempt to control his behaviour, rather than as encouragement as his parents had intended.

3. Rewards can represent conditional love.

Stevie was a sensitive child who craved her parents' love and acceptance. She was used to receiving rewards for her 'good' behaviour and depended on them to feel loved and valued. For her, staying on Santa's 'nice' list was a breeze. She always worked hard to be good and please her parents anyway.

However, one day, she didn't receive the reward she expected. This left her confused and hurt. Believing that her parents' love was conditional on her actions and behaviour, she became concerned that she had done something wrong. This assumption led her to believe she had to be not just good but perfect to receive love and acceptance. She became hyper-focused on the needs and wants of her parents, disregarding her own, which meant she couldn't be herself. As a result, she developed anxiety and stress.

4. Rewards can lead kids to find ineffective strategies.

Yasmin was growing increasingly frustrated with her daughter, Tharaki, for constantly answering back and being disrespectful. She felt like Tharaki wasn't listening to her and needed some kind of motivation to behave properly. Yasmin thought of a reward and told Tharaki that, if she spoke respectfully all week, she would take her out to buy the jeans she really wanted.

What Yasmin didn't realise was that Tharaki had been feeling misunderstood and frustrated herself. She didn't know how to communicate her feelings effectively. As a result, she had resorted to answering back in frustration. When Yasmin offered the reward, Tharaki saw it as a chance to prove herself and agreed to the terms. As the week went on, Tharaki tried her best to speak calmly to her mother. However, she found it difficult to communicate her thoughts and feelings. She felt like she was constantly walking on eggshells and didn't know how to approach her mother without the fear of losing out on her reward.

By the end of the week, Tharaki had managed to earn her reward, but she didn't feel any better about her relationship with her mother. She had come up with a strategy to win the reward that involved trying not to communicate with her mum at all. She stopped sharing her worries and concerns with her mother, choosing instead to keep them to herself. Yasmin was happy that Tharaki had managed to speak respectfully but didn't realise that it came at a cost. She didn't understand that the root causes of Tharaki's behaviour were a lack of communication skills and a feeling of being misunderstood.

5. Rewards can cause a 'what's in it for me?' attitude.

Oscar's parents used toys, sweets and other incentives as a way to bribe him to do what they wanted. For instance, they offered him dessert after he finished eating his vegetables, promised to buy him toys if he got good grades at school, offered a special reward if he behaved well during days out, granted screen time and video game privileges as a reward for completing homework, and brought him a new toy if he cleaned his room. He had come to expect these rewards and began to view everything as a transaction. Asking himself, *'What's in it for me?'* before agreeing to do anything.

Oscar's parents became more and more frustrated with him. They held him responsible for his attitude without realising that they were the ones who had conditioned him to anticipate rewards in the first place.

Relying on external incentives conditioned Oscar to prioritise his own interests and expect immediate rewards for his actions. This made it difficult for him to form friendships and build lasting connections. Others perceived him as self-centred since he struggled to grasp the importance of cooperation, empathy and trust in relationships.

6. Rewards can undermine intrinsic motivation.

Becca believed in encouraging her children to share, so she decided to reward her daughter whenever she shared her toys with her younger brother.

Brigid started to feel like sharing her toys was a chore, something that she had to do in order to receive the stickers, rather than an act of kindness towards her brother. Brigid's resentment towards the reward system grew, and it began to affect her relationship with her brother. She no longer shared her toys with him willingly but, instead, only did so when her mother was watching in order to receive the stickers.

Brigid's experience is a good example of how rewards can have unintended negative effects. While the reward system initially encouraged Brigid to share her toys, it eventually led her to feel manipulated and resentful. Plus, it sent the message that she needed to get stickers to share, so her natural generosity must not be enough. Brigid got that message.

Over time, Brigid felt like her mother didn't trust her to do the right thing on her own. This can be detrimental to a child's sense of autonomy and self-worth and can create a sense of resentment towards the person providing the rewards as well as the person they are supposed to be sharing with.

7. Rewards can feel manipulative.

Imagine yourself in Mary's shoes. Mary's husband gave her a beautiful necklace as a reward for being a 'good wife'. Later, he started reminding her that she didn't deserve the necklace if she couldn't do what he wanted. Mary tried to please him, but it was never enough. Instead of feeling cherished and appreciated, she felt manipulated, and the necklace became a weighty reminder of her husband's expectations.

Mary's story serves as a reminder that using gifts as rewards to control our loved one's behaviour, either before or after the gift is given, can feel manipulative. Gifts given with strings attached are not true gifts at all.

This is especially true with our children. Dangling the promise of a 'gift' to get our child to change their behaviour to earn it, or requiring specific behaviour afterwards to deserve it, attaches conditions to the 'gift' that make it a reward for 'good behaviour'.

Children who grow up this way carry it into adulthood. They may constantly seek validation and approval from others, believing that their worth is dependent upon meeting certain expectations or behaving in a certain manner. And, like Mary's husband, they often give gifts with strings attached because they don't know any other way.

WHY THREATS DON'T WORK

If you think threats don't work because you don't follow through, think again. There is a deeper problem that keeps them from working even when you do follow through. Here's an example:

April was tired of her boys Lucas and Noah constantly bickering over the PlayStation. One day, she decided that enough was enough. It was time to come up with a consequence for their behaviour.

She marched over to the TV, turned off the console, and unplugged it from the wall.

'That's it. I'm tired of you two fighting over the PlayStation. And from now on, every time you fight, no one will play. You have to learn!' April declared.

April didn't see the consequence as a threat, but the boys did as you can see by their reaction. They were angry, shouted, and slammed doors. Still, April assured herself that at least they'd learnt a lesson.

But did they?

Many parents believe that they are teaching their child a lesson by setting up artificial consequences so the child will feel the repercussions of their behaviour.

- ✗ *Fight in the car, no TV when you get home*
- ✗ *Hit your brother, no ice cream*
- ✗ *Don't behave at school, no iPad all week*

If threats of consequences like these are something that sound familiar, please know you're not alone. It's what so many of us have been told to do. But I'm going to share an uncomfortable truth with you.

There's no real purpose to creating consequences like these other than to inflict pain and inconvenience in the misguided belief it will motivate children to change their behaviour.

Used in that way, consequences are the same as punishments. When set up in advance, they act as standing threats: *'Don't do this, or else!'*

> If anyone lacks the ability to change their behaviour, no amount of consequences is going to teach them the skills they need to manage their own behaviour.

> When I used to shout at my kids, it was like thinking that threatening myself with 'No Netflix' would teach me a lesson and motivate me to stop shouting. It couldn't! I already wanted to stop shouting. The motivation was already there. What was missing were the skills and knowledge for me to be able change my behaviour.

April thought her consequences had worked as the fighting stopped, but beneath the surface, Lucas and Noah were developing unhealthy coping mechanisms. This is because managing behaviour with the threat of consequences often leaves children to figure out solutions on their own.

Lucas and Noah had been fighting over the PlayStation because Lucas believed he was a better player and didn't want to share the controller. Although Noah tried to defend himself, it often led to more fighting.

Noah learnt to give up trying because he felt like he never got what he wanted anyway. His brother always won, and his mother didn't listen to him, so he concluded that there was no point in standing up for himself anymore. This became his pattern of dealing with conflict in his other relationships with his friends as well.

And Lucas didn't learn appropriate ways of interacting with his brother, so he struggled to form positive relationships with others.

It's a scary thing for a child to feel like they have to figure things out on their own.

In this instance, the threat of no access to the PlayStation couldn't solve the problem of fighting in a productive way – it didn't teach the boys important skills like how to negotiate, communicate and work together as a team to prevent the fighting from happening again.

WHY PUNISHMENTS DON'T WORK

Your child is NOT focusing on their wrongdoings or what they can do differently next time. Their WHOLE focus is on this:

- ✗ How mean you are
- ✗ How they won't get caught next time
- ✗ How they must be a terrible person
- ✗ How mistakes are bad
- ✗ How you don't understand and won't try to see the good in them
- ✗ How, when they're feeling overwhelmed or upset, people don't want to be with them
- ✗ How they can get back at you
- ✗ How if someone doesn't do what you like, you make them suffer to teach them a lesson

No surprise that those thoughts and beliefs would push your child into acting out even more and into more of the behaviour you DON'T like.

It's a normal human reaction, isn't it? How would you, as an adult, react to someone you love punishing you, putting you in a timeout or confiscating your phone?

Do you remember being punished as a child?

What did the punishment teach you?

How did it leave you feeling about yourself and your parent?

How did it affect your relationship with your parent?

Did it motivate you to do better?

Did the punishments 'work' in the way your parents thought?

Did you know how to get your needs met or how to behave next time, or were you left trying to figure it out on your own?

NOTES

NO CHILD IS SITTING IN A TIME-OUT THINKING ABOUT THEIR WRONGDOINGS

'Gee Mummy! Thank you so much for putting me in a timeout. I really need time to reflect on my behaviour and how much I need to change my ways. You're so right! I was unkind. I shouldn't have shouted. I should have stopped what I was doing and listened to you.'

...Said NO child EVER!

So, what's the alternative to using rewards, threats or punishment to change your child's behaviour?

It can be a challenge for many adults to accept that a child may be unable to do something, whether it's due to their current abilities, the environment or other factors, especially if the adults were raised with rewards, threats or punishment themselves. By default, they might tend to assume that children are simply being difficult, stubborn or even naughty depending on the lessons their parents unintentionally taught them.

To help your child change their behaviour, it's important to first address your child's underlying feelings or needs and find a solution to resolve the root cause of the issue.

Throughout this workbook, you'll gain tools and strategies to coach your child to become more confident in their abilities, learn important skills, problem-solve and manage their own behaviour.

Think of a time when you used rewards, threats or punishments to change your child's behaviour. What were the apparent results?

What unintended lessons might your child have learnt?

It's time to RETHINK 'bad behaviour'

Before we can change unwanted behaviour, we have to understand it.

Misbehaviour isn't a sign of bad parenting or a sign that your child is 'bad' or 'naughty'.

We are so used to seeing behaviour as good or bad, but behaviour in our children is neither good nor bad.

A child's behaviour is an expression of their thoughts, emotions and reactions to others. Some expressions we like; others we don't.

For example, think of what behaviour you and your child show when you are feeling happy or joyful, curious, delighted, excited, loving or proud. These emotions feel good, and we often like the behaviour we see in ourselves and our children when we or they are feeling these emotions.

Now, think of what behaviour you and your child show when you're feeling sad or angry, annoyed, anxious, ashamed, fearful, helpless, hopeless, jealous, lonely, overwhelmed, scared, self-critical, unacceptable, unlovable or useless. These emotions don't feel good, and we often don't like the behaviour we see in ourselves and our children when we or they are feeling these emotions.

When human beings get annoyed, get overwhelmed, or feel hopeless or the thousands of other big emotions we feel, it's a normal human reaction to 'act out'. We're not being 'naughty' or 'giving attitude'. We're not even thinking about how we sound. We're triggered and acting from our reactive brain. In that moment, we're not choosing how to 'behave', thinking of future consequences or exhibiting empathy. These are not within our grasp.

When we look at misbehaviour as a sign of a child (or adult) in distress, having big emotions or experiencing a perceived threat or danger, it changes our focus and helps us respond with empathy and support.

Each time your child receives your loving guidance and calms down, you are effectively strengthening the connections between their brain cells – literally changing the physical structure of their brain. Their experiences shape their future responses for life, so they become better able to understand emotions, know how to get their emotional needs met, learn how to calm themselves down, and gain skills to respond to tricky situations rather than reacting.

BEHAVIOUR ICEBERG

What We See

Screaming
Crying   Hitting
Not listening   Biting
Running away   Kicking
Hiding   Sibling fighting
Avoidance   Threatening
Refusal   Verbal abuse

Angry, Anxious, Ashamed, Confused, Different,
Disappointed, Distrusted, Embarrassed,
Exhausted, Failing, Grieving, Helpless,
Hopeless, Hurt, Jealous, Lonely,
Nervous, Offended, Overwhelmed,
Rejected, Scared, Self-loathing,
Stressed, Tricked, Unloved,
Unsure, Untrusting,
Unwanted, Unworthy,
Worried,
etc

What we don't see: the underlying causes

COACH YOUR CHILD TOWARDS SELF-CONTROL

Instead of focusing your attention on trying to control your child's behaviour, I will show you how to coach your child to manage their OWN emotions and control their OWN behaviour.

Over the course of this workbook, you'll become a better coach for your child and gain a deeper understanding of why your child's (and your own) behaviour makes sense, even when you don't like it. You'll be able to support your child to meet their needs in ways you both like.

It's only when your child learns to manage their own emotions, meet their needs in healthy ways and access their self-control, that they will be able to control their own reactions and behaviour.

THE CONTROL CYCLE

As parents, it can be easy to fall into a pattern of focusing on 'surface' behaviour and trying to control the symptoms of what's going on.

Just as when we have a headache, it's easy to take painkillers to ease the symptoms. However, this doesn't address the root cause of the headache. It could be due to dehydration, lack of sleep, stress or illness. Similarly, when we only focus on surface-level behaviours in children, we may be treating the symptoms without addressing the root cause and may not be aware of the role our reactions play. This can lead to a recurring cycle of unwanted behaviour, worsening over time.

Focusing solely on the symptoms (our child's behaviour) can slowly deteriorate our relationship with our child. Our child may perceive that we no longer care about their needs and wants, which can lead to them disregard our needs and wants as well. As a result, guiding our child towards positive behaviour becomes extremely challenging. At this point, they may feel defensive and resentful, unwilling to accept guidance from us.

It's important to remember, our child is only open to our guidance when we have a strong and healthy connection with them.

So often, we fall into the trap of waiting for our child to change their behaviour first so we won't have to punish them.

But I believe that we've got it all back to front.

As the parent, we need to change OUR ways first. Our child's behaviour is a reaction to ours, so we need to be the one to break the cycle.

> I used to think, *'If only my daughter would listen, I wouldn't have to shout!'* I'm sure that if she could've articulated her thoughts, she would have said, *'If only my Mum wouldn't shout at me, then I would listen to her. But I'm not listening to a MEAN Mum!'*
>
> This powerful shift in perspective will help you see with new eyes. And just like magic, you'll see your child's behaviour change.

THE CYCLE WE CAN FALL INTO TRYING TO CORRECT UNWANTED BEHAVIOUR IN OUR CHILD

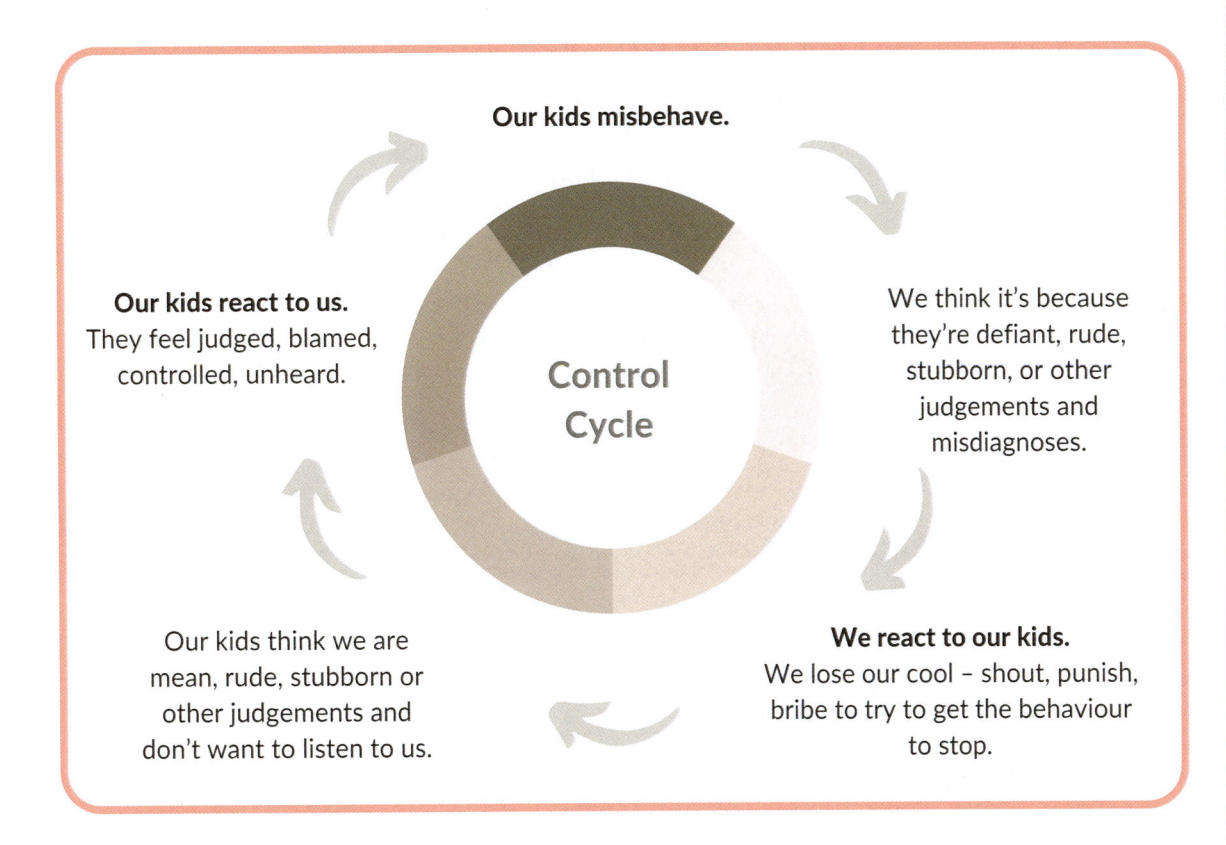

Control Cycle

- **Our kids misbehave.**
- We think it's because they're defiant, rude, stubborn, or other judgements and misdiagnoses.
- **We react to our kids.** We lose our cool – shout, punish, bribe to try to get the behaviour to stop.
- Our kids think we are mean, rude, stubborn or other judgements and don't want to listen to us.
- **Our kids react to us.** They feel judged, blamed, controlled, unheard.

In trying to resolve our child's unwanted behaviour, we can get stuck using punishments, threats and bribes. This cycle erodes the parent-child relationship. It's based on using shame and control to try to change a child's behaviour. External control only makes children angry and defensive, causing more unwanted behaviour.

When we find ourselves in this cycle, it doesn't feel good. It feels like we're against our child, which fuels resentment and despair on both sides.

If you find yourself in this cycle, it's not your fault. It can be so hard to break this cycle as doing so goes against the grain of what you have probably been told to do.

Understanding the control cycle is the key to breaking its chains and setting yourself free.

As you can see, there are two reactions occurring in the control cycle: your reaction to your child's behaviour and their reaction to yours. That means it's not just your child's behaviour that causes this cycle to spin out of control. Your response can keep it going or stop it too!

But first, if you have some resistance to changing your response, I want to reassure you that change does not mean letting your kids off the hook or not addressing behaviour you don't like.

This is not some kind of unhinged parenting where the kids run wild, or you mollycoddle them. YOU changing the way you respond to your child's unwanted behaviour puts YOU in control of the cycle. Being stuck doesn't feel good for you or your child. Breaking this cycle by changing YOUR response will change the way your child responds to you.

If you're sitting there thinking, '*No s**t Sherlock! But how do I do that? I need tools and strategies,*' hang in there. They're coming! I will give you the exact steps you need to break this cycle for good AND get you the behaviour you want.

NOTES

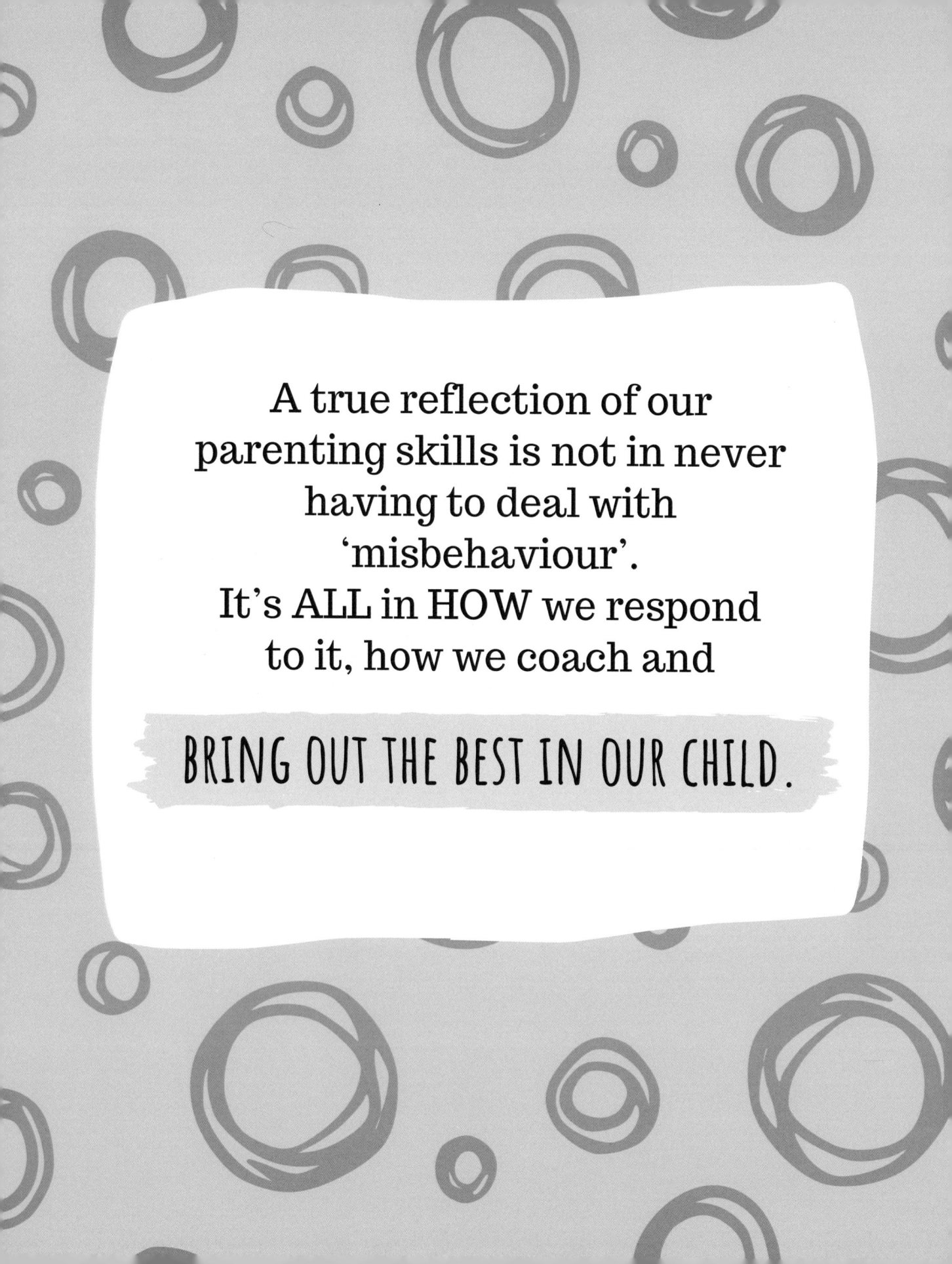

A true reflection of our parenting skills is not in never having to deal with 'misbehaviour'.
It's ALL in HOW we respond to it, how we coach and

BRING OUT THE BEST IN OUR CHILD.

Your child's behaviour is not a reflection of your parenting skills.

Read that line again! Let it sink in.

When my son was born, I thought I was an epic parent! Truly! I thought because he was an easy-going, never-had-a-tantrum, did-as-he-was-told kind of child, it was a reflection of my parenting. It was only when my daughter was born with a different temperament and personality that I had a wake-up call.

Since I kept to this faulty way of thinking, no wonder I felt like a failure as a parent. Her epic tantrums were a reflection of my parenting!

For far too long, we've focused on our child's behaviour as a benchmark for our parenting skills. If our child 'behaves', we use that as validation of how great a parent we are. And if they 'misbehave', we've somehow failed, and it's all our fault.

This is utter baloney! Our child's behaviour is not a reflection of our parenting skills. It's a reflection of their internal world, their emotions, their thoughts, and their self-regulation and communication skills.

A true reflection of our parenting skills is not in never having to deal with 'misbehaviour'. It's all in how we respond to it – how we coach, bring out the best in our child, and find the true solutions to our tricky situations.

When we see the world through our child's eyes, we get to have compassion and respond without judgement. That change allows our child's defenses to come down, so we are better able to guide them to behaviour we like.

Control cycle broken!

STEP INTO YOUR
CHILD'S WORLD

CHILDREN SEE THE WORLD VERY DIFFERENTLY

Understanding a child's perspective and their unique way of seeing the world helps you to empathise and connect with them. This allows for a better understanding of their innocence and ability to live in the present moment. It's what helps you laugh instead of cry, which makes overcoming tricky times a heck of a lot easier.

It's important to keep in mind that your child sees the world in a different way than you. They believe that Father Christmas flies around the world delivering presents. Their logic and reasoning are not the same as an adult's.

Avoid comparing your child's behaviour to what is considered appropriate for adults. It will stress you out and lead to expectations that are way, way off, leaving you and your child feeling miserable.

Children see the world so differently because a human brain does not fully develop until we're well into our 20's. The last part to develop is the executive function, what some people call the 'management system of the brain'. It's the part that helps us with logic, reasoning, impulse control, rational thinking, planning and empathy. Without these skills, it's hard to focus, follow directions, reflect on our behaviour and deal with emotions.

However, what our children come fully equipped to do is stay in the present moment. They live in the physical world of the here and now while we tend to live in our heads – full of the past or future and full of judgements, assumptions, expectations, predictions and fears.

Let's look at a typical example of how a child's lack of executive functioning skills affects their behaviour.

It's easy to get annoyed at a child who isn't getting dressed in the morning even after telling them multiple times. It can feel like they're not listening and being defiant on purpose. No wonder you feel frustrated!

But when you pause and look at the situation through age-appropriate brain development, you notice:

- ✗ They don't yet have the impulse control to stop playing and do what you ask.

- ✗ They don't have the time awareness to understand time restraints.

- ✗ They don't have planning skills to know what item of clothing goes on first.

- ✗ They don't have the capacity to understand another's perspective or how their behaviour affects others.

The magic of seeing the world through your child's eyes is that it gets you right back into the moment of what is actually happening. Children are experts at living in the here and now.

When you let go of judgements and see the way they make sense of their world, **you can step in to offer support and encouragement** instead of feeling frustrated and resorting to punishment. Your children need your loving guidance to develop their executive functioning skills in healthy ways.

Keep stepping into your child's world and trying to see things from their viewpoint.

HOW CHILDREN MAKE SENSE OF THE WORLD

Have you ever bought ice cream for your child at the park one time, and the next time you go back your child says, *'You always buy me ice cream'*?

Or have you taken them on trips to the park, swimming, play dates, the whole shebang, and a day later they complain, *'I never get to go anywhere'*?

It can be infuriating! It's easy to see them as ungrateful, always wanting their way, selfish or any of the other judgements we attach to our child's unwanted behaviour.

But it's none of that! Children live in the present moment much more than we do. They don't see the future and don't think about the past like we do. At this moment in time, 'now' is all there is! This is how children develop a relationship with their physical reality.

In a child's world, 'once' is always and 'not now' is never.

It's just HOW they see the world. It helps them create a sense of permanence.

Instead of responding to your child through your understanding of a situation, try seeing it through your child's eyes. Their reactions are showing you how they see the world.

That's why they get so upset if you say no to a toy at the toyshop – in their eyes, it's NEVER going to happen! Imagine really wanting something and not seeing the possibility of ever getting it. Now, you can understand their big reactions!

Understanding doesn't mean you have to buy them the toy or give them ice cream when you don't want to. It just helps you understand why your child has such big reactions to seemingly small things – they simply see the world differently from you.

Understanding helps you change how you respond.

Let's look at an example.

My 6-year-old daughter came out of school, begging for a playdate. I was busy, and it was not a good day to have friends around. My daughter started getting upset and demanding that I let her invite a friend to play.

'*I never get to have friends come over,*' she wailed, causing a scene at the school gates.

'*Wait a minute,*' I thought. '*She'd just had a playdate two days ago! What is she talking about?*'

Knowing that 'not now is never' helped me stay in the present moment. It would've been all too easy to slip into judgement, see my daughter as ungrateful or rude and try to fix a problem that wasn't there by trying to teach her to be grateful.

Staying in the moment and stepping onto my child's side, I saw a child who just loves having her friends over to play. She was 'right' for wanting a playdate, AND I was 'right' for not wanting to have a playdate. And as I'm the parent, I get to choose.

My conversation went like this:

SAY WHAT YOU SEE: '*You really want a playdate. You LOVE having friends around and wish they could come every single day. You're such a great friend. You just love having fun.*'

I acknowledged her and, at the same time, didn't agree with her demands.

CAN DO: '*And there's no playdate today. There must be something you can do to have fun at home.*'

I connected her to her core want, which was to have fun, and she didn't have to give up what she wanted to stay within my boundary.

Yes, she wasn't happy, AND we went home, baked cupcakes, and had fun together.

I then got the opportunity to point out her **STRENGTHs**: '*You got sad, worked through it, and found something fun to do. That shows you know how to calm down and find solutions. You're a problem-solver!*' My daughter got to see her **STRENGTHs** – what a great friend she is to want to have playdates AND how she is able to handle disappointment and find solutions within my boundaries.

You know how differently this interaction could have gone if I had got angry because I thought she was ungrateful or rude to me. Just one moment of seeing the situation through her eyes helped me stay firm with my boundary of no playdate, stay in the present moment and see the best in my daughter – she is a great friend and loves connecting with others. **What a different message my daughter got to hear about herself!**

YOUR TURN:

What about you? Can you see how your child sees the world differently from you? *Use this space to write down situations as seen through your child's eyes.*

THE WAY YOU SPEAK TO YOUR CHILD MATTERS

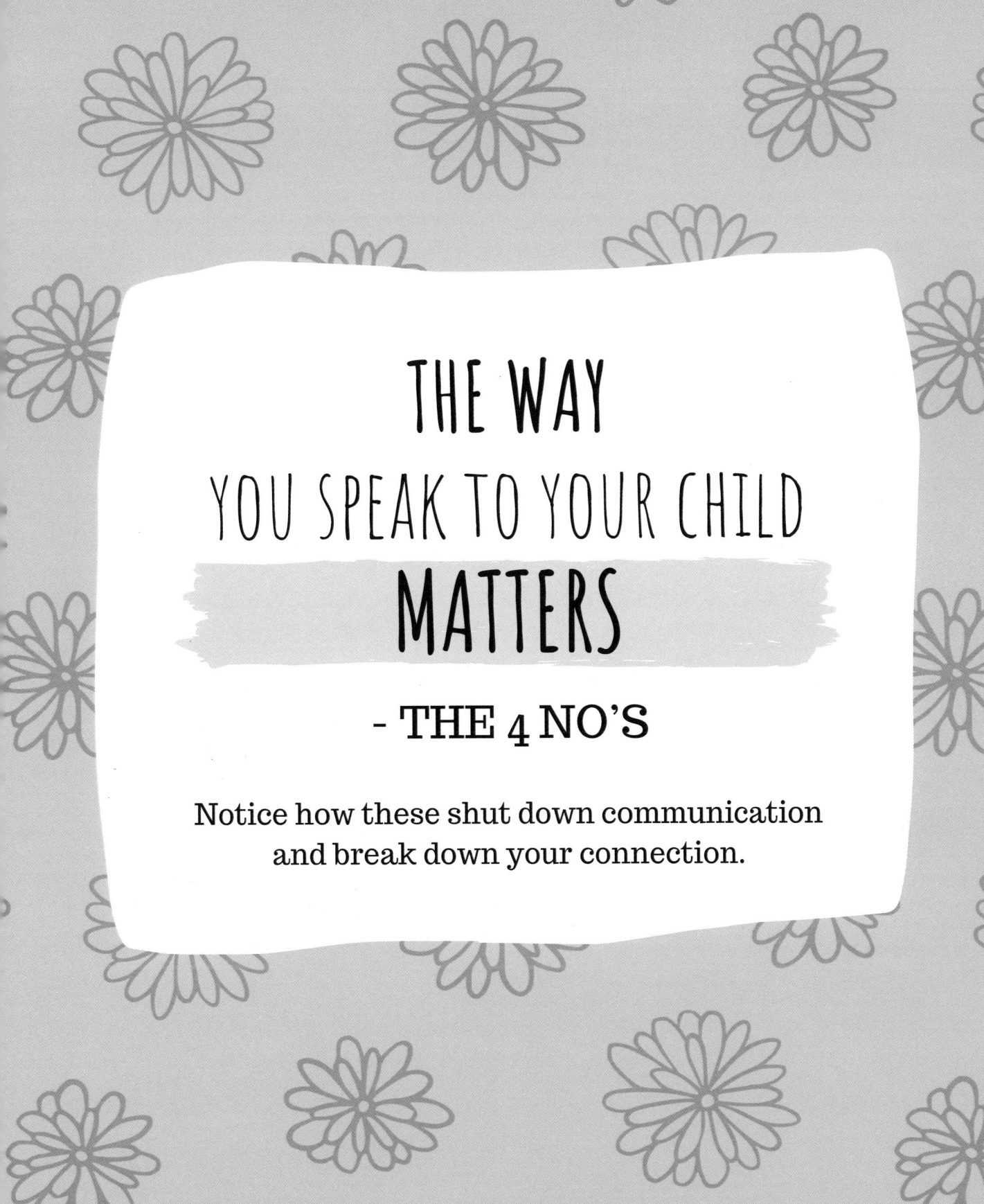

- THE 4 NO'S

Notice how these shut down communication and break down your connection.

NO JUDGING

Judging can sound like this:

- *'You're just not concentrating.'*
- *'You're being a baby.'*
- *'You're not trying.'*
- *'You're being lazy.'*
- *'That's not very kind.'*

Judgement in the form of criticism shuts down communication and puts children on the defensive. If you've experienced this type of judgement during your upbringing, you might not even realise when you are judging. Or if you do realise it and are finding it hard to stop, understanding why can help.

Primarily, we've been taught that being critical will motivate children to change their behaviour. It's probably what you experienced as a child. But the truth is, the tendency to judge others stems from our own insecurities and fears.

If we faced criticism or rejection for certain behaviours or traits in the past, as ironic as it sounds, we might judge our child to save them from being judged by others.

For example, if we were criticised for being a messy or disorganised child, we may criticise our child when it looks like they're developing those same habits. It would be really hard not to if it meant leaving them open to what we experienced – criticism and rejection by others.

It's important to recognise when we're judging and why we're doing it. By becoming more self-aware and compassionate, we can learn to let go of our judgements and treat children with understanding instead.

Every time we make a judgement about a child, what we're doing is attaching stories and interpretations to their actions that colour the way we see them and reflect how we see the world.

Imagine that a child has just grabbed a toy from his sibling and whacked him. If we ourselves were judged as bad, aggressive or mean as a child, we'd tend to judge that child the same way. When we've been taught to see behaviour through the lens of judgement, it's hard to stop to ask if any of it is true.

Without meaning to, we make a lot of assumptions. We see a snapshot of a moment in time in front of us and then fill in the missing information with our interpretation. Maybe that child's sibling grabbed the toy from him first, and he was trying to get it back; maybe the child feels defensive and resentful towards his sibling for earlier reasons; or maybe the child lacks skills to stand up for himself. When we stop judging, we open our minds to other possibilities and can coach our child to find solutions.

Judgements are based on our past experiences, assumptions, beliefs, and expectations rather than on what we observe or what is going on for the person we're judging.

Judging others trains our brains to find the bad in others, so we often forget to pause and become curious as to what is actually happening. That's one of the reasons I LOVE using SAY WHAT YOU SEE. It trains your brain to make neutral observations.

Let's look at an example.

When my daughter is upset and frustrated about something, she can speak in an ear-splitting voice. If I respond to her with judgement, it might sound something like: '*Stop being disrespectful. You sound rude.*'

In the past, I thought that by pointing out a judgement of my child's behaviour, it would motivate her to change her behaviour. But it doesn't work like that.

Judging my daughter's behaviour is counterproductive and leads to misunderstandings, disconnection and hurt feelings. When people feel judged, they tend to get defensive. Parents may misinterpret their child's reaction as rudeness or defiance, which can make things more complicated and create a whole new set of issues.

It becomes harder to find common ground and move forward in a positive way. Instead, it's far more effective to focus on understanding each other's perspectives and finding mutually agreeable solutions.

When my daughter speaks in an ear-splitting voice, it's likely that she's feeling overwhelmed or frustrated and, in that moment, finds it hard to express herself in a more constructive way.

One of the ways I support my daughter now is by providing her with a safe and non-judgemental environment in which to express herself. For instance, when she speaks to me in a way that seems out of character, I respond by saying something like, '*Wow! To speak to me like that, you must be feeling really upset.*' This helps her feel heard and understood and encourages her to open up to me in a way that judgements would never do.

When you approach your child's behaviour with understanding, it doesn't mean that you accept everything they do. Rather, you try to empathise with their perspective and take the time to understand the context and underlying factors that may be influencing their actions. By doing so, you address the root causes of their behaviour and help guide them towards the kind of behaviour you and they like better.

It's also important to model the behaviour you want to see from your child. If I speak to my daughter in a calm and respectful tone, she is more likely to follow my lead.

I want you to notice how making judgements can quickly shift the conversation away from productive problem-solving and straight into an argument of who is 'right' or 'wrong'. Look out for it. When you drop the judgements, you'll notice a huge reduction in your child's defensive reactions.

The next time you're about to judge or criticise, stop and start over by opening your heart, extending your curiosity and creating acceptance by seeing what's 'right' about the situation.

Help your child feel better about themselves, not worse.

PRACTISE 'NO JUDGING'

Do you find yourself using judgements in your interactions with your kids?

This week, focus on becoming more aware of how this language sounds, and remember to be gentle with yourself.

Can you identify specific instances where judgements are the first thing that come to mind? Consider how you can replace those judgements with neutral **SAY WHAT YOU SEE** statements?
Write down your thoughts and experiences.

NO FIXING

Fixing can sound like this:

- 'Why don't you...?'
- 'Here. Let me do that for you.'
- 'Just go and play with Sally. She's kind to you.'
- 'You know you'll have fun once you get to school. Don't be sad.'
- 'I'll talk to [friend/sibling/teacher] and sort things out. Don't worry.'
- 'I'll buy/get you [something] to make up for it.'

How do you react when your child is upset, uncomfortable, frustrated or angry? Like many of us, you may want to step in to fix things for them. It's a common dynamic. As parents, we naturally want to protect and support our children.

But did you know, these good intentions can sometimes lead to unintended consequences?

When we constantly intervene and 'fix' things for our child, it sends the message that we don't believe they can do it.

This can lead to a lack of confidence and reduced self-esteem. It can also make it harder for them to develop valuable life skills such as problem-solving and resilience.

It's important to strike a balance between providing support and allowing children to learn and grow through their own experiences and challenges. By doing so, we can help them build confidence, bring out their STRENGTHs, and become independent and capable individuals.

It's not about being hands-off or neglectful. Instead, it's about helping our kids become self-reliant by believing in their abilities while being there to guide and assist when necessary, all in a loving and supportive way. Striking the right balance between independence and support is essential for their growth and success.

It's about trusting them enough to figure things out on their own and giving them the space to learn, adapt and find their own solutions.

Let's look at an example.

Tony, a kind-hearted dad, knew his 15-year-old son Sammy got easily overwhelmed, and he wanted to shield him from life's challenges. His drive stemmed from Tony's own childhood experiences. He wished someone would have swooped in and made everything better when times got tough.

Tony wanted Sammy to feel happy and secure. He believed that stepping in and 'fixing' things for Sammy would achieve that goal, so he frequently gave in to his son's requests, relaxed rules and changed plans to prevent him from getting upset. This ultimately meant no helping around the house, no going to school if he didn't feel like it and endless hours of video games and TV in the comfort of his room.

Over time, Tony noticed a change in Sammy. There was something missing. He didn't seem happy or content. Tony realised his intentions had inadvertently hindered Sammy's growth. Sammy lacked a sense of responsibility and purpose. It was a turning point for Tony, and he understood it was time to help Sammy develop resilience rather than shield him from life's challenges.

If you're a parent who often finds themselves 'fixing' things for your kids out of love and kindness, don't worry, you're not alone. Your intentions are good. And the wonderful part is that you can continue to be that loving parent while also setting boundaries, offering guidance and supporting your child as they navigate the world… as the next example shows.

Here's another example.

One morning, my 5-year-old daughter came downstairs and asked if I would make her pancakes for breakfast. We were running late for school that morning, and it just wasn't going to happen. It was a toast or cereal kind of morning.

If I'd been afraid of her reaction, I might have tried to rush and make her pancakes even though I didn't want to, or I may have tried to talk her out of wanting pancakes. Instead, I stated my boundary: *'I'm not making pancakes this morning,'* and gave her time to work through her upset without trying to 'fix' it for her. That enabled her to quickly move on to find a solution.

'I know what I can make!' she said, and she hurried off to make this banana concoction she likes. (Don't ask! It involves bananas that are nuked in the microwave. But it works for her!)

I then replied by pointing out a STRENGTH: *'You found something you wanted for breakfast. You got upset, calmed yourself, and then made what YOU wanted all by yourself.'*

She was SO proud of herself, and I could see her standing tall. Best of all, she now quite frequently makes her own meals, including her own pancakes and scrambled eggs.

Children who are given this kind of autonomy grow up to be confident, capable and happy people who can handle challenges without getting overwhelmed or feeling like they have no control over their lives.

PRACTISE 'NO FIXING'

Do you find yourself rushing to fix things for your child to save them from challenges or feelings?

This week, take some time to consider where you feel compelled to intervene and solve problems for your child and why.

> Are there specific instances that come to mind where you tend to fix?
> Consider how you can replace fixing with giving your child space to try on their own so you know how much they are capable of. (You might be surprised.)
> *Write down your thoughts and experiences.*

NO TEACHING

Teaching can sound like this:

- *'You should do it this way, not that way. Let me show you.'*
- *'Be sure to take turns so that your friends get a chance to play.'*
- *'If you're feeling upset or angry, take a deep breath and count to ten before reacting.'*
- *'You need to hold on tight and put your feet right here. That's the way to do it!'*

I'm not saying you should never teach your children, just that there's a time and a place for it. It's about becoming aware of why and how often you try to teach. There are a few reasons why teaching isn't always the best response.

You know how it feels when you know how to do something, but someone still tries to teach you how to do it? It's really frustrating, isn't it? It feels insulting that they'd assume you don't already know. Or maybe they proceed to explain it in a way that sounds condescending. Or maybe they're trying to convince you to do something their way, and they jump in to tell you why your way (that you were quite happy with) won't work. Our children feel the same.

Or have you ever experienced making a mistake like burning dinner or accidentally breaking something? In those moments, being told what to do differently next time is frustrating and can feel kind of insulting. You already know you messed up and could have done things differently.

What you really need is for someone to acknowledge and validate your experience first, and then give you the space to come to your own conclusions about what you could do differently in the future. In this case, timing is everything! It helps you feel empowered and capable, rather than foolish and hopeless. Again, our children feel the same.

When we always teach, instruct or give advice to our children, it can send the message that we don't trust their knowledge or abilities and breed defensiveness. It can also prevent us from gaining valuable insights into their thoughts, perspectives and how their minds work. However, when we show curiosity about their experiences and listen first, it encourages children to open up and share more.

Our curiosity builds connection and empowers our children to cultivate a genuine love for learning.

Let's look at some examples.

Micromanaging:

Lisa and her teenage daughter, Mia, often found themselves caught in heated arguments while cooking. Lisa, with good intentions, wanted to teach Mia how to cook. But in her eagerness to teach, she tended to micromanage every step – how to chop an onion, how thin the tomato slices should be and how to stir the sauce – which left Mia feeling that her abilities were not trusted.

Mia's frustration grew. One day, during a disagreement, Mia firmly told her mum that she knew what she was doing. Lisa realised she had been too controlling in her teaching. *'You're absolutely right, Mia. I believe in your skills, and I should trust you more in the kitchen. Let's try cooking together differently from now on.'*

Lisa allowed Mia to take the lead while offering guidance only when needed. With this change, their kitchen transformed into a place of laughter and learning, strengthening their bond and boosting Mia's confidence. In the end, it was about nurturing independence and trust, rather than just teaching cooking skills.

Bad Timing:

When I was a child, my grandma taught me how to knit. I remember feeling so capable as I worked on my first project, making my way through each stitch with determination. Grandma smiled and gave me space to practise. Even though my work was clumsy with some slipped stitches here and there, I was proud of what I had created.

One day, I eagerly showed my knitting to my dad. As he looked at it, the first thing he did was start teaching me what I could do to do better next time. I knew he was only trying to help me improve, but it left me feeling discouraged and disheartened. After that day, I knew he wasn't the first person I wanted to share my knitting with. Grandma was.

Having space to process your mistakes often leads to ideas for what you could do differently in the future.

Here's another example.

I was eager to collect my 7-year-old daughter from school. I'd dropped her off that morning with her swimming bag packed for her first swim lesson at school. As I waited by the school gates, I watched her coming towards me. She didn't look as animated as I thought she would be – a bit wet and bedraggled, and not happy.

'So?' I asked.

'HMMFFF,' she replied.

'Wasn't good,' I presumed.

She was fighting back tears. *'It was terrible! We didn't even get to swim more than half a width!'*

'Oh!' I replied.

'My group just had to watch everyone else swim. It was SOOO annoying.'

'Oh sweetie, you were so excited, and you didn't get to swim! That is annoying!'

'SOOO annoying! Amy got moved up a group and spent the whole time bragging about it. I just had to sit on the benches with my group and watch everyone else swim and listen to Amy go on and on!!!'

'Oh! That must have been annoying. And then for your good friend to brag like that!'

On the way to the car with my daughter clearly upset, tears welling up, verging on a full-blown meltdown, my friends couldn't help but notice her distress.

Their comments went something like this:

- 'Ah, don't worry. Think of all the fun you'll have next week.'
- 'It's just this week when they work out the groups. Next week, I'm sure it will be fine. You'll see. You'll swim the whole time.'
- 'I'm sure if you practise more and concentrate, you will move up a group too!'
- 'It's nothing to cry about.'

We genuinely have good intentions. We don't want our kids to suffer, right? We aim to teach them, offer logical explanations and reassure them, all while trying to stop the crying and upsets as quickly as possible. It can be uncomfortable to witness our children cry, especially in public.

However, moments when our child is upset aren't the best times for teaching. Just like us, they need to feel heard before they can move forward. Listening and validating with **SAY WHAT YOU SEE** allows our child to effectively manage and work through their upsets and emotions in their own time.

This coaching skill also encourages our child to trust themselves and their feelings. Trusting their own emotions and instincts builds their self-esteem and resilience, and it helps them navigate through challenging situations with confidence.

PRACTISE 'NO TEACHING'

Do you do you find yourself frequently taking charge as the primary instructor?

This week, focus on becoming more aware of why and how frequently you try to teach your child.

> Are there specific situations where you try to teach your child something and hit resistance? Consider how you can replace teaching with trusting your child's abilities and pointing out their STRENGTHs.
> *Write down your thoughts and experiences.*

NO QUESTIONS

Questions can sound like this:

- *'Why would you do that?'*
- *'Did Bobby tell you why he didn't want to play with you?'*
- *'How was lunch at school today?'*

Questions are not the best way to build a relationship with a child. They automatically give us the upper hand by directing the conversation and setting up the expectation of an answer. Even open-ended questions can feel directive and trigger a defensive response, especially if the child isn't sure why we are asking or what kind of answer we want.

Again, we mean well. Maybe we're trying to get more information from our child, find out what happened between siblings or find out why our child didn't do something we asked.

But even when we're just trying to be supportive, a question like, *'Did Bobby tell you why he didn't want to play with you today?'* could prompt our child to wrack their brain to see if Bobby not wanting to play was their fault. A **SAY WHAT YOU SEE (SWYS)** statement like, *'You seem sad that Bobby didn't want to play,'* would avoid that and encourage your child to tell you more.

Likewise, asking *'How was lunch today?'* may seem like a simple question and be completely fine if our child isn't struggling with lunchtime at school. However, if they are, then it can feel like we're fishing for answers to solve/fix their problem, which can prompt a defensive reaction.

Other questions might be more of a way to vent our frustration.

- *'Why can't you just do as your told?'*
- *'What's the matter with you?'*
- *'When will you learn?'*

You might be surprised at how many judgements can be packed into these little words: Why/What/When + You. Questions that sound accusatory are especially troubling for children since they feel like attacks and convey distrust or doubt in the child's abilities and intentions. Children who feel misunderstood may lash out, shut down, feel stupid or feel like they have to justify their choices. None of those reactions will open communication or build a relationship.

Try **SWYS** instead. It's non-threatening, keeps the child in the lead and encourages communication.

- *'Why can't you just do as you're told?'* → **SWYS:** *'You're so busy playing that you didn't hear me.'*
- *'What's the matter with you?'* → **SWYS:** *'You're disappointed that I'm not buying that for you.'*
- *'When will you learn?'* → **SWYS:** *'You didn't mean for that to happen.'*

Without feeling accused or attacked, your child is far more likely to tell you more.

Let's look at an example.

Whenever Jacob felt frustrated or upset, he would hit his little sister. He didn't know why he did it. It just seemed to make him feel better in the moment.

Each time, his mum would ask him, '*Why would you do that, Jacob? What's the matter with you? When will you learn that hitting is naughty?*'

The questions put him on the spot, and he felt ashamed because he didn't have an answer. He already knew that hitting was bad. He didn't know why he was hurting his sister and didn't know how to stop.

The questions didn't help clarify anything for him or his mother. They were loaded with judgement, and that's the message Jacob got.

Jacob's mum tried SAY WHAT YOU SEE statements instead.

With **SWYS**, she was able to switch her responses to neutral observations like, '*You're upset and angry, and you hit your sister.*' That allowed Jacob to tell her more. He said things like, '*She looked at me,*' or '*I didn't want her there,*' which helped his mum realise that it wasn't about his sister at all.

Jacob was having a hard time dealing with his own emotions. He didn't have the skills to express them in healthy ways, so he was taking it out on his sister.

His mum also realised that no amount of questioning would help Jacob change his behaviour and find healthier ways to express himself. With her new coaching skills (that I will teach you later in this workbook), she was able to coach Jacob to find more acceptable ways to express his feelings and meet his NEEDS, and the hitting stopped.

Here's another example.

Every day, when Ethan returned home from school, his dad, Richard, would often ask questions like, *'Did you finish your homework?'* or *'Did you clean your room today?' 'Did you behave at school?'* Richard genuinely wanted to instil a sense of responsibility in Ethan, so he thought asking these questions would encourage him to be honest about his actions.

However, the questions felt accusatory, so Ethan felt defensive. He began to perceive his father's inquiries as tests. Every question seemed like an opportunity to either pass or fail, and Ethan didn't want to disappoint his dad or get into trouble. So, he started to clam up, even when he had nothing to hide.

Richard began to notice that Ethan was becoming more secretive. He couldn't understand why his well-intentioned efforts were backfiring. Then, one day, Ethan decided to open up and express his feelings to his dad. *'Dad,'* Ethan said hesitantly, *'I feel like you're always testing me with your questions. It feels like you're trying to catch me out.'*

Richard was taken aback. He realised that his approach, driven by good intentions, had led to the opposite result. Instead of encouraging Ethan to take accountability, Ethan felt pressured and defensive.

Richard stopped asking questions and instead started using **SWYS** + **STRENGTHs**.

'Looks like you finished your homework. That shows you're responsible.'
'You put your clothes away, your room looks tidy. That shows you know how to look after yourself. '
'You're ready for school on time and always try your best. That shows you're self-motivated.'

With this change, Ethan felt valued and respected, leading to more open communication and increased responsibility and accountability.

PRACTISE 'NO QUESTIONS'

Do you find yourself frequently using questions in your interactions with your child?

This week, focus on becoming more aware of how your questions might sound to your child, and remember to be gentle with yourself.

Are there situations where you ask questions and your child feels defensive?
Consider how you can replace those questions with neutral SWYS statements to create more open and supportive communication.
Write down your thoughts and experiences.

FROM JUDGEMENTS TO OBSERVATIONS

Let's look at an example.

When my daughter was 8, I took her and her best friend to see Little Mix at an open-air concert. It was an extra special occasion because it was their very first concert experience. Naturally, I wanted the day to be absolutely perfect. The tickets weren't cheap, and don't even get me started on the extortionate prices of the food and merchandise.

After we waited for hours, the group finally came on stage. I looked to see the girls' reaction only to hear them say: *'I want to go home!!! It's stupid.'* I had a split-second thought of *'OMG! After all I've arranged! How dare they be so spoilt and ungrateful.'* It's so easy to go down that route of judging and labelling our kids for their behaviour, isn't it?

As I took a pause, I chose to set aside the judgements and, instead, get curious and observe. After all the anticipation and excitement, I couldn't help but wonder, *'Why did they want to leave before we even had the chance to hear a single song?'* To find out, I used SAY WHAT YOU SEE.

Our conversation went like this:

SWYS: *'You don't like it!'*

Instantly, their response provided further insight: *'It's not that! We thought we would be able to see the stage.'*

Ah, it dawned on me in that moment. Of course! It was their first concert experience. Their only frame of reference was TV performances. Here, they were surrounded by a crowd with people obstructing their view and Little Mix appearing like tiny ants on the stage!

SWYS: *'Oh! You want to be able to see clearly.'*

CAN DO: *'Must be something we can do.'*

'Let's go and stand over by the side of the stage where we can see better,' they replied.

I took the opportunity to acknowledge their STRENGTHs: *'You knew what you wanted, and you found a solution. You're problem-solvers!'*

Poof! Drama over. We found a solution and had a great time dancing and singing along. As you can imagine, the entire situation would have taken a completely different turn if I had impulsively reacted by saying, *'Stop being so ungrateful!'* or *'What's the matter with you? Can't you just have fun!'* Instead of judging and labelling, I paused, observed, said what I saw, and...

I managed to turn this tricky situation around.

SWYS gave me the chance to step into their shoes. When I realised that they weren't spoilt or ungrateful, they were simply experiencing their very first concert and it wasn't what they expected, it was easy to stay calm and connected and concentrate on finding solutions.

WHEN JUDGEMENTS BECOME NEGATIVE LABELS

When we judge our child negatively, we stop looking for solutions to the real problem and start blaming our child instead. Negative labels reinforce our judgements and become who we think our child is. Since we can't 'fix' who a child is, this thinking keeps us and our child frustrated and stuck.

The words we use to describe our children are powerful. When we think of and refer to our child in a negative manner, it becomes easy to start treating them in negative ways.

When we think our child IS the problem, we don't spend time finding solutions to the real problems.

This is a list of negative labels we've been taught to attach to behaviour we don't like:

Anxious	Entitled	Rebellious
Argumentative	Explosive	Rude
Arrogant	Hyperactive	Selfish
Brat	Impatient	Spoilt
Bossy	Impulsive	Stubborn
Challenging	Inconsiderate	Uncaring
Cheeky Monkey	Insistent	Ungrateful
Defiant	Lazy	Unkind
Demanding	Liar	Unreliable
Dishonest	Loud	Untrustworthy
Disrespectful	Manipulative	
Drama Queen	Never Listens	

Circle the ones you've seen in your child.

Remember, this is NOT who your child is! It's a lens you're viewing their behaviour through.

NEGATIVE LABELS KEEP EVERYONE STUCK

Negative labels have a major impact on how children see themselves and on how they act.

Children tend to take our labels as facts about who they are. Once a child accepts a label, it can be difficult for them to change it. (However, the STRENGTH tool I'll be teaching you later in this workbook can help reverse it.)

> Review the list of negative labels on the previous page. Can you add any more?
> *List any that stuck with you from your childhood.*

All these thoughts would rush through my mind when my daughter was acting up.

- 'If she speaks to me like that now, she'll have no friends.'
- 'If she's like this now, what's she going to be like as a teenager?'
- 'After all I do for her, how dare she treat me like that?'
- 'I'm not good enough. I can't control my daughter.'

It was this thinking that kept me stuck. Let me explain why… **Because this changes everything!**

Our thoughts about a situation are just that – thoughts. In other words, they are our judgements and our interpretation of what is going on. We can't really SEE disrespect or stubbornness or rudeness even though we are sure we can. What we may SEE is red cheeks, kicking and howling.

Disrespect, stubbornness or rudeness are our judgements (thoughts) about what those actions mean seen through a particular lens – the lens of good or bad. That lens was passed on to us by our parents, which is why we so often react like they did even when we don't want to.

The way we, as parents, react to our child's behaviour through OUR lens of good or bad becomes how our children SEE themselves, others and the world.

Before children reach seven years old, they learn from us that:
'GOOD BEHAVIOUR = GOOD PERSON' AND 'BAD BEHAVIOUR = BAD PERSON'

I used to think my daughter was rude, defiant and stubborn. Can you see how these judgements become your child's character traits?

And what options do you have when you believe these judgements? You think you have a child who IS those things, and you think you are a failure, not good enough, so you focus your attention on changing these traits. The problem is these character traits aren't really there – they're only in our heads.

So why is it so important to know this when we are dealing with our child's unwanted behaviour?

When a child hears, *'You're so rude and stubborn. You only think of yourself. No wonder no one wants to be with you,'* or *'What's the matter with you? Your younger brother can behave. He's not a problem,'* or *'No one cares what you want. You're so stubborn,'* and you link these words to your child's behaviour as proof, it sets a belief in the child's subconscious that BEING rude and stubborn is WHO they are. That they are unworthy or not good enough. It becomes their inner voice and drives their future behaviour.

And we're the same. When we link our child's behaviour to our own self-worth, it sets a belief in our subconscious as to WHO we are. It becomes our inner voice and drives our future behaviour.

Our words matter.

The way we THINK about our child's behaviour determines our words and reactions. So next, I'll show you how we can sidestep judgements and coach our child to achieve the behaviour we want to see by changing what we think.

Trying to change your reactions is really, really hard. But when you change your perceptions, your reactions automatically change, easily and effortlessly.

How do you react when you see these behaviours?

- Your child acts rude, ungrateful, disrespectful?
- Your child acts bossy or aggressive?
- Your child seems to always want their own way?
- Your child throws a tantrum when they can't get what they want?
- Your child acts shy or anxious?

Trying to stop or ignore your reaction and become non-judgemental, curious and emotionally connected when you are triggered is next to impossible. Your perceptions of your child's behaviour, the meaning you give it and the stories you tell yourself about it run the show.

When you're positive that what you are seeing is a rude, stubborn, naughty or disrespectful child, of course you're quick to anger, use a harsh tone or tell off or punish them or yourself. It's a perfectly human reaction, isn't it?

THOUGHTS	EMOTIONS	REACTIONS
What you think – your assumptions, judgements, beliefs about a situation	Feelings triggered by your thoughts	Actions triggered by your thoughts and feelings

You can see that your reactions are a perfect human response to your emotions and thoughts. So rather than try to change your reactions, it's easier and way more effective to change your thoughts and the way you interpret behaviour. To do that, you need a new way to SEE.

Some new ways to see your child's behaviour

When your child speaks to you in a tone you don't like, instead of seeing them as rude, bratty, aggressive or disrespectful, what if you saw a child who feels misunderstood, unheard or is trying to get their point across in the only way they know how?

When your child hits a sibling, instead of 'naughty' or 'aggressive', what if you saw a child who wants to play with his sibling but lacks the skills to handle disappointment or frustration when his sibling doesn't want to play with him? Instead of seeing a child who's naughty, you'd see a child who loves their sibling and wants to play, yet lacks the ability to find another solution or has difficulty handling their emotions.

Of course you DON'T LIKE being spoken to like that and DON'T LIKE your children fighting, but instead of telling your child off, you can remain curious and step into your child's world.

When you see your child in this new way, you're likely to react with more empathy and understanding. From that place of connection, you're primed to offer loving guidance and coach your child to bring out their STRENGTHs so they can manage their own behaviour.

Changing what you see, changes what you think and 'triggers' feelings and actions you like!

DON'T BELIEVE EVERYTHING YOU THINK

YOUR THOUGHTS CAUSE YOUR REACTIONS

AHH! My daughters are so ungrateful. After all I do for them...

AHH! My son is so selfish! He never learns! He's going to end up with no friends.

AHH! My son is so disrespectful, rude, bratty and aggressive!

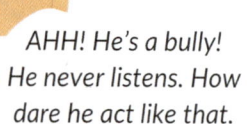

AHH! He's a bully! He never listens. How dare he act like that.

AHH! My kids are so naughty!

AHH! She's such a cry-baby. She has to learn!

YOUR THOUGHTS CAUSE YOUR REACTIONS

He feels misunderstood and unheard. He's trying to get his point across in the only way he knows how. With my coaching he will learn better skills.

My daughter is determined. She knows what she wants. That doesn't mean I have to get it for her. I can support her to get what she wants in another way.

It's OK to cry.

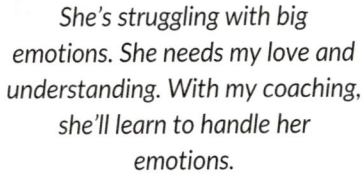

She's struggling with big emotions. She needs my love and understanding. With my coaching, she'll learn to handle her emotions.

My son is still learning. With my support, he will learn to manage his own behaviour.

By changing what you SEE, your thoughts and behaviour automatically change.

Jonny, a 3-year-old, is busy playing. He sees a toy his brother is playing with and grabs it.

What did you see in this scene? Because what you SEE affects how you respond and, in turn, the behaviour you get more of in the future.

If you see a mean boy who knows grabbing is naughty but does it anyway, you might want to punish him to teach him to be kind. You may say something like: *'You know grabbing is naughty! You wouldn't want someone to do that to you, would you?! I've already told you! If your brother is playing with a toy, you don't grab! That's not kind. Now, go and sit on the naughty step and think about what you did!'*

What if, instead, you SEE a kind boy who wants a toy his brother is playing with and doesn't know a kind way to get it? Understanding that kids are impulsive and do what works in the moment, you might think he just needs another solution that will work for him and his brother too.

Then your reply would be more like: *'Jonny, you want that toy, and it looks like Sammy hasn't finished playing with it yet. Hmmm. Two boys and one toy! There must be something you CAN DO!'*

If your children aren't used to solving their own problems, you may have to step in to guide them. And because you have not used shame, blame, or criticism, Jonny is likely to be more receptive to your guidance.

Then when the kids have found a solution like taking turns or playing with it together, you get to point out their STRENGTHs: *'You knew what to do. You found a way to make it work for both of you. That shows you're kind and a problem-solver!'*

Consider what message Jonny might take away from each situation:

'I'd better not grab toys because I fear what might happen if I do!'

OR

'When I want to play with a toy my brother's playing with, I know how to be kind. I'm a problem-solver!'

Which message would better guide him to the behaviour you want to see next time? And which message would improve his self-belief and connection with you?

Let's look at an example for an older child.

Toby, a 13-year-old, is using his phone in his bedroom well after the time he knows he shouldn't be. You walk in to find him trying to hide it under his pillow.

What did you see in this scene? Because what you SEE affects how you respond and the behaviour you get more of in the future.

If you SEE a child who should know better, who's pushing your boundaries and lying to you, you may say something like: *'What do you think you're doing?! You know better than that! How many times have I told you? That's so disrespectful of you. That's it! I can't trust you. No phone for a week. That should make you think.'*

Or if you SEE a child who is struggling, who knows your boundaries and, at the same time, doesn't want to miss out on a friend's group chat, and you remember that you also find it hard to come off your own phone, your reply would be more like: *'Toby, it's hard when all your friends are chatting after lights out. I know you don't want to miss out, AND no phones in the bedroom after 8.30. there must be something you* CAN DO *to keep in touch and be off your phone before 8.30. I know the pull of the phone is so tempting.'*

Then you would wait, giving your child the space to correct his own behaviour.

Chances are, as you've not blamed or criticised him, he will reply, *'Sorry mum! Here.'* and hand over his phone willingly. (And if not, you'd be on his side coaching him to deal with his frustration and disappointment.)

You'd then get a wonderful opportunity to point out his STRENGTHs: *'That took self-control and shows honesty.'*

I wonder what message Toby would take away from each situation. What would better guide him to the behaviour you want to see next time, and what decisions might Toby base his future actions on?

'Mum doesn't understand. She's so mean, I'm just going to sneak it next time.'

OR

'Mum understands it's hard to come off your phone. She's there to support me.'

Notice that, in both scenarios, the boundary DIDN'T change. It's how we communicate and enforce our boundaries and rules that has a significant impact on our child's response and future behaviour.

PRACTISE NOTICING YOUR THOUGHTS

By becoming aware of your thoughts, you can change them. The best place to start is right where you are.

When Jake's older son was acting boisterous and impulsive, he started to become aware that he thought of his son as the instigator, bully and troublemaker of the family. Jake became aware that these thoughts were causing him to feel angry and powerless. They made him feel like he was doing it all wrong and served as proof that he wasn't a good dad. He thought that if he couldn't control his son's behaviour, his son was going to grow up into a thug, have no friends and be a bully. (You can see how easily our thoughts can spiral out of control into future fears.)

It caused Jake to think that HE was the problem. If he could only 'fix' his son, then he would be a great dad, and his son would be saved. These thoughts and the responsibility they carried caused him to snap at, shout at, tell off, threaten and punish his son.

His son felt left alone with his feelings. He felt unheard, misunderstood and hurt. He thought that his dad preferred his younger brother. When his favourite things were taken away from him, he felt ashamed and unworthy. He learnt that he was 'bad' and that he couldn't control himself. He put on a front to protect himself and pretended he didn't care.

Then Jake interpreted that behaviour as defiant and aggressive, reacted to those additional thoughts, and tried to 'fix' his son more.

As he became aware of his thoughts, he could see the role they played in the Control Cycle (see page 42). For the first time, he had the chance to break both himself and his son free.

Seeing his son as hurt and defending himself instead of defiant and aggressive changed what he thought and how he responded, which turned the whole thing around.

> What kinds of unwanted behaviour are you seeing in your child?

EXAMPLE ONE

To change your reactions with ease, you need to get out of your head. Pay attention to your thoughts, beliefs and assumptions, and begin to question them.

Every time you react in a way you don't like, start by questioning how you're seeing the situation:

Questions	An example of Jake's responses
What actually happened? What did you see or hear?	I was in the kitchen, and I heard my boys fighting. The older one was yelling and younger one was telling him to go away.
What do you think you are seeing? (your perception and story about what happened)	I automatically think my older son is instigating the fight and being a bully. I think the younger one is a victim and needs rescuing.
What are your emotions and additional thoughts in reaction to what you think you are seeing?	I feel my heart racing and my head throbbing. I feel like I've failed. Why can't I get them to stop fighting? I'm useless. He's a bully. I need to teach him a lesson. My younger son needs me to stand up for him. I feel mad.
What actions do you take in reaction to your emotions and thoughts?	I race into the sitting room and tell off my older son. I shout, 'Why do you have to be such a bully, yelling at your younger brother? What's the matter with you?' Then I take away his iPad.
How can you see the behaviour you don't like in a new way?	They are just kids. Of course they're fighting! My boys are learning how to get along. My sons are both kind. The younger one doesn't want to play, and the older one does. He wants to play with his little brother! Of course he'd yell. He feels rejected and angry. He needs my support to handle his emotions and bring out his self-control and problem-solving skills. I've got this!
How might your actions change if you didn't believe your initial thoughts?	I could take a pause and step in to support both children and bring out their strengths.
How might your child's actions change if you acted differently?	Both my children would feel heard and understood. My older son would feel I was on his side supporting him too. He most likely would want to listen to me more.

EXAMPLE TWO

To change your reactions with ease, you need to get out of your head. Pay attention to your thoughts, beliefs and assumptions and begin to question them.

Every time you react in a way you don't like, start by questioning how you're seeing the situation:

Questions	An example of typical responses
What actually happened? What did you see or hear?	I said no more TV, and my child had a tantrum.
What do you think you are seeing? (your perception and story about what happened)	I think my child can't accept that I said 'no', so it must be my parenting. It's my fault she's upset. I made her cry.
What are your emotions and additional thoughts in reaction to what you think you are seeing?	I feel bad. I feel tense and resentful that she is making me feel like this. I think if she wouldn't fuss, then I wouldn't feel so emotional. I start doubting my decision. Maybe I should just let her watch more TV.
What actions do you take in reaction to your emotions and thoughts?	I give in to her demands, and her fussing stops for the moment.
How can you see the behaviour you don't like in a new way?	I'm a good mum for saying 'no' to more TV. I want my daughter to play outside more. Her reaction is not a reflection of my parenting; it's her way to handle big feelings.
How might your actions change if you didn't believe your initial thoughts?	I could learn to coach my child through her emotions and still say 'no' to more TV time.
How might your child's actions change if you acted differently?	My daughter would learn to handle disappointment and know it's OK to feel big emotions. She could learn she has self-control and manage her own behaviour.

YOU HAVE A GO

To change your reactions with ease, you need to get out of your head. Pay attention to your thoughts, beliefs and assumptions and begin to question them.

Every time you react in a way you don't like, start by questioning how you're seeing the situation:

Questions	Your responses
What actually happened? What did you see or hear?	
What do you think you are seeing? (your perception and story about what happened)	
What are your emotions and additional thoughts in reaction to what you think you are seeing?	
What actions do you take in reaction to your emotions and thoughts?	
How can you see the behaviour you don't like in a new way?	
How might your actions change if you didn't believe your initial thoughts?	
How might your child's actions change if you acted differently?	

IT'S ALL IN THE PAUSE

Before you react, PAUSE!

Even when it feels like there is no time, there is always a moment to pause… even if just for 30 seconds. Unless your child is about to be hit by a bus, there's always time!

Start to watch your thoughts and separate yourself from them. When you become aware of them objectively, you can become curious as to where your mind goes and how it thinks. You can start to watch and observe your thoughts, emotions and actions.

Pausing before you react stops your impulses and creates new neurological pathways. You have more opportunity to respond rather than react.

This is not something that changes overnight. It takes effort to change your default thinking. The great thing is that the more you practise, the easier it gets. That's because the more you practise, the more you literally change the synapses in your brain, forming new neural pathways. And before you know it, you'll be creating new ways of responding.

Visualising a calm path through a field can help train your brain to respond instead of react in challenging situations. By consistently pausing and taking the calm path, your old pathway becomes overgrown and obsolete, just like the old neural pathways in your brain. The calm path becomes your default reaction, replacing the previous behaviour.

CONFIRMATION BIAS

Confirmation bias is a tendency to seek out and interpret information in a way that confirms our pre-existing beliefs and opinions. This results in a filtered view of reality where we overlook information that contradicts our beliefs. It's like wearing a pair of invisible goggles.

When applied to parenting, this can result in interpreting our child's behaviour in a way that confirms negative beliefs and opinions about our child.

> ### How it works
>
> I used to believe my daughter was stubborn and never listened, so I missed out on seeing other aspects of her personality and behaviour that did not fit my belief. As a result, I treated her in a way that reinforced her stubbornness and made it harder for her to listen.

To break this cycle, it's important to question your beliefs and try to see situations objectively.

It's easy to gather evidence to prove yourself correct: *'You see? She doesn't listen. You see? She's a brat. You see? She's defiant...'* When, in fact, I could interpret her behaviour in a completely different way.

When you hold on to a belief or judgement about your child, it affects how you perceive and respond to their behaviour. Over time, this can lead to a disconnection between you and your child as you start to see them only through the lens of your bias.

To maintain a healthy and strong relationship with your child, it is important to be aware of and challenge these biases and work to see your child in a more positive light.

It takes work and awareness to challenge and alter your established beliefs and biases.

It starts by changing the way you gather proof and make sense of your child's behaviour.

CHECK YOUR CONFIRMATION BIAS

Which of your child's behaviours are you seeing through your pair of invisible goggles?

My confirmation bias had me see my daughter's as stubborn and gather proof of all the ways she behaved that confirmed that belief. I didn't notice that she was struggling with adapting to new situations or that she had a hard time seeing things from someone else perspective.

What are some of your pre-existing beliefs and opinions about your child?
Use this space to become aware of your confirmation bias.

What proof have you gathered?

What aspects of your child's personality might you have missed out on?

DOUBLE-STANDARD BIAS

At the times when you're snappy, stubborn or quick to shout, notice what you think. Perhaps you think you're in a grumpy mood because you're tired, feel unheard or feel rushed off your feet...

However, when your child is in a grumpy mood, snappy, stubborn or quick to shout, notice what you think. Is it because they're ungrateful, rude, sassy etc? If so, you would be attributing their behaviour to a character flaw but yours to circumstances even though the behaviours are the same.

That's called a double standard – a common way of thinking about our children's behaviour differently from our own. It's important to become aware of our double-standard biases and treat our children with the same understanding and compassion that we would want for ourselves.

Look out for a double standard at play and make a note of it here.
A double standard is a hidden bias, so it's super easy to be unaware of it.

THE FIRST STEP IN YOUR COACHING MODEL:

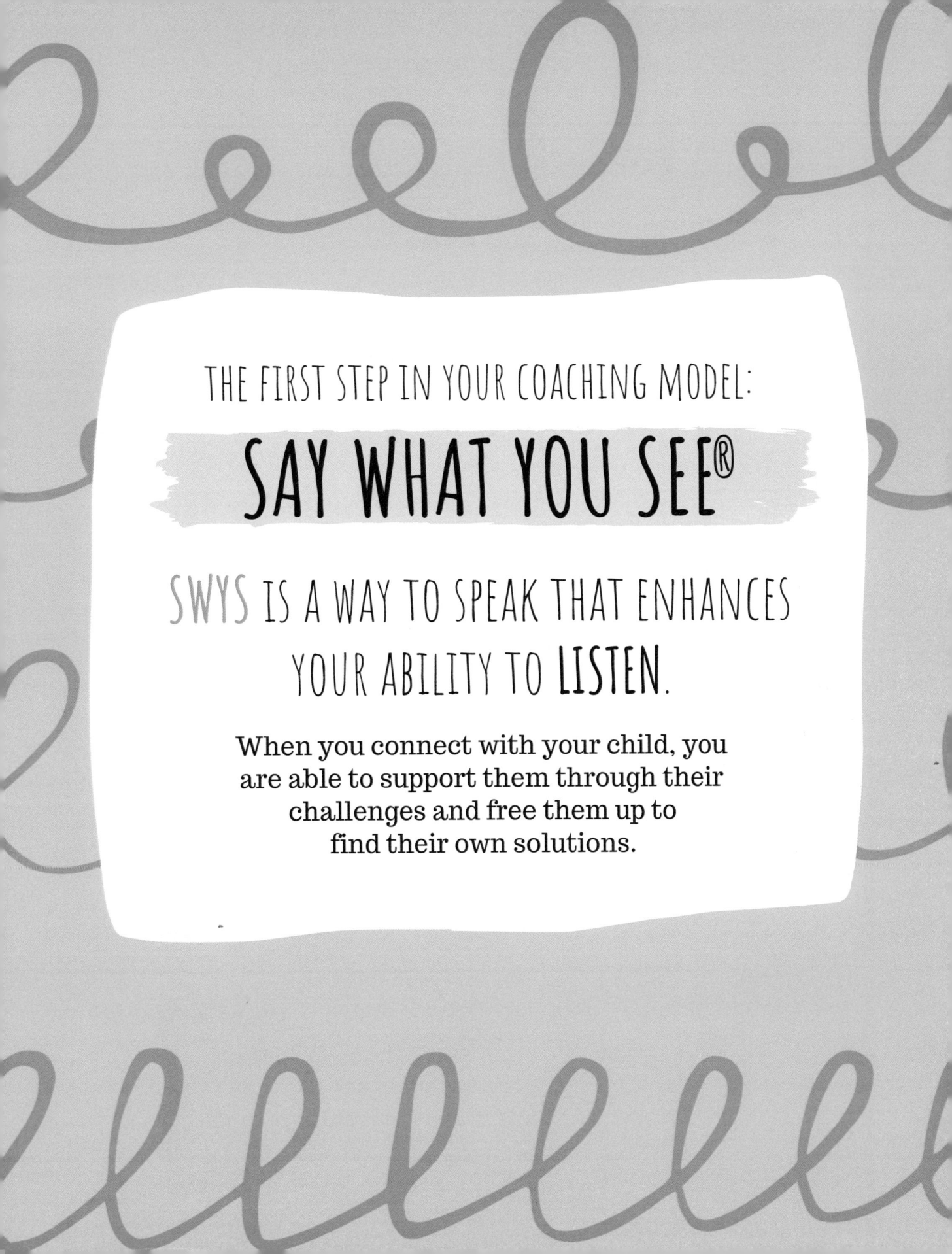

SAY WHAT YOU SEE®

SWYS IS A WAY TO SPEAK THAT ENHANCES YOUR ABILITY TO **LISTEN**.

When you connect with your child, you are able to support them through their challenges and free them up to find their own solutions.

SAY WHAT YOU SEE

The first step in the coaching model I will teach you is all about connection. It's the most overlooked step in parenting – the step of connection, understanding and validation.

The coaching tool is called SAY WHAT YOU SEE because you literally just say what is right there in front of you. You say out loud what your child is doing, saying, feeling or thinking.

It's the first thing you do every time you have an interaction with your child. It allows you to stay in the present moment and observe. Just pause a moment before you react, and SAY WHAT YOU SEE.

It changes how you SEE and interact with your child. It helps you reinterpret situations and SEE your child's behaviour in new ways.

Normally, in an interaction with your child, you see things your way, and they see things theirs. SWYS gets you out of your head into the neutral space in the middle where you can meet your child in the physical world of the here and now and, from there, step into guidance.

When I was really struggling with my daughter's out of control behaviour, I started using SWYS and saw changes almost immediately. As I stepped into her perspective, I saw my daughter in a new light. She wasn't just a child acting out; she had her own struggles and worries. I had been so focused on my point of view that I had missed hers entirely.

During a calm moment, I asked her why she had started to listen to me, and she replied, *'Because you get me mummy. You understand me.'*

It is ONLY when your child feels that you 'get' them that they will be able to move on, accept your guidance and find solutions that work for the both of you.

The general purpose of SAY WHAT YOU SEE is to understand and connect.

The reason this is so important is because:

> 'Everything children do and say is a communication. Children must continue to communicate until they're heard.'

This is the first premise of Language of Listening. What it tells you is that children cannot listen unless they're heard first.

Ever notice your child getting louder, whining more, stamping their feet, back chatting? That's your child acting out a communication, a message to you. And if you don't listen and **SAY WHAT YOU SEE**, you give your child no other option than to escalate their behaviour.

So often, we dismiss this behaviour as manipulative, just our child trying to get their way. I like looking at it as our child just trying to feel heard and understood.

I call this the broken loop because, if you don't close the loop, if you don't hear what your child is trying to communicate, you give your child no other option than to increase the whining, crying, fussing or backchat to make their point.

When your child feels heard, the acting out can stop, and your child can move on. That is why **SWYS** is always, always the first thing you do. It gets your child heard.

It's the most important step.

It's the first step to understanding your child. You can and should still hold your boundaries, but if you start by acknowledging your child's wants, you'll be surprised at the difference it makes.

So many of my clients tell me that using this first step drastically changes their child's unwanted behaviour in moments.

Plus, this **SWYS** step of connection sets you up for success with the two guidance steps of your 3-step coaching model: **CAN DOs** and **STRENGTHs**. I'll show you how to use those later in the workbook.

How the 3 steps sound with young children

2-year-old Polly and 4-year-old Bertie were having a kerfuffle over a pair of swimming goggles. Bertie wanted the goggles his little sister was wearing. *'I want them!'* he said and tried to grab them from her. She started screeching. He tried to grab them again.

SWYS: *'You want the goggles. They look fun!'* I said.

'Yes!' Bertie replied.

SWYS: *'Your sister is wearing them.'*

> Remember to always start with **SWYS**. It helps you to remove judgement and build connection, so your child is open to your guidance.

Then comes the all-purpose **CAN DO** statement: *'Hmm, there must be something you can do to have a turn.'*

'Can I have a turn?' He asks his sister. *'No!'* she screeches again.

SWYS + **CAN DO**: *'Hmm! She wants to wear them. Must be something else you can do.'*

He runs off to look in the swimming bag and holds up another pair of goggles. *'You can have these,'* he says to his sister.

'OK!' she says smiling and willingly takes her pair off. *'Here, I'll help you put them on,'* he says to his sister. They swap goggles, laugh and play together.

I concluded by pointing out his **STRENGTHs**: *'You knew what you wanted, and you found a way to get it. That shows you're a problem-solver. And you looked after your sister. That shows how thoughtful you are.'*

This last step is so important since pointing out **STRENGTHs** is what helps your child gain proof of their abilities. Children decide who they are based on what they do, so that proof also changes who they think they are and their inner voice. (Your inner voice is what you say to yourself as your self-talk. It reveals what you think about yourself and the world, and influences your decisions, reactions and emotions.)

Bertie's now sounds like this: *'I know what I want and how to get it in a way that works for everyone. I'm a problem-solver. I'm thoughtful.'* And that inner voice will help guide his actions next time.

You know that moment could have gone a completely different way. If I had tried to manage his behaviour with threats or warnings or tried to teach him a lesson about how grabbing wasn't kind, he probably would have learnt that he was not kind and that he just needed to get better at not getting caught next time.

But by using coaching skills instead, I was able to quickly and easily put him in touch with who he really was and set him on a new path that he immediately began following naturally on his own.

How the 3 steps sound with older children and teens

Although what you say is slightly different when interacting with older children, your responses are still based on the same 3 steps. Your goal is to be authentic, connect and find solutions together.

Here are a few examples of interactions with my 14-year-old daughter and 16-year-old son.

Example of getting ready for school on time:

SWYS + STRENGTH: *'I noticed you always make it to the car on time. That shows you're responsible.'*

SWYS: *'AND I've noticed you love staying in bed for as long as possible.'*

BOUNDARY / CAN DO: *'When you leave coming downstairs to the last minute, getting to the car becomes hectic and things are sometimes forgotten. I'm wondering if there's something you can do to have a few minutes buffer so you're not leaving it to the last minute.'*

We discuss possible CAN DO solutions. Now, she leaves a spare tie and hairbrush in the car! Notice how I didn't change her wish of staying in bed as long as possible? She came up with an idea that worked for her, and my boundary of leaving the house on time was honoured.

Example of screen time and homework:

STRENGTH: *'Your friends mean a lot to you. You love playing together.'*

SWYS: *'Playing video games is one of the ways you connect and have fun together.'*

BOUNDARY / CAN DO: *'AND I've noticed homework is being pushed back to nearly bedtime and being rushed. There must be another way to get homework done and not miss out on playing with your friends.'*

He came up with a solution to split his homework in two so he had less to do after dinner.

Notice how I stated a STRENGTH before the boundary? Pointing out a STRENGTH first allows you to see what your child is doing right in that situation and connects them with their best intentions and character strengths.

> Pointing out a STRENGTH is essential with older children. This step meets their need for power, demonstrates respect, puts you on their side, and leads straight into problem-solving.
>
> It also models how to see the best in each other. Over time, you'll find that they repeat that back to you and show you the same respect.

A quick example with a teen:

'I'm not staying here! I can't believe there's NOOOO internet. How am I going to listen to music or speak to my friends?! This is stupid!' My 13-year-old daughter stormed off to the car.

We'd just arrived at the campsite after a long drive, and this was NOT what I was in the mood to deal with.

I had flashes of disaster as I was putting the tent up, imagining her refusing to do anything we had planned on our camping trip or being in a sulk the whole time. I so wanted us to have a fun family trip together.

In the past, I would have said something like: *'Do you know how ungrateful you are?'* or even *'You're ruining it for everyone. It's no big deal you don't have good wi-fi.'* But I knew those words would just add fuel to the fire and cause more of the behaviour I didn't want.

And if I had responded to her behaviour through the eyes of judgement, I wouldn't have seen my struggling girl. I would have felt annoyed and resentful and had a compulsion to control her or fix the situation.

Instead, I reminded myself that this was a tough transition for my children who are used to being hooked up to wi-fi 24/7.

So how did I respond? I used SAY WHAT YOU SEE.

SWYS: *'That sucks! You hate not being in contact with your friends.'*

As I watched, she kicked her legs up on the dashboard, her tears begin to flow as she felt safe to let out her frustrations and upsets, and she began to adapt to the situation. Within 10 minutes, she jumped out of the car, gave me a massive hug, and without waiting to be asked, started to unload the car!

With kids of any age, this step has the amazing ability to help you stay out of judgement. It helps you see the world through your child's eyes.

SAY WHAT YOU SEE helps children adapt.

When we give our children permission to be, when we don't jump in to fix the situation or use guilt or shame to change their behaviour, we give them the space they need to adapt.

Look out and see how relaxed and content your child looks after crying (when they are allowed to get it all out). Then remember to SAY WHAT YOU SEE and point out the STRENGTH:

SWYS: *'You got all your tears out, and now you're smiling.'*

STRENGTH: *'You knew just what you needed to calm yourself.'*

When you finish your interaction by pointing out STRENGTHs, it helps your child recognise their greatness. It leaves your child feeling great about who they are.

They get to have an inner voice that says, *'I can trust myself. I know exactly what I need to calm myself. I can handle any big emotion. I'm resilient!'*

And not to mention, you will have a much calmer and simpler time holding your boundaries than you would if you were trying to control or fix things for your child.

A quick example with a young child:

My 5-year-old son shouted, *'I'm not doing it! You can't make me. I've changed my mind!'*

After waiting almost an hour in line for a rollercoaster at Lego Land, he decided to refuse just as our turn approached. Great!

A well-meaning family member started saying things like: *'You'll be OK. Come on! we came here for you. We waited in line for hours, and you're not going?! Really?! Don't be a scaredy-cat.'*

Well, that tactic didn't go down well. (Using guilt and shame is never a good motivator.) Tears welled up, and my son refused even more.

So how did I respond? I immediately validated his experience with SAY WHAT YOU SEE.

SWYS: *'We've been waiting in line, and all you can hear is the squeaky wheels going round the tracks and people screaming. No wonder you're a bit apprehensive. You're wondering, "Do I or don't I go!"'*

'YES!' he replied. *'Let me take a breath! OK! let's go! I can do it!'* And he leapt into the next car.

That's the magic of SWYS. When children don't need to justify how they feel, they don't escalate their reactions to prove to you how right they are. It allows them to move forward more freely.

Here are a few more examples of SAY WHAT YOU SEE.

Use this list as ideas for what you can say. The more you communicate this way, the easier it becomes to make **SWYS** your own.

SAY WHAT YOU SEE helps you focus on what IS happening because you can't **SEE** something that is NOT happening.

For example, you can't see 'not sharing'. Not sharing is what you THINK is happening. Sharing might be what you wish would be happening, but what IS your child doing? Are they busy playing?

INSTEAD OF... *'You're NOT sharing.'*
    SWYS: *'You're busy playing.'*

INSTEAD OF... *'How many times do I have to tell you to stop messing around and get your shoes on?!'*
    SWYS: *'One shoe on. You're halfway! Only one more shoe to go.'*

INSTEAD OF... *'Will you two just cut it out? You're always fighting!'*
    SWYS: *'You're fighting over whose turn it is. Looks like you both want a turn.'*

INSTEAD OF... *'Stop snatching toys! That's not kind.'*
    SWYS: *'You want the toy, and Sally is playing with it.'*

INSTEAD OF... *'That's not nice! Stop whining. You're making mummy sad.'*
    SWYS: *'You have something important to tell me. You don't think I understand.'*

INSTEAD OF... *'I don't care. We're leaving the park now! We come here all the time. What's the big deal? Don't fuss. If you stop crying now, you can have ice cream after dinner!'*
    SWYS: *'You want to keep playing. It's hard to leave. You wish we could stay here all day.'*

INSTEAD OF... *'Don't you give me attitude! You will listen to me right now!'*
    SWYS: *'Wow! To speak to me like that you must be feeling really frustrated.'*

INSTEAD OF... *'You know the rules! Cut it out. I'm not interested in what you've got to say.'*
    SWYS: *'You're so mad! You're finding it hard to stop yourself.'*

INSTEAD OF... *'No new toys today! You're so spoilt! How many times do I have to tell you "NO"?!'*
    SWYS: *'You're showing me with your tears how much you want that toy. You're so disappointed.'*

INSTEAD OF... *'How many times do I have to shout for you to do as I ask?'*
    SWYS: *'It seems like we're both feeling unheard.'*

INSTEAD OF... *'Sit down, and stop fussing.'*
    SWYS: *'You've finished eating. You want to get up and play.'*

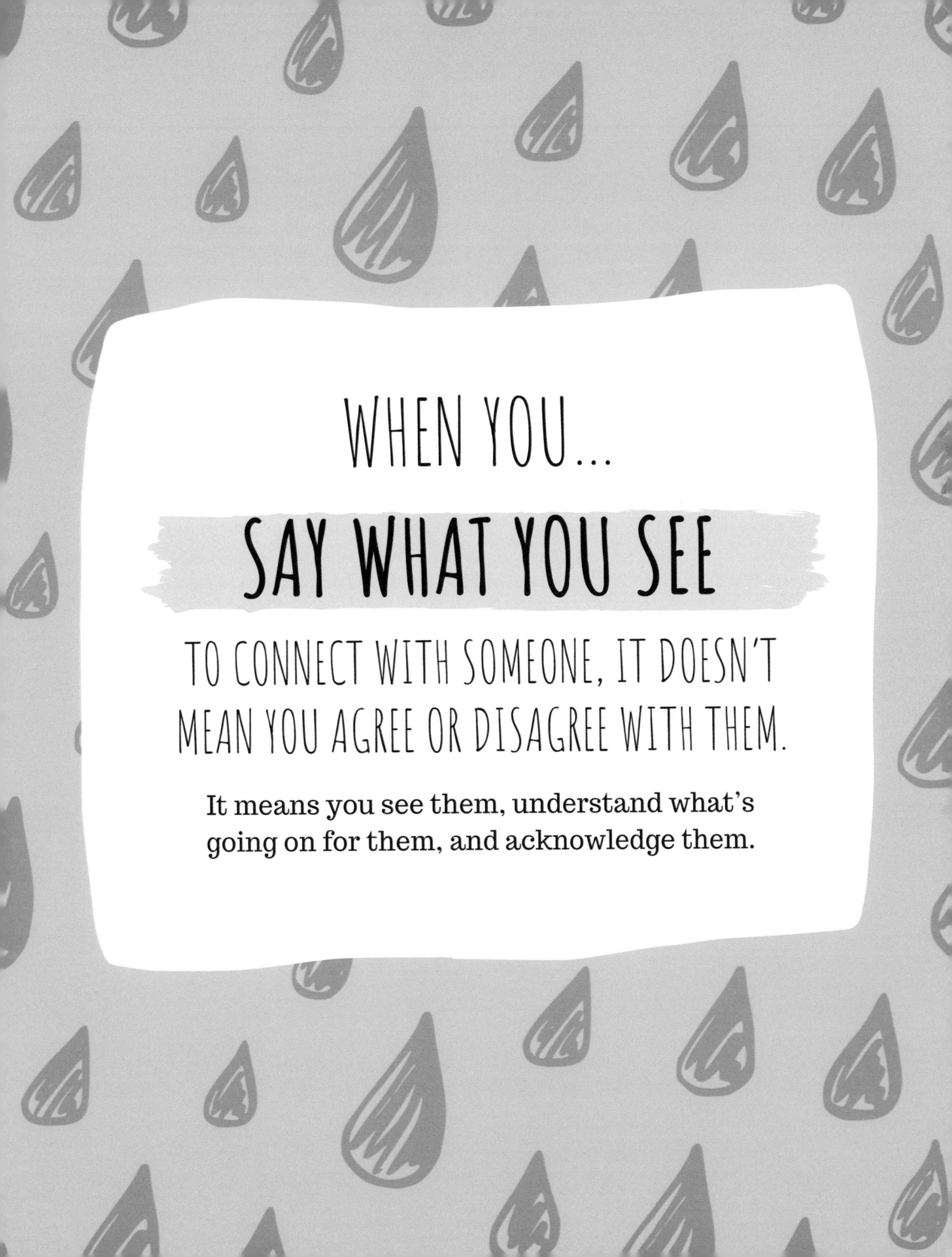

WHEN YOU...
SAY WHAT YOU SEE
TO CONNECT WITH SOMEONE, IT DOESN'T MEAN YOU AGREE OR DISAGREE WITH THEM.

It means you see them, understand what's going on for them, and acknowledge them.

FOUR TYPES OF
SAY WHAT YOU SEE RESPONSES

SAY WHAT YOU SEE your child DOING.

Describe what your child is doing as if you're a sportscaster giving a running commentary.

'You found something to do.'
'You're putting your PJs on. Only one thing left to do till story time.'
'You're practising your dance routine; you're determined to get it right.'
'You found a way to solve that tricky maths problem.'
'You're fighting over whose turn it is.'
'You're waiting, and you hate it! Feels like it's never going to happen!'
'You're grabbing the toy, and it belongs to someone else.'
'You've set the table.'
'You found a way to make that work.'

> **Practise SWYS your child DOING.** *Notice if your neutral description helps you stay calm or helps you see your child's actions from their perspective.*
>
> 1) Picture your child doing something you like, and without judgement, describe what they are DOING. Start your commentary with *'You…'*
>
> 2) Repeat the exercise several times.
>
> 3) Repeat steps 1 and 2, picturing your child doing something you **don't** like.

SAY WHAT YOU SEE your child SAYING.

Repeat back what your child is saying or only repeat the important words. Watch for their reaction – a nod, a smile of recognition, telling you more etc. If you hear a message (want, wish, intention) behind your child's words, you can say that.

'You picked these flowers just for me.' OR say: *'Just for me!'*
'You're letting me know you'd really like to read this book first.' OR: *'This book first!'*
'Oh, you offered to help your friend with their homework.'
'You wanted to have a turn.' OR: *'A turn. Of course you did!'*
'You wish you didn't have to go to school.'
'You don't want to get wet and have a bath.'
'You don't want to share. Sounds like you might not be done playing with it yet.'
'You're shouting to make sure I hear you! You must be angry to speak to me like that!'

Practise SWYS your child SAYING. *Notice if repeating their words helps you stay calm or helps you understand the message behind their words.*

1) Picture your child saying something you like, and without judgement, repeat what they are SAYING, just the important words, or the message behind it. Start your commentary with *'You...'* except when only repeating the important words.

2) Repeat the exercise several times.

3) Repeat steps 1 and 2 picturing your child saying something you **don't** like.

SAY WHAT YOU SEE your child FEELING.

Pay attention to your child's facial expression and body language, and name the feeling to validate it. Use a range of emotion words and match the intensity of your child's feelings with your response.

'You're so frustrated, and you just want to do your own thing.'
'You feel so proud because you remembered this time!'
'You're feeling scared of the dark.'
'You're so annoyed! You want to keep watching, and it's Sophie's turn to choose a show.'
'You're all cosy in bed, and you don't want to get up.'
'You are so disappointed you can't have it.'
'You just need to be sad about it for a little while.'
'You're feeling happy. You like that!'

> **Practise SWYS your child FEELING.** Notice if naming the feeling helps you stay calm or helps you allow your child to feel what they are feeling. (I'll teach you how to help your child find acceptable ways to express their feelings with CAN DOs later.)
>
> 1) Picture your child feeling an emotion you like, and without judgement, name what they are FEELING. Start your response with 'You...'
>
> 2) Repeat the exercise several times.
>
> 3) Repeat steps 1 and 2, picturing your child feeling an emotion you **don't** like.

SAY WHAT YOU SEE your child THINKING.

You can't go wrong here. If you say what you think your child is thinking, they will be sure to let you know if you are wrong. Keep going because understanding builds a deep connection with your child.

'Looks like you're not stopping until you're done.'
'Looks like you are planning to go somewhere.'
'Sounds like you find that really tricky.'
'Sounds like you want to tell me something first.'
'Feels like a big challenge for you.'
'Feels like you think that's really unfair. You wish that hadn't happened.'
'Seems like you're always being told what to do, and you want to choose for once.'
'Seems like, to you, your brother is always in your way.'

> **Practise SWYS your child THINKING.** Notice if looking for what they might be thinking helps you stay calm or helps you understand your child's intentions or perspective better.
>
> 1) Picture your child doing, saying, or feeling something you like, and without judgement, say what they might be thinking about it. Start your commentary with *'Looks like…'*, *'Sounds like…'*, *'Feels like…'*, or *'Seems like…'*
>
> 2) Repeat the exercise several times.
>
> 3) Repeat steps 1 and 2, picturing your child doing, saying, or feeling something you **don't** like.

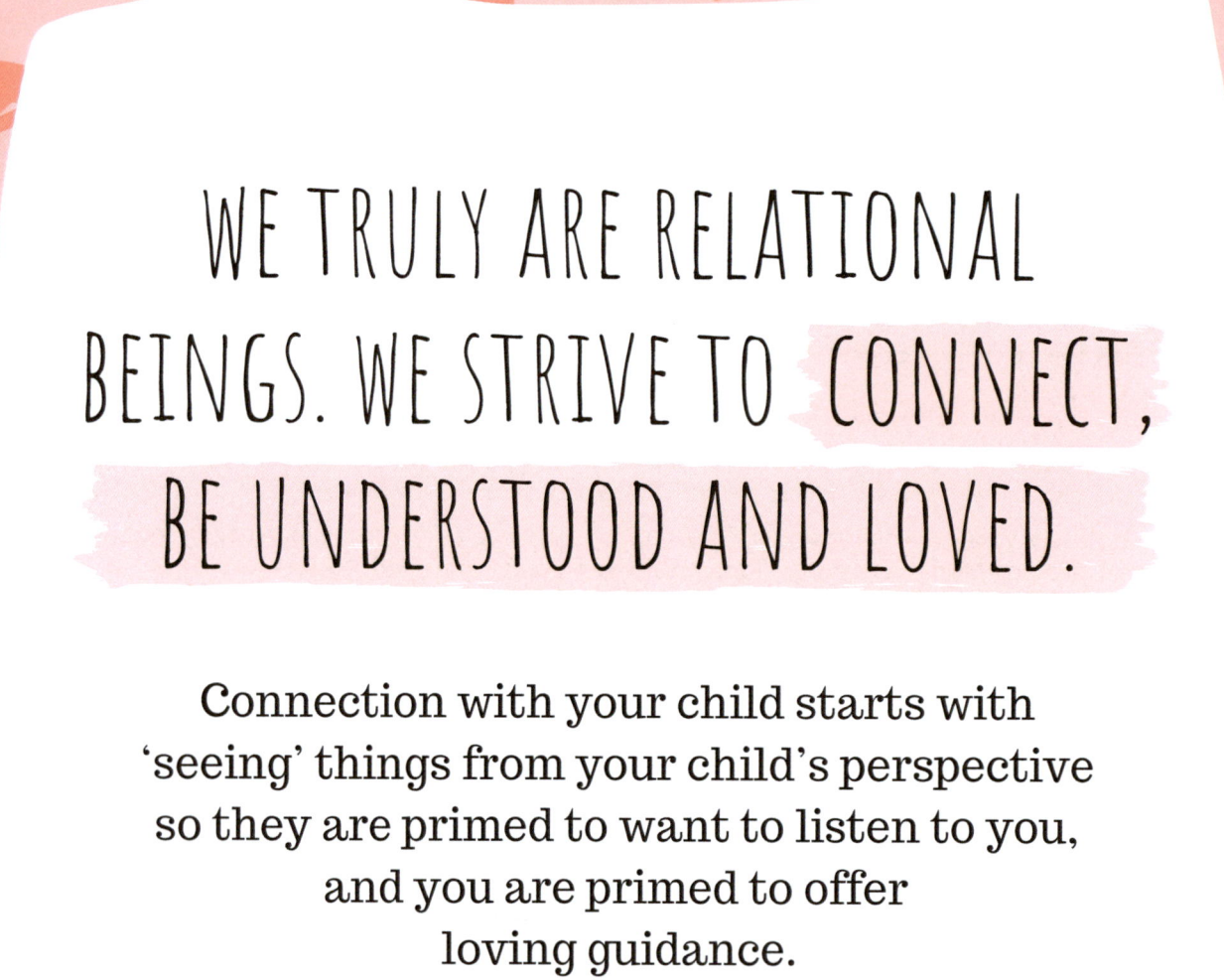

WE TRULY ARE RELATIONAL BEINGS. WE STRIVE TO CONNECT, BE UNDERSTOOD AND LOVED.

Connection with your child starts with 'seeing' things from your child's perspective so they are primed to want to listen to you, and you are primed to offer loving guidance.

Validating your child's feelings, wishes, wants and way of seeing the world means acknowledging your child in the moment.

Validation is not about fixing, correcting, teaching a lesson or advising.

Validation is about understanding your child, seeing things from their point of view and acknowledging their experiences. **SAYing WHAT YOU SEE** is the quickest way to help your child feel seen, heard and understood. It's this that builds deep connection and trust with your child.

All four types of **SWYS** responses can be connective at any age. Just follow your child's focus. If they are focused on what they are **doing**, say that. If they are focused on what they are **saying**, say that. The same with **feeling or thinking**. If they switch back and forth, you do too.

When you follow your child's focus, you will meet them right where they are. Over time, you will likely see what I've seen – the older kids get, the more they want the deeper connection that comes from having what they **feel** and **think** validated. (Trust me. This becomes easier with practice!)

Validation with SWYS can sound like this:

'Oh, no! You really want that cup, and we left it at Grandma's.'

'Oh, you want to have a bath, and you don't want to get wet.'

'You wish those peas weren't even on your plate.'

'You're so frustrated that your brother keeps bugging you to play with him. You don't like that.'

'You've had a five-minute warning, and you're still watching TV. Looks like it's hard to stop.'

'You wish you'd got ten out of ten in your spelling test.'

'You feel like you don't get enough time alone with me.'

'Seems like you don't like the decision I made. You wish I would change my mind.'

'You didn't think that would happen.'

'School starts so early. You hate early mornings.'

'You're a homebody! You'd rather stay at home.'

'That's annoying.'

'That's frustrating!'

'You wish...'

'You want...'

'You don't like that...'

SAY WHAT YOU SEE REMINDERS

Learning a new language takes time.

If you're validating your child with SAY WHAT YOU SEE, following the steps, trying your best, and not seeing quick results, you may feel like giving up or like it isn't for you. Please don't stop!

This takes time. It's called **Language of Listening** for a reason; it truly is a new language. And on top of that, you probably have years of old conditioning. Your brain has not been programmed to think or see things this way, so speaking this language can feel like mental gymnastics.

Learning is a process. It takes time. If your child isn't listening, it doesn't mean you're failing; it means you have more practice to do. And the great thing is, your kids will give you lots of chances!

SWYS is for you.

If you find yourself thinking, *'I've said what you told me to say, and it's not "working". My child isn't listening or doing what I ask,'* it could be that you're trying to use SWYS to get your child to DO something. No wonder it feels frustrating! This step is NOT meant to be used to get your child to DO anything. (That's what the guidance steps I'll teach you later are for – CAN DOs and STRENGTHs.)

SWYS is more for YOU. It's about changing what YOU see and how YOU respond. It's about walking around inside your child's world. Staying neutral and descriptive can help you feel calmer and more confident. Start to notice how YOU feel. If you don't feel different yet, that's OK. Pause, keep practising, and pay attention to your thoughts and intentions.

Practise SWYS in the easy moments.

If you find it hard to SWYS in the heat of a tricky situation, practise when all is calm. Print out the examples and stick them up somewhere you can see them daily. Start training your brain to look for what IS happening, not what is NOT happening or your thoughts or fears about it.

Do-overs retrain your brain.

It's OK to stop yourself mid-sentence. *'Zip your lip,'* as my kids call it! Then start again. Do-overs retrain your brain. You can say, *'Oops! That didn't come out quite right. Let's start over.'*

Starting over when things don't go to plan is also great modelling for your child. And it shows you noticed! Awareness is the first step towards change. Before picking up this workbook, I bet another way to respond wasn't even in your subconscious. And now, you know how – SWYS.

It's OK for your child to be upset.

If your child is upset, tantrums, cries, slams doors, shouts at you etc, it's not a failure or a reflection on your parenting. With your support and coaching, your child will gain the skills they need to manage their own behaviour.

Repetition changes habits.

If you're finding being present in the moment with your child tricky and feel yourself slipping back to telling off, threats and punishments, remember this is normal. Your brain likes predictability; it likes what feels familiar.

Repetition is how you make long-lasting change. The more you practise staying in the moment and seeing things through your child's eyes, the easier it becomes. You're literally reprogramming your brain.

Do the groundwork. It takes time to change your habits. Remember, you don't react to your child and the situation, you react to your beliefs and assumptions. Spend time becoming aware of your thoughts and judgements, and you'll find that using the tools becomes more natural.

Parenting is a marathon, not a sprint. You are giving your child skills for life, not just controlling the moment.

Keep reading. There's more to come!

Reading through this workbook gives you new knowledge that, by itself, is superficial. It takes implementing, talking about and practising these new ideas and tools for them to become wired into your brain and part of your biology. As you integrate them, you'll gain new insights and more awareness.

Learning Language of Listening is a journey. You now have an idea of where you're heading and the path you want to take. Think of this workbook as your guidebook. Sometimes, you're going to get off the path, take a detour, slip up and fall off the wagon. This doesn't mean you've failed. It means you need to jump back on the wagon and get back on the path. The more proof you gain that your new tools are making a difference, the easier it will be to stay on the path.

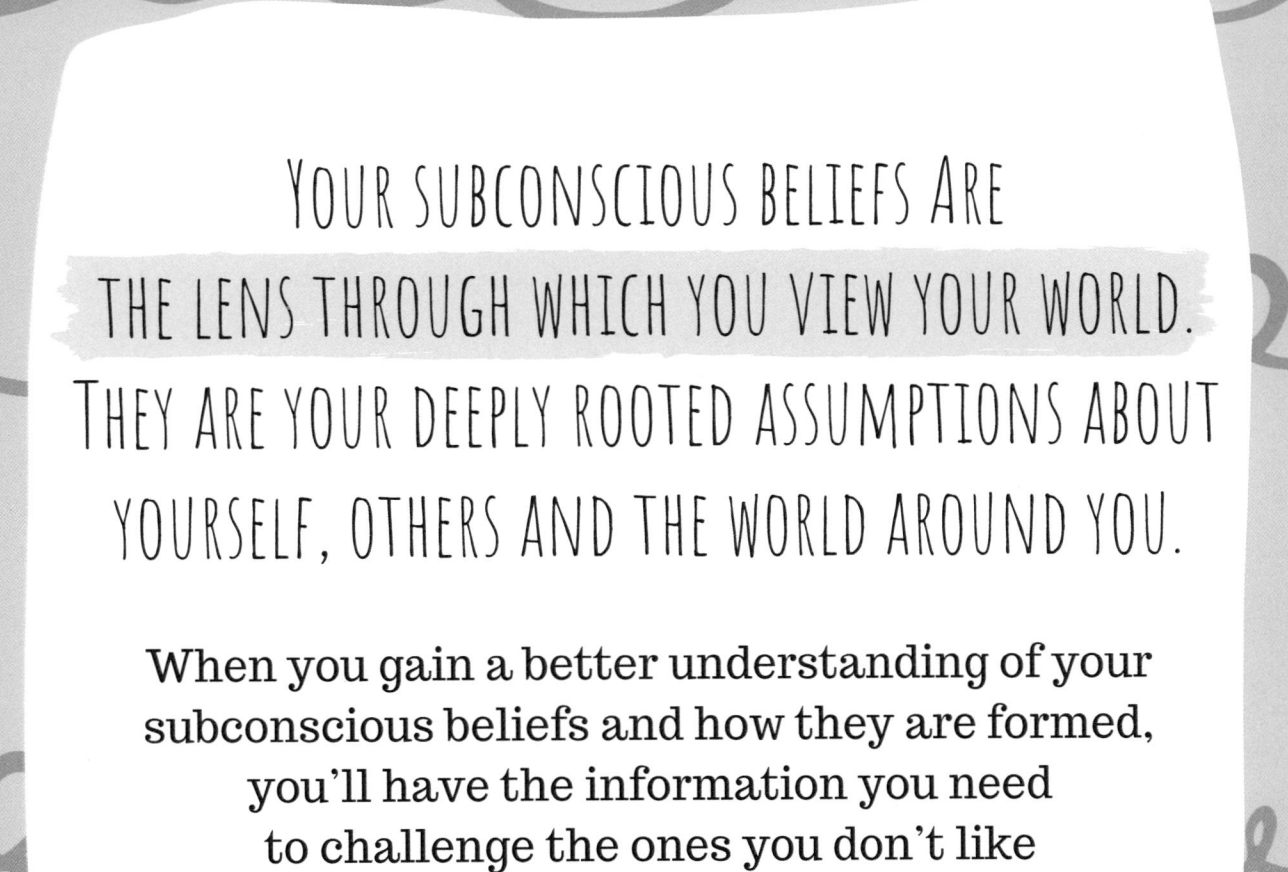

Your subconscious beliefs Are the lens through which you view your world. They are your deeply rooted assumptions about yourself, others and the world around you.

When you gain a better understanding of your subconscious beliefs and how they are formed, you'll have the information you need to challenge the ones you don't like and develop healthier ones.

HOW BELIEFS ARE FORMED

Little Ava was jumping up and down, refusing to go down the big slide. *'I don't want to!'* she wailed. *'I'm scared.'*

'Don't be a silly billy! Slide, and I'll catch you!' Her daddy replied. *'You just need to concentrate. Be brave.'*

These little interactions fascinate me. Little snippets of life, little interactions that seem so insignificant by themselves, yet collectively, how we respond to our children forms the foundation of their beliefs.

When we're young, we believe what we are told. We lack the ability to recognise the difference between truths and untruths. We have a different kind of logic and reasoning – very present-minded and literal. I remember my son looking at my wedding photos. He got upset when he couldn't see himself in the photos even though he hadn't been born yet! Remember, to a child, 'now' is all there is!

Our interactions and experiences shape our beliefs, values, and perception of the world and ourselves.

> Beliefs can be beliefs we like (positive) or beliefs we don't like (negative). Beliefs are typically formed in two ways:
>
> - Based on our childhood thoughts and conclusions about our experiences and the things we see other people do.
>
> - By accepting what other people tell us to be true.

Let's look at how negative beliefs become fixed as our 'truths.'

In the big slide example, Ava is scared of sliding down. She has that funny feeling in her tummy warning her that something doesn't feel right. She doesn't understand that her daddy is just trying to reassure and encourage her. All she hears with her child logic is that she's being silly. There's nothing to be scared of.

And at other times, when she doesn't want to wear her coat, she's told everyone else is cold, so she must be too. When her food burns her mouth, she's told her food can't be that hot. When she doesn't want to kiss Grandma, she's told don't be silly. It's Grandma's house; you have to do what she wants.

Every time her parents respond to her in this way, even though she doesn't quite like it, she starts to take what they say to be the truth. She starts to build a picture of who she is and the 'rules' of life. This is how she sows the seeds of a negative belief, a belief she doesn't like.

She starts to believe that being scared is silly, that she can't trust how she feels or even the messages her body sends her about hot and cold, and that others know better.

Each time she overrides her feelings and body messages and pushes away her own needs, she's praised by her parents for it. So, she starts to believe that ignoring her internal guidance is required to be loved and accepted. The more these experiences happen, the more firmly ingrained her beliefs become. And the more Ava accepts those beliefs to be true about herself, the more they are reinforced in her subconscious mind.

Once formed, our early beliefs become firmly fixed. They become absolute truths and just 'the way things are'. In fact, our early beliefs are so convincing that, as we grow, our mind gathers evidence to prove them right. They become the unconscious lens through which we see and experience life (see Confirmation Bias, page 89).

Here's another example of how negative beliefs are formed.

Oliver grew up with a very controlling mother. He wasn't allowed to make his own choices, and if he shared an opinion or expressed his big emotions, he was told he was being disrespectful.

Oliver's mother repeated what her parents did to parent her. She would take away his favourite toys, tell him he was naughty and send him to his room as punishment. Oliver learnt it wasn't safe to share his emotions or wants with his mother.

In order to feel safe, children often use ineffective coping mechanisms to manage their parents' behaviour. On the surface, Oliver's mother may think he's being a 'good boy', but in fact, he's learnt to adapt his behaviour to please his mother and stay out of trouble.

Each time he's corrected or punished, Oliver learns not to trust his decisions and detach from what he wants and desires. He learns to hide his emotions and needs. He acts a certain way with his mother to try to gain her approval. At a subconscious level, he concludes that he's not good enough and that his wants and needs don't matter.

Fear-based beliefs like these are planted when children interpret their parent's behaviour as their own fault. 'If I were good enough, then my mother would love me.'

Oliver, like all children, didn't think his parents' actions were the problem. He thought it was his fault. This is how children begin to sow the seeds of negative beliefs.

As a result, this became Oliver's inner voice:
- ✗ *'I am not good enough.'*
- ✗ *'I'm not worthy of love.'*
- ✗ *'What I want doesn't matter.'*
- ✗ *'I'm bad.'*
- ✗ *'People will reject me if I show them my true feelings, wants or needs.'*

Our childhood beliefs carry into adulthood.

Oliver's subconscious beliefs acquired in childhood became the lens through which he viewed his world. With those in place, when he became a parent himself, he found it hard to deal with his children's big emotions because he'd never learnt to deal with his own.

While others could view a child expressing big emotions as a child learning to handle disappointment and frustration, Oliver viewed his child's display of big emotions as proof that he was not a good enough parent and unworthy. He felt rejected. He believed that his own children weren't good enough, were naughty and needed to be punished to learn self-control, so he repeated the same cycle of punishments with his children that he'd experienced.

In other areas of his life, Oliver found it hard to have deep, meaningful relationships. He withdrew from conflict and found it difficult to stand up for himself. When he felt big emotions, he shut down and wanted to hide, just like when he was a child being sent to his room. He stuffed his emotions down by overeating and drinking.

As you can see from Oliver's story, our beliefs are powerful. Our beliefs can impact our reactions and behaviour in different situations. Even when those situations are not directly related to our past experiences, beliefs in our subconscious can affect every aspect of our lives.

By becoming aware of our ingrained thought patterns and replacing them with fresh insights about our own capabilities, we can become conscious of our negative beliefs, shift our perceptions, and open up and change the lens through which we view the world.

Let's look at an example of how positive beliefs are formed.

Our interactions with our children can sow the seeds of positive beliefs. Sarah grew up with supportive parents, they nurtured her independence and loved her unconditionally.

Her parents coached her:
- To get her needs met in healthy ways
- To handle her emotions and not be scared of them
- To regulate her emotions and feel them fully
- To problem-solve and find solutions
- To see the possibilities in life
- To see the best in herself and gain confidence in her abilities

Her parents sowed the seeds of positive beliefs.

As a result, Sarah developed a positive inner voice:
- 'I am good enough.'
- 'I'm worthy of love, even when I've got big emotions and act in ways I later regret.'
- 'What I want matters, and I know how to find solutions to get what I want.'
- 'People will listen and support me when I show them my true feelings, wants or needs.'

She learnt to bring out her self-control and manage her own behaviour. She shared her true wants and desires with her parents. She became effective at problem-solving, going after what she wanted in life and seeing the best in herself.

As you can see from Sarah's story, early subconscious beliefs are powerful. They became the lens through which she viewed her world and set her on the road to success, happiness and a more enriched life as an adult. When she became a parent, she was able to pass them on to her daughter as her parents had done for her.

Our subconscious beliefs, positive or negative, get passed on to our child.

Our subconscious beliefs and underlying assumptions send messages to our brain telling us who we are and how the world works. They are hidden beneath our thoughts. Often, they are so well hidden that we're unaware we even have them.

But as you can see from Oliver's and Sarah's examples, positive and negative beliefs formed in childhood carry into adulthood. When we become parents, we unknowingly project them onto our child in the form of our judgments and assumptions, and automatically react to those thoughts as if they are real.

Then from our reactions, our children decide who they are and how the world works... That's how our subconscious beliefs get passed on from generation to generation.

In order to raise healthy, self-worthy and confident children, we need to become aware of and question our negative beliefs.

> **You can recognise a negative belief by your reaction. When you react in a way you don't like, pause and reflect on the thought behind it.**
>
> **Questioning your assumptions and beliefs helps you dig deeper. Simply recognising that childhood is the source of a negative belief can help you change it.**

As you grow your awareness of your subconscious beliefs, you'll be able to appreciate your positive beliefs more and react from your negative beliefs less.

Notice how our subconscious beliefs are the lens through which we view our world.

They affect the way we make sense of our experiences and how we react to them. Our reactions then prove our beliefs are correct, and on and on this cycle plays out in our lives:

MISTAKEN NEGATIVE BELIEFS

I'm not good enough

I can't cope

I'm powerless

I don't matter

I'm doing it wrong

PARENT'S THOUGHT PROCESS

Everyone else finds it easy; what's the matter with me?

I'm always messing things up; I'm so stupid for making that mistake; I can't do anything right

My child is manipulating me

I'm a failure

BELIEFS PROJECTED ONTO CHILD

My child is bad, naughty, needs to be punished or taught a lesson

My child is out of control, needs to be controlled

My child can't cope

PARENT'S BEHAVIOUR

No confidence making decisions or setting boundaries

No emotional regulation skills to pass on to child – child doesn't learn to cope, feels powerless over his feelings and escalates to tantrum level

Reacts with anger or anxiety, reinforcing existing beliefs

Avoids conflict

Oliver's Example: Oliver developed a subconscious belief that he was never good enough, so no matter what he did, he was never able to please anyone.

When Oliver had his own son, he was determined to be the kind of parent that he never had. He wanted to give his son all the love and support that he never received. However, when his son began to display challenging behaviour, Oliver found it difficult to understand the reasons for these actions.

Despite his best efforts to be a good father, Oliver couldn't shake the feeling that he wasn't good enough. He projected his subconscious belief onto his son, which led him to perceive his child as naughty and not good enough. In his eyes, his son's behaviour was confirmation that he was a bad parent.

Notice the difference in how the projection cycle plays out when the subconscious beliefs are positive.

POSITIVE BELIEFS

I'm good enough

I'm a problem-solver

I can trust myself

What I want matters

PARENT'S THOUGHT PROCESS

I wonder why my child would react like this?

I can find ways to support my child

What my child wants matter too

BELIEFS PROJECTED ONTO CHILD

My child is good enough

My child can learn to solve her own problems

My child can trust herself

PARENT'S BEHAVIOUR

Tries to understand what child needs

Uses coaching skills – child gains self-control, finds acceptable ways to meet her own needs

Reacts calmly with confidence, reinforcing existing beliefs

Sarah's Example: Sarah developed a subconscious belief that she was always good enough. She saw the best in herself, so it was natural for her to see the best in others.

When Sarah had her own daughter and her daughter had challenging behaviour, she didn't take it personally. She knew that her daughter's behaviour was a normal part of child development, and she trusted in her daughter's ability to work through it.

Rather than getting frustrated or anxious, Sarah became curious about her daughter's behaviour, trying to understand what was causing the outbursts and how best she could support her.

Sarah's daughter could sense that her mother trusted her and believed in her, which helped her feel more secure and loved. As Sarah coached her daughter, she was modelling problem-solving skills and emotional intelligence. By watching Sarah stay calm and patient, her daughter learnt how to do the same.

Do any of these resonate?

Put a tick next to the ones that stand out for you.

Negative Beliefs	Negative beliefs projected onto my child
☐ I'm worthless, not loveable.	☐ My child doesn't respect or care about me.
☐ I can't trust myself; others know better.	☐ My child can't be trusted, is manipulative.
☐ I'm not good enough.	☐ My child isn't good enough, should do more.
☐ I don't matter.	☐ My child is arrogant to think they matter.
☐ My wants don't matter; I have to give in.	☐ My child always wants their own way.
☐ You can't always get what you want.	☐ My child is stubborn, unrealistic.
☐ I'm doing it wrong.	☐ My child is doing it wrong, has to learn.
☐ Everything is my fault; I've ruined my child.	☐ My child is ruined, needs me to save them.
☐ I'm powerless, helpless.	☐ My child is helpless, needs me to fix things.
☐ I'm out of control; I need others to reign me in.	☐ My child is out of control, needs to be controlled.
☐ I can't cope.	☐ My child can't cope.
☐ I don't deserve love or good things in my life.	☐ My child has to earn love and gifts.
☐ I'm a bad person, bad parent etc., nothing I do works	☐ My child is bad, naughty, needs to be punished or taught a lesson.
☐ People will reject me if I show them my true appearance/feelings/thoughts/wants.	☐ My child's behaviour/appearance/feelings/thoughts/wants make them unacceptable.
☐ I have to make others happy or they won't want to spend time with me.	☐ My child has to change to please others, be liked, have friends.

Do any of these resonate?

Put a tick next to the ones that stand out for you.

Positive Beliefs	Positive beliefs projected onto my child
☐ I have value, am loveable.	☐ My child is respectful, cares about me.
☐ I trust myself.	☐ My child is trustworthy.
☐ I'm good enough.	☐ My child is good enough.
☐ I matter.	☐ My child knows what they want out of life.
☐ My wants matter.	☐ My child's wants matter (and so do mine).
☐ Mistakes mean I'm learning.	☐ My child is learning; mistakes are normal.
☐ I'm a problem-solver.	☐ My child is a problem-solver.
☐ I deserve to be treated with love, respect and understanding.	☐ My child deserves to be treated with love, respect and understanding.
☐ I'm interesting, beautiful, clever etc.	☐ My child is interesting, beautiful, clever etc.
☐ I'm extraordinary.	☐ My child is extraordinary.
☐ People like being with me.	☐ People like being with my child (so do I).

TAKE TIME TO REFLECT

Can you identify the influence your parents or caregivers had upon how you view yourself and your world?

Can you think back to any situations in your childhood that sowed the seeds of a negative subconscious belief for you?

Can you think back to any situations in your childhood that sowed the seeds of a positive subconscious belief for you?

NOTES

SELF-COMPASSION

Treating yourself and your kids with kindness and connection in the face of tricky situations allows you to respond with non-judgemental curiosity and emotional warmth.

Just like ALL human beings...

- We mess up and make mistakes.
- We have tricky, stressful situations.
- We have big emotions that highjack our brains.
- We can act in ways we later regret.

There is no escaping this reality. It's part of the human experience.

What's important is the way we give meaning to and judge our behaviour. Instead of seeing actions as proof we are not good enough or unworthy, we can see them as simply part of being human.

Unfortunately, the way many of us respond to our mistakes is by beating ourselves up and being self-critical.

Do any of these phrases whirl round inside your head?

- *What's the matter with you?*
- *You can't cope.*
- *You should have known better.*
- *You're stupid.*
- *You're not good enough.*
- *You'll never learn.*
- *You're acting like a baby.*
- *If you act like that, no one will like you.*

The way we talk to ourselves is influenced by our childhood and often happens automatically without us realising it. This can lead to negative feelings of not being good enough.

By ditching the negative self-talk, you can break the cycle and keep it from being passing down to your children. Responding to your own mistakes with compassion and empathy can change your inner voice for the rest of your life. How cool is that?!

It's the foundation for your future success and happiness. It helps you see you and your child's greatness and moves you on to find solutions.

When things don't go to plan, or you have a tricky situation, imagine speaking to yourself and your child with kindness, understanding, self-acceptance, love and respect.

SELF-ACCEPTANCE

You can do so much more from a place of understanding, compassion and acceptance than from
blame, shame and guilt.

Many people believe that acceptance is a sign of indifference or not taking action. It's actually the complete opposite.

Acceptance of yourself and your child does not mean you turn a blind eye to unwanted behaviour or that you resign yourself to your current situation even though you wish for things to change.

In fact, accepting yourself and your child means seeking to understand why a great person like you or your child would do something the way you do.

Let's imagine, you're struggling to get the kids to listen. Frustrations build, and you find yourself shouting at your kids. As soon as you've lost your cool, you feel guilty and annoyed with yourself.

Self-acceptance doesn't mean you ignore the guilt and carry on shouting at your kids. It means that you acknowledge that parenting is hard, relentless and exhausting, and that you don't want to shout at your kids. Then you validate yourself the same way I would validate you as your coach: *'Of course you'd shout. You felt unheard, rushed for time and powerless to get the kids out the door. Shouting is the normal human reaction to feeling stressed and powerless, and you don't like it. You want something else that works!'*

When you know that you'd like to stop shouting at the kids, instead of beating yourself up and being self-critical, you can come up with a strategy for a more peaceful school run. You can become aware of the moment just before you lose your cool and take steps to change your reaction to one you do like. (Keep reading! This workbook will give you the actionable steps and strategies.)

Now, let's imagine your child has difficulty managing their big emotions. They throw epic tantrums, refuse to do as you ask, answer you back, fight with their sibling...

Acceptance does not mean that you like, want or support the unwanted behaviour. Of course you want the behaviour to change. But before you can change any situation, you must understand what is actually happening. When you see how it makes sense, it's easy to accept, as in, *'Now I get it!'*

When you criticise, compare, blame, find fault, threaten, punish or judge your child, you're focusing on what they did wrong. Focusing on wrong things keeps you stuck. It stops you moving towards growth and acceptance.

Acceptance means you acknowledge your child for who they are and become curious about why your wonderful child would behave in that way.

It's this understanding that helps you find real solutions and support your child to grow and manage their own behaviour.

All growth is through acceptance.

The biggest breakthrough for me was accepting that my daughter had a hard time managing big emotions. There wasn't something wrong with her; I didn't need to fix her; it wasn't that I was causing it; and it wasn't a reflection of my parenting. None of that!

Accepting her for who she was helped me accept her behaviour, as in: '*Of course she would act that way. She has a hard time managing big emotions.*' That helped me acknowledge her amazingness and see her superpowers of being determined and self-directed.

Then I realised that, with my support and coaching, there would be no chance that she wouldn't learn how to regulate her emotions, calm herself down and gain confidence in her abilities. This allowed me to enjoy the journey, notice all the small steps in the right direction and rejoice in my daughter's successes.

When you watch your child's progress through the lens of acceptance, you'll see your child sets exactly the right level of challenge for their growth. In fact, you can't stop your child growing. You just have to learn to spot the small successes along the way that are taking them in the right direction and coach them to bring out their best.

Validating, understanding and seeing the greatness: This method helps us accept 'what is' to create a healthy foundation for problem-solving.

Acceptance creates the experience of love, safety and connection for children. It's the foundation for supporting and coaching your child. Practising acceptance expands your capacity to handle tricky situations, find true solutions and build deep connected relationships.

Acceptance is where true change comes from. It allows you to move forward with baby steps to build momentum for massive change.

Understanding this really sets you free:

Your job as your child's life coach is simply to facilitate and create possibilities that allow your child to grow into the best version of themselves.

Before you can coach your child to speak to themselves with compassion and acceptance, it's important to become aware of the way you speak to yourself.

Use this page to identify your judgements and criticisms of yourself when things don't go to plan. What's your inner voice telling you, and how is it speaking to you?

Example:

I noticed that my mind would go into a complete spiral of despair and self-criticism when I shouted at my children. It sounded like this:

'When you shout, it shows you're useless. It's proof you're a bad mum, and you're not good enough. You can't do this. It looks so easy for others. What's the matter with you? Your daughter is out of control. You can't control her. You need her to behave to feel better about yourself, to feel in control. How selfish is that? If you can't take it anymore, you should just give up…'

Your turn:

Begin by observing your thoughts and emotions without judgement or criticism.

Observe your thoughts as if you're watching another person. A good reminder is to WATCH your thoughts, not BE your thoughts. You're mission is to spot your critical inner voice and stop the spiral of negative thoughts.

I can't begin to tell you how important this step is. Bringing awareness to your thoughts and emotions is the first step to changing them.

What you tell yourself in tricky times and in happy times is a direct link to your subconscious. Self-talk reveals your beliefs about yourself and your child. If you find the following questions tricky, go back to the section on Subconscious Beliefs and untangle them (see page 111).

Notice how your thoughts change when you first focus on validating, understanding and finding your beliefs in tricky situations. You'll be amazed at how much easier it is to find real solutions to tricky situations.

What's a tricky situation you often find yourself in?

What happened?
I shouted at my daughter.

What didn't go to plan?
My daughter spoke to me in a rude tone, and I lost it.

What are you making this mean about yourself?
I'm making it mean that I can't cope and that I'm not good enough. When I hear that tone, I feel like I don't matter.

What are you making this mean about your child?
I'm making it mean that she's rude and ungrateful and that I am raising a brat.

You know this NOT to be true about yourself and your child because…
I do matter, and I don't need my child to prove my worth to me. My child IS good. She's learning.

It makes sense it didn't go to plan because you were thinking…
I was thinking that my child not listening to me and sounding rude was proof I didn't matter. I was fearful she was a brat.

Of course you reacted like you did. Your past experiences cause you to believe…
They cause me to believe what I want doesn't matter. Logically, I know this is not true. I DO matter. My emotions take over in the moment, triggered by past experiences. Of course I shouted at my daughter; my brain is wired to protect me when I think I don't matter and to protect my daughter from becoming a brat.

What is a possible solution for next time?
Pause, notice where I feel my emotions in my body, and catch my thought. Next time, I'm going to stop talking and go get a glass of water to reset my nervous system.

YOUR TURN:

What happened?

What didn't go to plan?

What are you making this mean about yourself?

What are you making this mean about your child?

You know this NOT to be true about yourself and your child because…

It makes sense it didn't go to plan because you were thinking…

Of course you reacted like you did. Your past experiences cause you to believe…

What is a possible solution for next time?

NOTES

Authentic self-esteem occurs when you believe you are competent and have worth.

When you have low self-esteem, you put little value on yourself and your capabilities and don't see yourself as worthy of other's love and respect.

When you have healthy self-esteem, you feel good about yourself and see yourself as worthy, capable, and deserving of the love and respect of others.

Self-esteem is confidence that comes from believing in your own abilities and value.

As a parent, you probably know how important healthy self-esteem is for children. It affects everything – how they think, how they behave, their view of the world and their place in it. Self-esteem has a massive impact on their mental health and their future success.

You also probably know that with healthy self-esteem, children generally feel more self-confident, have more self-respect, and are more able to handle whatever life throws at them.

No wonder it feels so hard to watch children suffer with low self-esteem.

Building self-esteem in your child is not always straightforward. This is because self-esteem is something that's not based on logic or rational thinking. It's also *not* something that you can give your child because it's formed very deep in their subconscious mind.

Essentially, self-esteem is the relationship that a person has with themselves – how they view themselves, how they value themselves, how they think other's judge them, how capable they feel.

Self-esteem is a combination of subconscious beliefs and years and years of experience and conditioning.

These subconscious beliefs are so deeply rooted and so lacking in adult logic and reasoning that trying to help somebody bring out their self-esteem can be tricky. But never fear! Your coaching skills will make it much easier to do, especially pointing out STRENGTHs. (I'll teach you more about how to use that tool later.)

As you will see, bringing out your child's self-esteem happens in stages. Remember, it's confidence that comes from believing in their own ability and value, so each time you point out a STRENGTH, you'll be helping your child connect and identify with who they really are.

You can think of it as wiring (or re-wiring) your child's brain.

The work you just completed on how subconscious beliefs are formed is your foundation for helping your child build healthy self-esteem.

5 WAYS YOU CAN SUPPORT YOUR CHILD TO DEVELOP HEALTHY SELF-ESTEEM

It starts with you seeing your child as the best version of themselves.

When you choose and decide that you are going to see your child as their best self, they have much more of an opportunity to see themselves as their best self too.

1. Teach your child they are worthy of love.

Give love unconditionally so they feel worthy of being loved for WHO they are. Don't have any strings attached to your love and affection. Let them know you love them for who they are, not what they do.

One of the most powerful questions you can ask your child is: *'What do you have to DO to make me love you?'* **and get them to reply:** *'Nothing! Just BE me.'* **Let them know this answer is the truth.**

> Don't listen to advice that tells you to ignore the 'bad' and praise the 'good'. Praise as a reward is the opposite of unconditional love. It's a loud message to your child that love is a commodity that has to be earned. From it, they learn to base their self-worth and 'goodness' on pleasing others. This reduces their self-esteem as they learn to look to others for their value and stop trusting that they are good enough and worthy of love just for BEING themselves.

2. Teach your child to trust themselves.

As self-esteem is the relationship that a person has with themselves, your child needs to know that they can trust themselves. It starts with us trusting them when they tell us how they feel and how they experience the world.

When they have an emotion, teach them to recognise and feel it. Validate it for them and help them find acceptable ways to express it so they feel in control of themselves. The more they trust themselves, the more empowered they will feel.

Use the SAY WHAT YOU SEE tool to validate your child's experience.

> Don't say things like: *'Don't be silly, there's nothing to fuss about! Don't cry, or I'll give you something to cry about.'* Those are the opposite of validation and undermine your child's self-trust. Try SWYS instead, like: *'You're crying. You're sad. Something must be troubling you.'*

3. Teach your child to feel confident in their abilities.

Children gain confidence from practising problem-solving, trying new things and assessing their skills. Confidence is a necessary quality for becoming a fully functioning adult with healthy self-esteem. Your goal as your child's life coach is to prepare your child for life so they know whatever life throws at them, they have the skills and confidence to handle it.

Use the CAN DO tool to hold healthy boundaries and help your child gain problem-solving skills, learn how to meet their needs in healthy ways and go after what they want in life.

> Don't use punishment and rewards. Remember, NO amount of time-outs, consequences or bribes are going to teach your child the skills they need to feel confident in their abilities.

4. Teach your child it's important to know themselves.

Take pleasure in the things they delight in. Let them share their dreams with you. Let them know that their preferences (what they like and want) matter to you. This doesn't mean you have to give your child everything they want. It simply means validating that they are right to like or want it. Your child's preferences are an expression of who they are. When they feel secure in who they are, they can see the importance of holding healthy boundaries. They can grow up trusting themselves and seeing the possibilities in life.

Use the STRENGTH tool to help your child see their preferences as STRENGTHs. Pay attention to their interests.

> Don't try to convince your child to change what they like or want, or to see things your way. This is the opposite of allowing your child to trust who they are. No wonder so many of us grow up not knowing who we are or what we want out of life! We've learnt to detach from our preferences and hide our true selves to please others and belong.

5. Teach your child to see their STRENGTHs.

When you prove to your child they have a STRENGTH, they naturally change their own behaviour to reflect it. As self-esteem is all about how they view themselves, changing how your child sees themselves from the inside out is the perfect way to help them build their self-esteem.

Use the STRENGTH tool to help your child to see their greatness and gain confidence in their abilities.

> Don't focus on your child's faults. Rather than helping them change their behaviour, the opposite is true. They start believing that's who they are and learn to see themselves in a negative way. Focusing on their STRENGTHs turns that around.

Don't poke the bear

DEFINITION: to do something that might provoke someone into becoming angry and cause more problems.

DON'T POKE THE BEAR

Your response either escalates or de-escalates a situation. Your response is one of the most important factors in de-escalating a situation with your child. You can't control everything your child says and does, but with practice, you can control your own response. This is not always easy, but it's far easier than dealing with the reactions of a proverbial bear that's been poked!

Have you ever got tired of having arguments and screaming matches with your child? You probably swear it isn't you that starts the fights, so it must be your child. And if they start the fights, it has to be your child that stops them, right? After all, if they just did as they were told, then you wouldn't have to lose your cool and could calm down!

At least that's how it seems...

When you become aware of the way you respond and what it communicates to your child, you'll realise that your response is often the catalyst for your child's big explosions.

Have a read through the next couple of pages. The typical ways we've been taught to respond are akin to poking an angry bear or throwing a big splash of fuel on the fire. Changing what you say can do the opposite.

When you change the way you respond to your child, you'll see a massive change in how they respond back to you.

RESPONSES THAT 'POKE THE BEAR'

BLAMING: *'Well, if you'd just have listened, then I wouldn't have shouted.'*

We blame our children for our own actions, but the truth is, no one makes you shout. That's your reaction. Blaming your child for your reactions and needing your child to change their behaviour first, puts the responsibility for changing *your* reactions on your child. Ownership returns responsibility to you.

DEMANDING: *'Come here right now!'*

Demands send the message that your child's needs, wants or feelings are not important. They communicate a lack of interest in your child and what they're experiencing. When a child's need for experience, connection or power is high, demanding that they meet your need first adds to their feeling of powerlessness, further fuelling unwanted behaviour. SAYing WHAT YOU SEE is a better way to start.

DEVALUING YOUR CHILD'S PERSPECTIVE: *'That's not happening. That's a silly idea.'*

We often say things like that because we want our child to see it our way. We think if they could just see it our way, then maybe they wouldn't fuss and tantrum. But it actually leads to disconnection and powerlessness. Instead, SWYS helps them adapt when what they want can't happen.

FIXING: *'Oh! Go on then. What's the matter? Let me make it better for you.'*

By fixing things for your child, you're unintentionally telling them you don't think they can do it. Solving their problems, giving advice or suggestions, and offering your own ideas and answers all fuel the belief that they can't solve their own problems. Instead, CAN DOs turn problem-solving over to the child.

IGNORING: *'I don't want to be with you until you've calmed down.'*

During times of misbehaviour such as tantrums, the last thing a child needs is to be ignored. They desperately need your full and dedicated attention in those moments! Don't withhold your love when your child is acting out. Instead, offer your support starting with SWYS, and only step away if you need to calm yourself down or if your child asks you to so they can calm themselves down.

JUDGING: *'You're spoilt. You're so lazy. You're too sensitive. You're so selfish.'*

Judgements never de-escalate situations because the whole conversation shifts to your child defending themselves against criticism, fuelling more unwanted behaviour. Judgements can result in your child feeling defensive, unheard and unsupported. Use SWYS to understand your child's behaviour and CAN DOs to find real solutions to tricky situations.

LOGIC AND REASONING: *'If you'd just gone to bed when I told you, then you wouldn't be so tired.'*

Anytime you use logic and reasons to try to persuade your child to change their behaviour, your child hears, *'You are wrong, and I am right.'* So they naturally dig in their heels to prove they are right and you are wrong. The need for connection and power increases, and an argument ensues. Instead, SWYS and compassion melt arguments away.

PUNISHMENTS/THREATS: *'That's it! Stop now, or you won't have your iPad.'*

Punishment is all about control. It increases your child's powerlessness and fuels the cycle. Your child doesn't need a deterrent to change their ways. Instead, SWYS, CAN DOs and STRENGTHs help your child calm themselves, stop themselves, and find acceptable ways to meet their needs without the fear of punishment.

RESTATING A BOUNDARY: *'You know the rules. You know it's bedtime.'*

This one might seem strange, but this 'poke' really riles up the bear! You know your child already knows the rules, so repeating them won't solve the problem. Plus, it focuses your child on what they don't want, which increases their resistance. Instead, CAN DOs focus your child on what they do want and what is possible within your boundary, and lead to solutions that work for you both.

SHAMING: *'You're rude. That's mean. You're ungrateful. I'm disappointed in you.'*

Any time you judge or criticise your child, you are shaming them to try to change their behaviour. Shame quickly reduces your child's self-esteem and self-worth and can be very long-lasting. Your child's beliefs and self-talk echo what they hear from you. Your child takes what you say as truth and starts seeing themselves in that way. Your child never needs shaming. They already want to calm down, act kind, express their appreciation etc, and they feel proud of themselves when they do. They just need you to see the best in them first and point it out to them as a STRENGTH.

TEACHING: *'You can't always win. You have to learn how to share.'*

If you try to teach your child a 'lesson' they don't like or a view, opinion or fact that contradicts theirs, insisting you are right will create more defensiveness and resistance. Instead, use SWYS to let them 'teach' you what they think first. When you listen to them with interest, it's easier for them to listen to you. And sometimes, you may even discover that they are right!

TELLING OFF: *'That's very naughty. You know better than that.'*

When you tell your child off, it's all about your judgements and your perception of the situation. For example, when you try to change your child's behaviour by telling them it's naughty, you may be trying to convey that their behaviour is naughty (again, that's just your judgement of their behaviour), but your child is likely to take it to mean that they THEMSELVES are naughty because children decide who they are based on what they do. When you judge what they DO (their behaviour), whether through your words or your reactions, your child takes it as a statement of who they ARE... And they believe you! Instead, use SWYS and offer solutions with CAN DOs that can lead to more constructive outcomes.

QUESTIONS: *'Why did you do that? What were you thinking?'*

Asking your child questions can trigger defensive reactions as it often makes them feel accused or judged. Your child may perceive your questions as a reflection on their character or as accusations, which can lead to feelings of shame and defensiveness. Instead, use SWYS and offer solutions with CAN DOs to encourage open and constructive communication without invoking defensiveness.

WHEN VALIDATION AND CONNECTION ARE NOT ENOUGH

It's easy to think that validation and connection should be enough to change a child's behaviour. I wish it were that simple, but it's not. Validation and connection are just the starting point.

Often we listen to our child, repeating over and over how they feel, expecting things to change. Then we try to impart our reasons and logic to change our child's point of view or get buy-in from them. We end up losing our patience and dishing out a threat as that's the only thing that works to change their behaviour in the moment.

On the surface, Language of Listening might seem the same as other parenting models, yet it is so different!

Yes, we have the **SAY WHAT YOU SEE** step of connection, but your role as your child's coach is different. It's not to calm down your child, get them to like your boundary, understand why you have a boundary in the first place or see things your way. (I'll be talking more about boundaries later in the workbook.)

With your coaching skills, you're always on your child's side, helping them figure out what they **CAN DO** within your boundary or helping them handle their feelings of disappointment with **SWYS**.

When your boundary is *'this is just how it is'*, not something to defend, explain or negotiate, offering a **CAN DO** helps you gain the willing cooperation you're after and helps your child gain problem-solving skills and self-control. You can help your child build upon their existing skills, get on their side, and help them find alternatives that work for everyone.

Let's look at an example in action.

Here's what getting on your child's side with your new coaching skills can look like. As you'll see, **CAN DOs** will help you guide your child, often with little or no resistance. (I'll teach you more about using the **CAN DO** tool in the next section.)

My 13-year-old daughter wanted to go to the big city, an hour's drive away on the weekend. My husband and I agreed that we both just wanted a chilled weekend. We definitely weren't going. My daughter started trying to convince us to go. I used **SWYS** to acknowledge how much she loves going and that's it's her favourite thing to do.

She started whining and fussing. I didn't get into a debate, defend my decision, or talk about her emotions. I side-stepped judgement too. I was still on her side as I wasn't trying to change her mind or tell her she was wrong for wanting to go.

Notice how I didn't try to give reasons like: *'You go all the time. I just took you a few weeks ago.'*

We mean well by trying to dissuade our child and reminding them that they do often go. However, when we do that, we are implying that they're wrong to want to go now, or that they're spoilt somehow.

Or we go into fixing the situation: *'I'll take you next weekend. You'll get to go, I promise, just not today. Let's go and do something else fun…'* Again, we mean well, but often, our urge to make it better for them comes from feeling guilty that they are upset, which implies that their feelings are our responsibility.

Or we go into defending our decision: *'I'm tired, and I don't want to spend the money, and I don't want to sit in traffic…'* They then come back with all their counter-defenses: *'Well, I'll give you a massage, and you can sit in a café, and you don't have to spend any money since I just want to look at the shops, and we can go by train…'* and on and on the argument goes.

I didn't give reasons, try to fix the situation or defend my decision. Instead, solid in my boundary, I turned the problem-solving over to her with a **CAN DO**:

'There must be something you can do to have fun this weekend.' And just like that, she found a way to have fun that was still within my boundary. She went for a walk with a friend!

Later that day, we went to the supermarket together. She huffed in the car, *'Humfff, we didn't get to go into town today!'*

So, I got a chance to point out a **STRENGTH**: *'And you still found a way to have fun!'*

Clearly, this whole situation could have taken a lot longer to navigate. I'm not going to kid you that it always runs so smoothly. My daughter used to have the most epic tantrums, and calming down wasn't her forte. She had to practise coming up against solid boundaries, calming herself down and finding **CAN DOs** that worked for us both. But look at her now! Altogether, that whole interaction took no more than ten minutes!

If you think your child isn't there yet, don't worry. I'll teach you the amazing **STRENGTHs** tool. You can use it to build upon your child's success to prove to them that they **CAN** calm down, **DO** have self-control and **CAN** find ways to meet their needs within your boundaries. When you **SEE** the best in them, you can teach your children by pointing out their **STRENGTHs**. It's what allows you to teach them through success rather than failure.

No more repeating over and over how your child feels and expecting things to change.

The coaching skills you're learning create true win-wins where both you and your child come away feeling good about yourselves.

4 STEPS WHEN YOUR CHILD SAYS 'NO!' AND REFUSES TO LISTEN TO REASON

Is your child forever saying 'No!' to your every request?

You know the drill. It's bath time. Your child knows it's bath time, and yet, the first thing out of their mouth is *'No!'* You want the TV off for dinner so you can sit at the table and have family time, and your child says, *'No!'* You're trying to get out of the house on time, shoes on and bags packed, and your child says, *'No!'* You want your child to play nicely at the playground, and yet, they're screaming the place down.

Oh my! I can relate. Moments like these trigger us!

FIRST STEP: Pay attention to WHAT you're thinking.

When my daughter was little, my every request was met by a big, fat *'NO!'*

'Why does my daughter have to be so stubborn? Why does she always have to push my boundaries? Why can't she be more like her brother? He just listens and gets on with it. Why, oh why, does every request have to be a battle?' were the thoughts spinning round my head.

Can you relate?! Have you noticed similar thoughts?

It's these thoughts that leave you feeling powerless and most probably reacting to your child in a way that causes them not to want to listen to you!

It's completely normal when you're triggered to only see two options:
- Give in to your child's demands.
- Threaten, bribe or punish them to get compliance.

No wonder it's exhausting! Either you have to give up what you want, or you have to fight to hold your ground. This may be hard to believe… but guess what?

That *'No!'* is not defiance or your child always wanting their way. And it doesn't mean that you have a 'strong-willed' child on your hands.

That *'No!'* is your child sharing their likes/dislikes and their wants/wishes with you. They're simply stating their preferences, loud and clear!

(Remember, they don't have to get what they want.)

SECOND STEP: Pay attention to WHAT you're saying. Remember that children must continue to communicate until they feel heard.

This is so important to understand as our usual responses typically escalate the situation. Because when we look at that 'No!' as a challenge, what do most of us do?

We reply with things like:

- **Logic/Reasoning:** 'Come on! You know you like bath time. Once you're in, you'll love it!'
- **Threats:** 'If you don't listen right now, there'll be no story time (or screen time) later.'
- **Demands:** 'Come here right now! That behaviour is unacceptable.'
- **Judgements:** 'Now, you're just being silly.'
- **Teaching:** 'You can't always have what you want.'
- **Shame/Guilt:** 'You're making me sad. Stop being so naughty. You know better than that.'

As you can see, our typical responses just don't hit the mark. More than anything, your child wants to feel heard and validated. That doesn't mean you have to change your boundary.

THIRD STEP: When your child is shouting 'No!' and not listening, go immediately into saying what they do WANT.

The purpose of **SAY WHAT YOU SEE** is validation. Seeing the wish or want behind their behaviour gets your child heard and closes the communication loop. This is so important because once your child feels heard, they don't have to escalate their behaviour to show you how much what they want means to them.

It also helps you understand your child's perspective. It's here that they start to open up to your guidance.

SWYS: 'You **want** to keep playing. The last thing you want to do is get wet and have a bath!'
CAN DO: 'There must be some way to play AND have a bath.'

SWYS: 'You **want** to finish that show. It's hard to turn the TV off and come sit at the table.'
CAN DO: 'There must be some way to watch the rest of your show AND come to the table for dinner.'

SWYS: 'You **want** that toy and so does your friend. You haven't finished with it yet.'
CAN DO: 'There must be some way you can both get to play with it.'

The wonderful result here is that you're not battling with your child. You're on the same side, stepping into your child's world for a moment and seeing what's 'right' with their 'No!'

Often, a child who feels validated and knows that what they want matters to you is then able to move on, cooperate with your wishes and find solutions within your boundaries. If you've offered **CAN DOs**, and your child still isn't cooperating, don't worry, there's a fourth step...

FOURTH STEP: Step in and be the boundary for your child.

If you can see the situation with your child is about to kick off and go pear-shaped, don't wait! Take action early to help your child be successful. Your intention to help them succeed puts you on their side.

Examples:
- *'I won't let you hit,'* and block your child's arm. (Help them be successful by not hitting again.)
- *'I don't like being spoken to like that. We can carry on speaking when we're both calm.'*
- *'Looks like you're having a hard time. I'm taking the toy away for now. You can try again later.'*
- *'We're going home. It's too much for you now.'* (This is not a threat. You're helping your child be successful by taking them to a place they can handle.)
- *'Running off down the road isn't safe. You can go into the buggy.'* (This is not a punishment. You're helping your child succeed in staying safe.)
- *'It's time for the TV to go off. You can do it, or I can help you.'* (This is a sincere offer of help, not a threat.)

It's OK for your child to be upset, have a tantrum, shout or stamp their feet. It does not mean you have got anything wrong or are not doing it correctly. Your child has to be given the chance to calm themselves down to learn they have self-control and the other STRENGTHs they need to manage their own behaviour in tricky situations.

Also, it can feel tricky for you at the moment because you only have a few pieces of the puzzle. There are a lot more tools and strategies to implement that I will teach you later.

For now, I want you to focus on the fact you got through a tricky situation as quickly as possible with a solid boundary despite your child's protests. That is progress!

NOTES

The second step in your coaching model:

The CAN DO Tool

The CAN DO Tool

Of course as parents, we all want to see the type of behaviour that we like. It can be frustrating trying to get our kids to behave or do what we ask. Especially if we've been given conflicting advice, it leaves us pulling our hair out.

Maybe you've tried banning screen time, hung up a few sticker charts or dished out threats with the hope that your child will be motivated enough to change their unwanted behaviour without a fight.

And that might work for a while… But boy, constantly managing your child's behaviour is exhausting, isn't it?

After a few days, the sticker charts are forgotten; your child has lost the use of the iPad again; and you're left wondering what else to do.

As we discussed earlier, it's not your fault because all the usual tools you've been taught assume that your child needs external motivation to change their ways. This misses the true cause.

Children do NOT need motivation to change their behaviour. Remember, your child already wants to behave. They don't need external motivation or a deterrent. What they need is to gain skills to manage their own behaviour and meet their needs in healthy ways.

And no number of time-outs, consequences or bribes are going to teach your child the skills they need to control their OWN behaviour.

But the **CAN DO** tool does! It connects children with their own internal motivation and provides them with the skills they need to succeed in managing themselves.

So with SAY WHAT YOU SEE (SWYS) + CAN DOs, you end up with self-motivated children who WANT to listen to you and WANT to manage their OWN behaviour!

Sound impossible? Not when you understand the premise behind this coaching tool.

The Language of Listening premise behind CAN DOs tells us:

> 'All behaviours are driven by 3 healthy needs: experience, connection, power.
> Whatever children are doing is already meeting their needs.'

So when your child is meeting their needs in ways you don't like, you can use the **CAN DO** tool to help them find ways that work for you both.

With the **CAN DO** tool and the coaching skills I will teach you in this section of your workbook, your children really will be able to connect with their internal motivation and start managing their own behaviour so you don't have to!

NO rewards.
NO threats of consequences.
NO punishments.

And willing cooperation. What's not to LOVE?

Swap out rewards, threats and punishments for **CAN DOs** that work!

CAN DO TOOL IN ACTION

CAN DOs are a simple way to meet both your own and your child's needs.

Typically, we're advised to stand firm and provide logical reasons why our child can't have what they want. When that doesn't work, we default to responses we don't like such as dismissal, *'It's not happening,'* or threats, *'Stop asking or no screen time!'* etc. to shut down their repeated pleas.

However, with a coaching approach, we begin with **SWYS** to empathise with our child and understand their perspective. Then, instead of simply denying our child's request, we offer **CAN DOs** to encourage them to find an alternative solution.

Here's a quick example of how CAN DOs work.

One day my 6-year-old son asked, *'Mum, can I have some ice cream, please?!!'*

I knew I didn't want him to have more sugar that day, and I could have easily delivered a flat *'NO.'* But instead, I stepped into his world with empathy and said, *'It seems like you're in the mood for something sweet, and ice cream isn't OK with me. There must be something you* **can do** *to satisfy your sweet craving with a healthier option.'*

By acknowledging his desire without dismissing it, my son felt heard and understood. I refrained from simply shutting down his request, opting instead to encourage him to find an alternative that could meet his needs while respecting my boundary.

He couldn't think of any healthy options he wanted, so I suggested a few: *'How about a banana with yogurt or some fresh fruit?'*

This helped him realise that, while he couldn't have ice cream, there were other alternatives available to him that he liked. So he chose the one closest to ice cream – a banana with yogurt.

By supporting my son in finding a solution within my boundary, I conveyed a powerful message: *'What you want matters to me. I value your needs. I won't simply dictate to you, but I won't compromise on my boundaries either.'*

How differently things could have unfolded had I had resorted to traditional methods of reasoning, lecturing or imposing my viewpoint without considering my son's wishes.

Our connection and collaboration resulted in a win-win outcome – a satisfied sweet craving for my boy and a maintained boundary for me.

If you're reading this and thinking, *'Yeah! That won't work for my kid! No way will they accept my boundary without massive push back,'* I want to tell you, it's not that your boundary doesn't 'work'; it's that your child needs more practice handling frustration and disappointment, and coming up with their own solutions so you can point out their **STRENGTHs**. Don't worry! We'll cover that later.

THE REASON CAN DOS WORK

The CAN DO tool gives you a constructive and collaborative way to address your child's behaviour.

The reason **CAN DOs** work so well is that they put you on your child's side. They help you identify and address the underlying reasons for your child's unwanted behaviour – unmet needs – and help your child get them met.

It's the most effective strategy for helping your child change their own behaviour while also strengthening your relationship with them.

Coaching your child to meet their needs in healthy ways involves listening, setting clear boundaries, and teaching problem-solving and coping skills.

By working together with your child in a collaborative and supportive way, you'll be able to help them stay inside your boundaries, develop a sense of self-worth and resilience, and gain confidence in their abilities to navigate challenging situations productively, both now and in the future.

Not to mention, the **CAN DO** tool is what gets you the willing cooperation you're after. It's what I call the Holy Grail of parenting – kids who *want* to listen and follow your lead!

These are some of the results switching to CAN DOs can produce:

- ✓ Children willingly cooperate and collaborate with you and others.
- ✓ Children become problem-solvers and find solutions within your boundaries.
- ✓ Children know how to get their NEEDS meet in healthy ways.
- ✓ Children understand that mistakes are opportunities to learn.
- ✓ Children see the possibilities in life and know how to find solutions.
- ✓ Children take personal responsibility and ownership of their lives.
- ✓ Children are intrinsically motivated.
- ✓ Children focus on what to do instead of reacting negatively to rewards, threats or punishments.

MORE EXAMPLES OF CAN DOS IN ACTION

A **CAN DO** is an alternative to your child's current behaviour that is OK with you. For example, if your child is jumping on the sofa, you can say, 'Looks like you want to jump. You can jump on these floor cushions.'

It's simply a way that your child can do something they want within your boundaries. Don't confuse this with going past your boundary: a **CAN DO** is something your child can do *that is still within your boundary.*

> *'You want to play with water, AND the kitchen floor is not the place to get all wet. There must be somewhere you can get wet and play with water.'*
>
> *'You want to jump, AND jumping on the bed is not OK. Must be something you can jump on.'*
>
> *'You want to run and run, AND running here isn't safe. Must be some way you can get all that energy out and stay safe.'*
>
> *'You are so mad at your brother, AND hitting hurts. There must be another way to tell him.'*
>
> *'You want go shopping with friends, AND it's not safe without an adult. There must be some other way to have fun with your friends.'*
>
> *'You want to share a secret with your friend, AND gossiping about others is not respectful. There must be a more positive way to connect and build trust.'*

Now, your turn: **Use SAY WHAT YOU SEE + CAN DOs**

SAY WHAT YOU SEE
Train your brain to spot what your child wants first.

CAN DO
Then ask yourself, what CAN my child do that's OK with me?

CAN DOs are a completely different way to meet needs, your child's and your own.

You CAN have your boundaries. In fact, you can have exactly the SAME boundaries you have right now AND coach your child to meet their needs inside them.

Here's another quick example.

George told his daughter to turn off the TV and get dressed for school.

'*Nooooooo!*' his daughter replied.

George was feeling challenged and ready for battle, but he paused and used SWYS.

He stepped into his child's world and offered her connection, understanding and validation:
'*You want to keep watching TV. You're all snuggly on the sofa.*'

George then followed up with an all-purpose CAN DO statement: '*There must be something you can do to keep snuggly and get dressed.*'

Because his daughter didn't have to give up what she wanted (keeping snuggly in front of the TV), she was able to move straight to a solution.

His daughter replied, '*Yes! I'll finish dressing under the blanket. Can you get me my clothes, please?*'

George started to see that his daughter's 'no' was only his daughter expressing her wants. She wasn't being defiant or trying to boss him around. His daughter needed to know that what she wanted mattered to her dad. George was OK with passing clothes to his daughter, and his daughter got dressed happily.

By helping his daughter get her needs met within his boundary, George sent a message to his daughter: '*I care what you want. I am not going to overpower you, and I'm not going to change my boundary either.*'

You can see how differently this situation would have played out if George had gone straight to threats to try to get his daughter to comply. You know that situation would have ended in tears and the battle George had anticipated.

Instead, George used his coaching skills to first step into his daughter's world, and then hold his boundary and consider his daughter's needs. Win-win!

If you're reading this and panic is setting in as you can't see this way working when time is short, just let me reassure you that working WITH your child takes less time, not more, and gets you out the door faster with everyone in a better mood.

Here's another quick example.

Sophie and her 15-year-old son's relationship had become increasingly strained. One evening, as Sophie was preparing dinner, she noticed Ricky was glued to his phone.

'Ricky!' Sophie said, 'It's time to set the table.'

'Mum, can't you see I'm busy? I'll do it later.' Ricky replied, not even looking up from his phone.

Sophie felt her patience wearing thin, and she was tempted to insist that he obey her immediately or she would take his phone away. But instead, she took a deep breath and decided to use a different approach.

She sat down at the table facing Ricky and tried **SWYS**: 'It looks you're busy with something important.'

Ricky seemed surprised by her change in tone. 'I'm chatting with my friends, We're making plans for the weekend.'

Sophie nodded and smiled. *'That sounds fun.'* She then followed up with an all-purpose **CAN DO** statement. *'The table still needs to be set. Must be something you can do to finish up your conversation and set the table.'*

Ricky was surprised by his mother's understanding. 'OK, Mum, I can do that.'

(I bet you just laughed at his reply, thinking, 'No way would my child say that!' But, I promise, the more you use this approach, the more your child will surprise you just like that.)

While setting the table, they discussed his weekend plans and deepened their connection and relationship. Sophie's acknowledgment of what was important to Ricky fostered mutual respect. It's this that builds trust and openness, promoting willing cooperation and pleasant interactions.

You can easily imagine how this situation might have played out if Sophie had taken her son's phone to make him comply. In that scenario, her son might have begrudgingly obeyed simply to avoid losing his phone, or alternatively, the evening might have turned into a series of arguments and power struggles.

Here's a crucial question to consider: *why* do your kids do what you ask? Is it because they feel compelled by threats or consequences, or is it because they genuinely want to help and cooperate? Consider what truly motivates YOU to be cooperative. It's a question worth pondering.

In contrast, when you use **CAN DOs**, you not only keep your boundaries but also actively support your child in finding possible solutions that work for the both you. The outcome is genuine, willing cooperation and a more effortless and harmonious family life.

NOTES

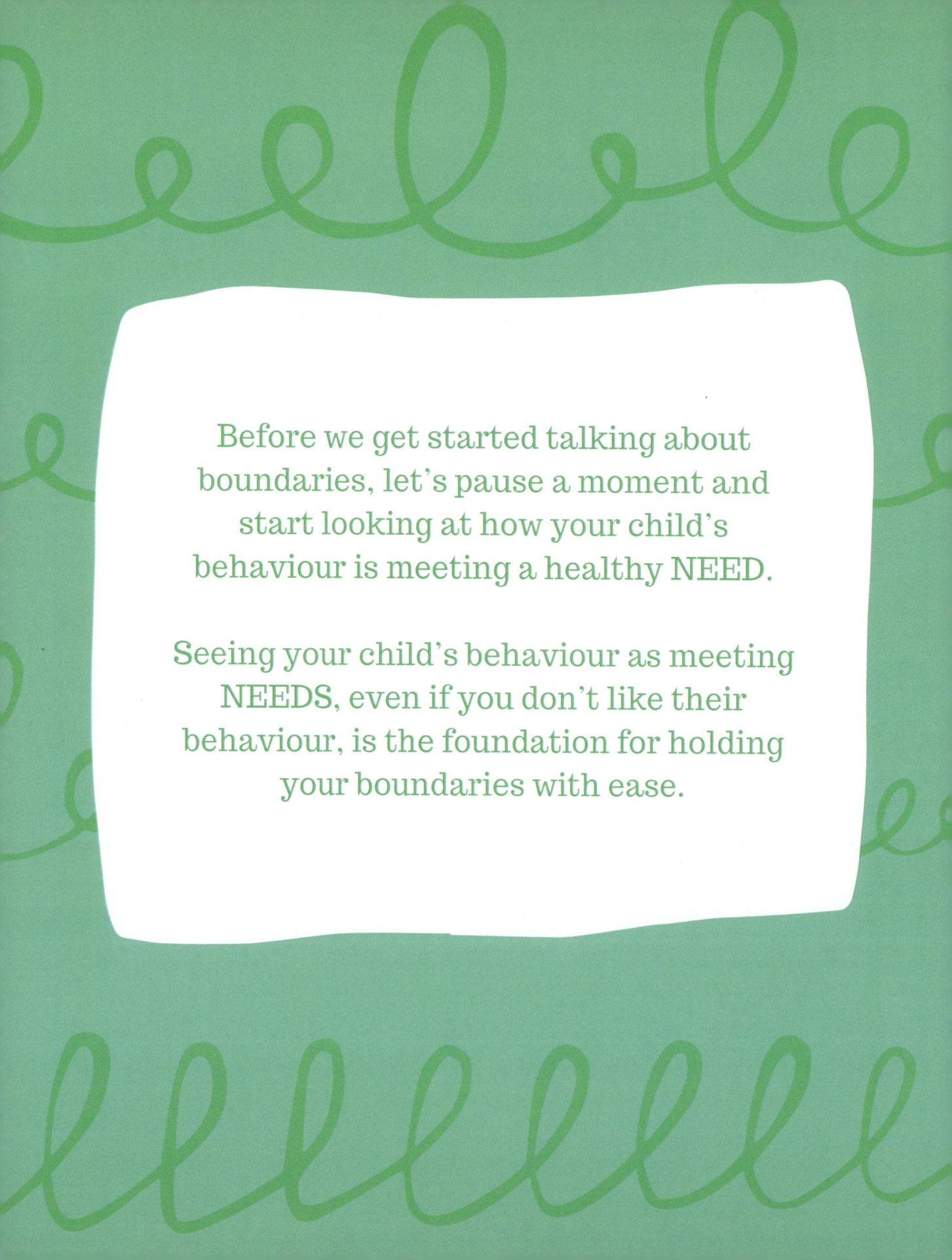

Before we get started talking about boundaries, let's pause a moment and start looking at how your child's behaviour is meeting a healthy NEED.

Seeing your child's behaviour as meeting NEEDS, even if you don't like their behaviour, is the foundation for holding your boundaries with ease.

WHAT IS A NEED?

We all have natural survival needs: food, water, clothing, shelter and safety. If those needs weren't met, we'd be in real distress, spending every waking moment trying to meet them.

Our natural psychological and developmental needs work the same way. In the Language of Listening coaching model, we break them down into three easy to remember needs.

THE 3 BASIC NEEDS FOR GROWTH

The NEED for CONNECTION:
Feeling noticed, understood, validated, loved, important, like you belong etc

The NEED for EXPERIENCE:
Sensory exploration, physical movement, playing, physical challenges, visiting new places etc

The NEED for POWER:
Feeling confident, in control of oneself, able to make an impact on the world etc

The 3 Basic Needs for Growth are all healthy needs. Just like our survival needs of food, clothing, shelter etc, when unmet, our healthy needs for growth lead to distress, so we automatically take action to try to meet them. This is true for adults and children.

When we don't support our child in getting their needs met, what we're really doing is prolonging their distress. That sends the message that their needs aren't important or worthy and leaves them to meet their needs on their own... which they automatically do, often in ways we don't like.

Unmet needs lead to feeling angry, ashamed, dejected, defensive, desperate, threatened, sad, unaccepted, unhappy, unsafe, worried, worthless... The list goes on. And what's the normal human reaction to feeling these emotions? Behaviours you might call anxious, aggressive, defiant, naughty, rude etc. As undesirable as those behaviours are, they are your child's automatic ways to try to meet their needs. I'll explain more about that in the following pages.

When you understand what is really going on when children behave in ways you don't like, you will realise that not only do most of the ways you've been told to respond just prolong your child's distress and the undesirable behaviour that follows, but they also don't teach your child how to get their needs met in ways that you do like. No wonder you feel like you're dealing with the same unwanted behaviour every single day!

Understanding the 3 Basic Needs for Growth helps us understand that requesting what we need is not selfish. When our needs are met, our best self emerges. Coaching children to meet their needs in ways you like reduces distress and leads to healthier communication, healthier relationships and a more enriched life.

Children have an innate, unwavering drive to get their needs met.

Unfortunately, children's strategies for getting their needs met are often not strategies we like.

No child wants to act out. When your child's needs are not met, they will go into action to meet them – oftentimes in ways you don't like!

I'm sure you don't like your kids whining, tantruming, not listening… But whether you like those behaviours or not, they are meeting the need for connection and power.

And unless you coach your child to get their needs met in ways you do like… well, the behaviour keeps on coming or escalates as your child still has needs that just have to be met!

And if you leave it up to your child to try to figure out how to meet their needs, they often learn really ineffective coping strategies that have long-term, detrimental effects.

I'm going to teach you to **SEE** your child's behaviour in a new way. When you learn to spot the needs behind your child's behaviour, you will start to notice that you have a whole new understanding of behaviour in general and that your child is naturally meeting their needs in everything they do.

Learning to see how your child is already in action meeting his or her own needs will help you trust your child more and use your coaching skills to facilitate your child's growth rather than struggle to manage their behaviour.

When you focus on helping your child meet their needs, you effortlessly bring out the best in yourself and your child. That's why it's so important for you to coach your child to get their needs met in ways you do like and that are within your boundaries.

Let's look at some actions children take.

Knowing how to spot the three healthy needs behind any behaviour changes how you SEE that behaviour, which then changes how you react to it.

Look at the illustration below. All of those behaviours actually DO meet your child's NEEDS even though some may be ways you don't like. Instead of controlling your child to keep them within your boundaries, coaching your child with CAN DOs allows you to offer ways you do like for your child to meet their needs. Your child gets their needs met; you get your boundaries met.

EXPERIENCE

You can spot this need in a child who wants to touch everything, jump, run, wrestle, play with their toys, stay out late, stay up late, build dens, make things, explore, can't sit still etc.

CONNECTION

You can spot this need in a child who wants your attention, wants to play with you, clings to you, acts up to get your attention, cries sadly or fusses whenever you leave, always wants more time with friends etc.

POWER

You can spot this need in a child who is bossy, aggressive, stubborn, demanding, perfectionist, refuses to do as you ask, shouts loudly, throws tantrums etc

Coach your child to find healthy ways to meet their needs

When your child is acting in a way you don't like...

First, spot the NEED behind your child's behaviour, and then guide your child to meet that same need in a way you DO LIKE. When a **CAN DO** really does meet your child's need as well as or better than the behaviour you don't like, your child will find it easy to switch.

Ask yourself: 'How CAN my child meet their NEED in a way that is OK with me?'

There are plenty of ways that your child can meet their needs that could work for you too. Try a few things out and come up with solutions that work for both of you. When you hand over the problem-solving to your child, you'll be amazed at how creative they can be.

Remember to start with **SAY WHAT YOU SEE**. You literally say what you see your child doing, saying, feeling or thinking as taught in the first section of this workbook. The magic of **SWYS** is that it's the quickest way to get your child feeling heard, understood and connected. It's only from a place of connection that your child can open up to your guidance.

> **Take a look at the bedtime example on the opposite page.**
>
> By first identifying the underlying NEED behind unwanted behaviour, you'll be better equipped to discover true solutions and coach your child in meeting their needs in ways that are OK with you.

Let's look at a bedtime example.

CONNECTION

If your child is trying to meet their need for connection by crying when you start to leave, clinging, starting deep conversations just as the lights go out, getting out of bed to come see you etc:

SWYS. Then offer **CAN DOs** to help them feel more connected and drift peacefully off to sleep.
- *Can you help them get ready for bed in a way that feels connective for you both?*
- *Can you read books together and let them choose the books (which will also help meet the need for power)?*
- *Can you offer a back rub or talk them through a relaxing guided meditation (which will also help meet the need for experience)?*

EXPERIENCE

If your child is trying to meet their need for experience by continuing to play, running around etc:

SWYS. Then help your child find some physical or sensory things they **CAN DO**.
Can they start the bedtime routine slightly earlier so they have a chance to potter around their room and finish their Lego or drawing? (Staying with them using **SWYS** *will also meet their need for connection.)*
- *Can they set up an assault course in another room to get the last bit of energy out before bed?*
- *Can you offer a fireman's lift or fly them into bed (which will also meet the need for connection)?*
- *Can they put lavender under their pillow or find a snuggly toy to cuddle as they fall asleep?*

POWER

If your child is trying to meet their need for power by refusing to get ready for bed, fighting you etc:

SWYS. Then help your child find things they can control within your boundaries. Coaching your child to find a **CAN DO** while holding your boundaries allows your child to practise stopping themselves and solving problems creatively, revealing **STRENGTHs** that meet their need for power naturally.
- *Can you let your child choose the order of bedtime preparations? ('Teeth or pyjamas first?' etc)*
- *Can they decide what light stays on, what music to listen to etc.*
- *Can they decide how long you will stay as in '3 minutes or 5?'*

Spotting NEEDS

Practise reframing how you perceive your child's behaviour. Instead of labelling it as good or bad, focus on identifying the unmet needs behind their actions. This shift in perspective can lead to more effective problem-solving.

> **Example:** My 16-year-old had been going out with friends after school and often didn't check in to let me know where he was. In trying to understand the NEEDS behind his actions, I've realised that he is meeting his need for CONNECTION and POWER. He wants the freedom to spend time with friends and make his own decisions.
>
> I want to support him to meet his needs while also ensuring his safety. Instead of constantly demanding that he checks in, I've started using **SWYS** + **CAN DOs**: *'You want to go out with friends and have some independence. You want me to trust you, and I want peace of mind for your safety. There must be something you can do to let me know when you reach your friend's house or let me know if your plans change.'* He came up with the solution of sending me a text to keep me updated.
>
> Since he came up with it, he actually follows through, which gives me the chance to point out his **STRENGTHs** – how responsible and trustworthy he is. (I'll teach you how to do that later.)

> **Your turn:** Practise noticing the NEEDS behind your child's behaviour and use **SWYS** + **CAN DOs** to help your child meet their NEEDS in ways you like.
> *Think of a specific behaviour your child has displayed recently that you found challenging or frustrating. It could be anything from tantrums to not following instructions.*

Use unwanted behaviour as a red flag, an opportunity to understand that your child's needs are not met. Helping your child meet their needs is the most effective way to help them change their OWN behaviour.

Focusing your attention on coaching your child to meet their needs (within your boundaries) helps you gain willing cooperation and helps your child gain problem-solving skills and self-control.

Your job is to help your child meet **THEIR** needs in a way that you **DO** like.

All behaviour is meeting a NEED in a way you either DO or DON'T like.

CONNECTION

Behaviour you probably don't like:	Behaviour you probably do like:
Arguing or talking back	Communicating clearly, discussing
Bragging, showing off	Sharing accomplishments, showing you their strengths
Hitting for attention, lashing out for attention	High five, gentle touching or patting, asking you to listen
Jealousy, sibling rivalry	Spending time alone with you; playing together as a family
Spending too much time on screens connecting with friends	Spending time playing with friends off screens, connecting in other ways

EXPERIENCE

Behaviour you probably don't like:	Behaviour you probably do like:
Climbing on furniture	Climbing trees or playground equipment
Getting into things	Exploring, experimenting etc
Playful screaming, swearing	Squealing joyfully outdoors, appropriate use of swear words
Sneaking out	Going out with friends and exploring with permission
Throwing things	Playing catch with balls, stuffed animals, etc.

POWER

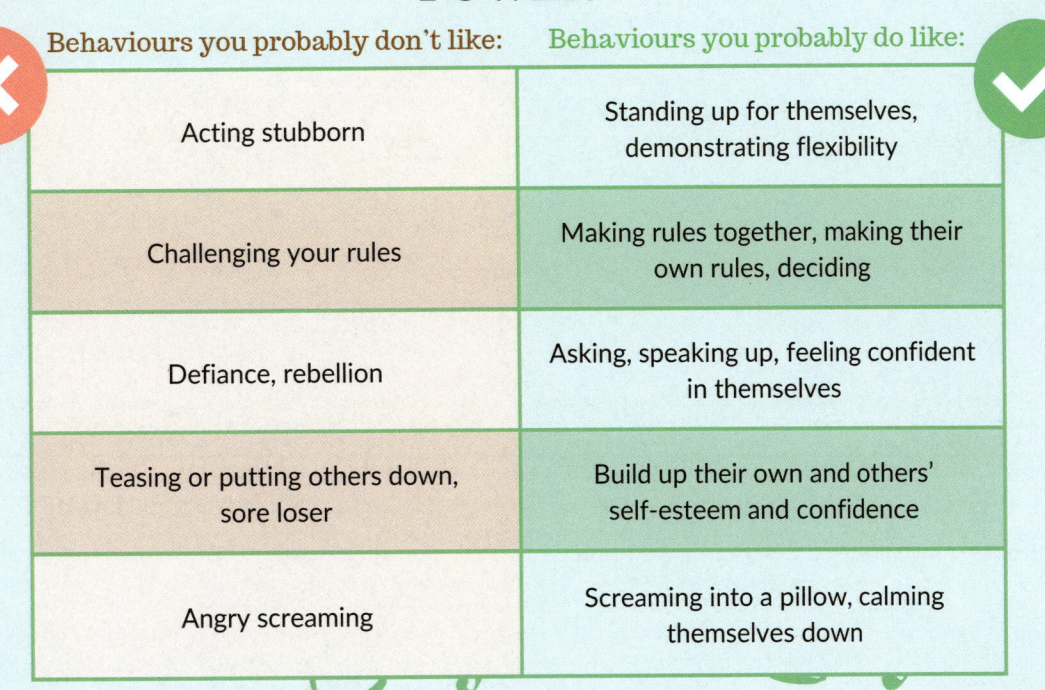

❌ Behaviours you probably don't like:	✅ Behaviours you probably do like:
Acting stubborn	Standing up for themselves, demonstrating flexibility
Challenging your rules	Making rules together, making their own rules, deciding
Defiance, rebellion	Asking, speaking up, feeling confident in themselves
Teasing or putting others down, sore loser	Build up their own and others' self-esteem and confidence
Angry screaming	Screaming into a pillow, calming themselves down

Notice the many ways your child meets their needs.

Refer to the behaviour charts on the previous two pages.

How is your child currently meeting their need for **CONNECTION** in ways you **DON'T LIKE**?

How is your child currently meeting their need for **CONNECTION** in ways you **DO LIKE**?

How is your child currently meeting their need for **EXPERIENCE** in ways you **DON'T LIKE**?

How is your child currently meeting their need for **EXPERIENCE** in ways you **DO LIKE**?

How is your child currently meeting their need for **POWER** in ways you **DON'T LIKE**?

How is your child currently meeting their need for **POWER** in ways you **DO LIKE**?

How do YOU feel and act when your needs are NOT met?

Do you see any similarities between your actions and your child's?

How are *YOU* currently meeting your need for **CONNECTION**, **EXPERIENCE** AND **POWER** in ways you **DON'T LIKE**?

How are *YOU* currently meeting your need for **CONNECTION**, **EXPERIENCE** AND **POWER** in ways you **DO LIKE**?

Help your child change their own behaviour by understanding what is driving it.

If you start your inquiry from a place of already knowing that your child IS good, that something must have got in their way to result in them behaving in a way you don't like, you can stay present and curious.

Refer to the behaviour charts to find the needs behind your child's behaviour.

What did my child do? What actually happened?

Why would my GREAT child do that? What NEED is my child trying to meet?

Let's take a pause.

Before we dive deeper into the topic of boundaries, let's pause and take a moment to check in.

Drawing on my years of coaching experience I understand that this stage can be a tricky one for many parents. I've gained valuable insights into what might be going on for you at this moment, so I want to let you know it's not uncommon for parents to feel on the verge of giving up.

It's totally normal to feel panic creeping in. You might have 101 reasons why you think these methods won't work for you or your child. Maybe you have thoughts like: *'This is NEVER going to work!'* or *'My child will just ignore me if I try a* **CAN DO** *approach.'* or *'It's all well and good if I have time, but I don't have time to use these tools all day; I've got to get to work and out the door in the morning.'*

Or you might feel blamed or judged, whether it's from others scrutinising your parenting choices or your own critical inner voice adding to the challenge. It can feel tough trying a new parenting approach, so be gentle with yourself during this time of transition.

If you're feeling triggered, anxious, or tempted to toss this book across the room, take a moment. Return to this page and practise SWYS for yourself, reminding yourself that all your thoughts are valid.

One reason things might feel particularly challenging right now is that your brain craves predictability. It thrives on knowing how to do things, so when you attempt to change your habits, it feels clunky and awkward, and your brain can take that as proof that you're not getting it right, or it's too hard.

Change may seem out of reach because your brain prefers the easy, familiar path and will conjure up countless reasons why new approaches won't work. It's almost as if your brain is trying to trick you into maintaining what's 'normal' for you.

Remember, you don't yet have all the pieces of the puzzle. This is the messy middle! Just like when you learnt to drive – at first it took effort, and now it's second nature. This moment is all about practicing and making changes. It's supposed to feel challenging; you're re-wiring your brain!

Change is a gradual process. Believing change is possible is the starting point for transformation, and you wouldn't be reading this workbook if you didn't think things could change. Next, you gain insights by understanding the dynamics at play. Then, you move on to problem-solving and addressing challenges in new ways. The progression leads to implementation, applying newfound knowledge for positive change in your parenting. And soon, this way will become your new normal.

Embracing this as your new normal will feel like flipping a switch. Life is about to become brighter, a tad easier and a whole lot more enjoyable with a Language of Listening magic sprinkled in.

DIVING DEEPER INTO
BOUNDARIES

COACHING INSTEAD OF CONTROLLING

When my daughter was little and I was struggling with her out-of-control behaviour, I thought I only had two options for boundaries:

- Come down hard to show her who's boss.
- Give in to her demands.

It never occurred to me that there could be another way. These were the only boundary strategies that were modelled for me as I grew up. No wonder I had a hard time holding boundaries… until I learnt that boundaries weren't about winning or losing.

When you become a life coach for your child, your whole perception changes and new options arise.

Instead of using boundaries to control your child, you use boundaries to bring out your child's **STRENGTHs** and help them get what they want or need in ways that work for you both.

The **CAN DO** tool helps you get on your child's side and bring out their problem-solving skills, self-control, ability to handle big emotions and so much more. These are the **STRENGTHs** that enable your child to manage their own behaviour.

Here's what getting on your child's side with coaching sounds like compared to the traditional approach of control.

Typically, when a child wants something that's not OK with the parent, like more screen time, the parent responds with their boundary: *'No more screen time. You've had your lot today!'*

The usual kerfuffle begins because the child won't give up what they want and the parent won't give up what they want! The child pushes against the boundary. The parent pushes back from the other side to hold the boundary in place. This is a classic example of a power struggle.

'But I want more screen time,' the child yells.

'I said no more screen time. You're addicted! Too much screen time is bad for you,' The parent replies. *'But I need more screen time. I don't play that much. All my friends are playing. I want to play with them,'* the child snaps back.

The child and parent both start getting frustrated; the situation escalates; threats, shouting and demands get thrown around; and either the child or parent has a meltdown.

That's the traditional win-lose model we learnt in childhood.

With coaching skills and the same boundary, it sounds like this...

The child wants more screen time, and that's not OK with the parent. So there's the boundary again. But this time, the parent starts the conversation with a SAY WHAT YOU SEE response:

'Of course you want more screen time. You really like playing with your friends, AND playing now is not OK. Oh! Having to stop is so annoying!'

Same boundary, but using SWYS and validating what the child likes and wants puts the parent on the same side as their child. The parent looks at the boundary from their child's perspective and then helps them try to figure out a CAN DO that meets their needs within it.

In this example, the needs screen time meets could be the need for connection with friends, the need for experience to unwind after school and the need for power by being great at something to build confidence before tackling homework.

If more screen time after homework and dinner is OK with you, your coaching might sound like this: *'Let's see. No more screen time now, AND you want to play with your friends. Must be something you can do to make sure you have time to play with your friends online after homework and dinner.'*

You can feel how that sets up a win-win. Your boundary is just the way it is, and you're on your child's side looking at the boundary together, helping them figure out what they CAN DO.

You're not offering the CAN DO to stop your child from getting what they want. You're offering it to help them get what they want or need inside your boundaries.

Read that again! This is one of the biggest shifts to make as a parent.

You skip the struggle because, with coaching skills, you're always on your child's side helping them figure out what they CAN DO or helping them handle their feelings of disappointment with SWYS.

Wants – our true motivation in life

Did you grow up thinking that wanting things for yourself is selfish or takes away from others? Or maybe you've heard that it's your job as a parent to teach your kids that they can't always get what they want in life.

But have you ever questioned who taught you these things? Because they simply aren't true!

It's completely natural for all of us to have our own desires and motivations. Knowing what we want, trusting ourselves and being able to see the possibilities in life are what motivates us to take action and achieve our goals.

And guess what? Going after what we want doesn't mean we have to ignore what others want!

With the **CAN DO** approach, we raise children who know how to trust their inner drive and achieve their goals, all while staying within OUR boundaries.

I can't overstate the importance of raising children who trust their inner drive. Uncertainty about our preferences and desires stops us from taking action because it's difficult to make decisions and take action when we're not clear about what we truly like or want and don't see any possibility to get it.

CAN DOs create 'win-win' situations where children can practise going after what they want in life while respecting other people's boundaries at the same time.

We don't want to stifle our child's natural desire to succeed and chase their dreams. By supporting our children from a young age to get what they want within our boundaries, we can raise self-motivated children who know how to pursue their goals.

You know something else? We don't have to micromanage them; we can just step back and watch their inner drive lead them towards success.

Most motivational experts agree that the key to success is knowing what you want and going after it. It's not what other people say you should want, but what YOU really want!

Unfortunately, many of us were raised to believe that wanting what we want is wrong or that it's impossible to achieve what we desire in life. As a result, some of us became adults who are unsure of what we want. We feel powerless to go after our desires, or we disconnect from them entirely, which can lead to feelings of hopelessness or despair. It's no surprise that many of us lose faith in ourselves and our dreams.

That's not what we want for our children. We want our kids to feel empowered to pursue their dreams while being considerate of others.

Your boundaries are all about what YOU want and are willing to do, not about stopping your child or being right or wrong.

Here's an example.

After spending a few days in London, I was utterly exhausted and keen to get back to my own bed. When we got home, my 13-year-old daughter was invited to the movies with her friends. She asked me if I could drive her there.

'I'm not driving anywhere. I'm not even taking you to the station. I'm too tired,' I told her.

My daughter walked away, muttering under her breath. But a few moments later, she returned with a new proposal.

'If I can get collected and dropped off at home again, can I go?' she asked.

'Of course,' I replied.

If I had simply told my daughter that she couldn't go because I didn't feel like driving her or had tried to convince her that going to the movies wasn't a good idea, I would have missed out on the opportunity to encourage her to do her own problem-solving and experience herself as resourceful.

My daughter immediately went to work on finding a solution that respected my boundary and got her what she wanted. She called her friend and arranged for her friend's mum to pick her up and drop her off. She even had her friend's mum buy her a ticket and promptly paid her back.

By holding boundaries in this way, we help program our children's brains to look for solutions and become more independent problem-solvers. We show them they can go after what they want while respecting other people's boundaries.

This is the win-win of coaching where we get to hold our boundaries while also supporting our children to find solutions within our boundaries.

A SIMPLE AND EFFECTIVE WAY TO GAIN WILLING COOPERATION

Always start a CAN DO with SAY WHAT YOU SEE.

For many of us, this way can seem alien. Our brain is programmed to think that by helping our child get what they want or need, we are giving in to our child's demands at the cost of our own wants or needs.

If that's where your brain goes, notice how your old programming of seeing things as winning or losing is showing up.

To get willing cooperation, you need to look for the win-win. You hold your boundary AND, at the same time, help your child meet their needs within your boundary.

'You want to run and run, AND *running here isn't safe.* Must be some way you can get all that energy out and stay safe.'

Starting with SWYS before stating your boundary or adding a CAN DO helps your child feel heard and understood first. This is so important! Children must feel heard and understood before they can effectively listen and respond to you. That's what frees them up to listen to your guidance.

Responding with SWYS first also helps you keep your focus on what your child wants. Remember, this way is NOT about stopping your child from getting what they want; it's about coaching them to get what they want **within** your boundary.

Starting with SWYS meets your child's NEED for connection. You'll notice your child will naturally decrease their defensiveness and reactiveness, the major causes of power struggles. With you on their side, your child will be primed to find CAN DOs that meet their needs inside your boundaries.

I know this way will lead to noticeable differences for both you and your child. It has to since you're working together on the same team and seeing the best in each other.

CAN DOs help your child meet their own needs and wants (their personal boundaries) inside your boundaries. Mutual respect is the result.

Always start with SAY WHAT YOU SEE, and then add a CAN DO.

Examples:

'You WANT to play, AND it's bath time. Must be something you CAN DO to play and get ready for your bath.'

'You WANT to play with the toy and it belongs to someone else, AND they get to decide. Hmm, must be something you CAN DO to have a turn.'

'You WANT to hit something, AND I'm not for hitting. Must be something you CAN DO to get your anger out without hurting anyone or anything!'

'You WANT to go home with your friend after school today, AND I haven't met their parents yet. Must be something you CAN DO to spend time together that would be OK with me.'

'You WANT to stay out late with friends, AND I'm concerned about your safety. Must be something you CAN DO to have fun while also letting me know your whereabouts and honouring a reasonable curfew.'

'You WANT more free time, AND I want to stick to the schedule. Must be something you CAN DO to manage your responsibilities while still having time for yourself.'

Your turn:

State your child's WANTS first.

As you read in the last few pages, the **CAN DO** tool is all about redirecting your focus to what your child wants or likes and how they can get it within your boundary. Without it, you'll likely end up in power struggles that weaken your connection and undermine the willing cooperation you're after.

Even in the midst of a busy schedule and tasks that need to be completed, you can state your child's wants first. This is how you help them harness their true motivation and gain willing cooperation.

This way is the win-win of coaching. No one has to give up what they want.

> To help you transition from coercive reward and punishment statements to supportive **CAN DOs**, you can try conditional **CAN DOs**. They automatically shift your focus to what your child wants:
>
> - 'You **want** dessert. You can have that as soon as you clean up.'
> - 'You **want** your iPad. You can have it as soon as you've finished your homework.'
> - 'You **want** to go to the park. You can go as soon as you've tidied your room.'

When phrased as a way for them to get what they want, your child will hear that you are on their side. **CAN DO** statements like that are clearly conditional but shift the tone. They keep the focus on what the child wants, and wants are more internally motivating and inspiring for your child than avoiding things they don't want.

Hello, willing cooperation!

What You Want matters!

State your child's WANTS first.

And whether you realise it or not, hearing what your child (or others) wants is inspiring for you too. Because being helpful is in your nature, it inspires you to WANT to help them succeed.

By contrast, rules phrased like threats, *'Do this thing you don't want to do or no goodies,'* place the focus on what the child doesn't want to do and on you doing something you don't want to do like withholding or removing something your child wants.

Though rules like that and the conditional **CAN DOs** I'm offering may seem like two ways of saying the same thing, it's harder to see the win-win in the 'do this or else' example. Even when the child does what you want, they are complying because they fear the consequences.

While language doesn't necessarily change the situation (your child does something and gets what they want, or doesn't do something and doesn't get what they want), it can change the outcome since it puts the power to get what the child wants in the child's hands. The empowering nature of a **CAN DO**, even a conditional one, shifts the way you and your child see and experience the situation.

A client of mine said to her son, *'You want cake. You can have that as soon as you finish your dinner.'* Her son had a bit of a moan, and within moments, he was back at the table eating his dinner! The moan tells you he wasn't completely willing (remember this is only a transitional step to get you from coercion to coaching), but his mum's focus on what he wanted helped them both succeed.

I'll teach you how to use unconditional **CAN DOs** next, but for now, practising these conditional **CAN DOs** will help you focus more easily on what your child wants. For proof that you can do it, look for examples where it helps your children comply. The more you focus on what your child wants and how they can get it within your boundary, the more this new way will start to feel like *'This is just what I do.'*

YOUR TURN:

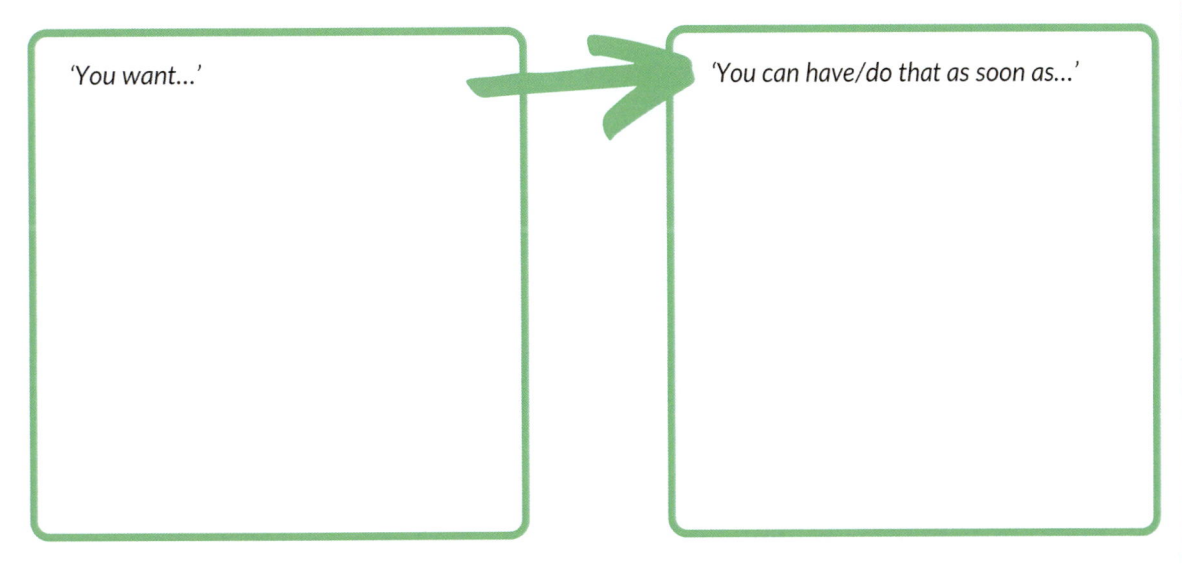

'You want...'	'You can have/do that as soon as...'

Why it's so important to start with SAY WHAT YOU SEE before adding a CAN DO boundary.

Saying what your child wants, wishes, or the intention behind their actions is what helps you shift your perception and puts you on your child's side. It keeps you focused on finding solutions that work for you and your child.

- It helps you understand the healthy need behind your child's behaviour (connection, experience or power).
- It helps you understand what your child wants or wishes.
- It helps you see the best in your child and reflect it back to them, which naturally meets their need for power and connection and primes them to want to listen to your guidance.
- It helps you get more willing cooperation because you connect your child directly to their own internal motivation.

If you are having a hard time spotting the wants and wishes behind your child's actions, check out the Hidden STRENGTHs tool in the third section of this workbook (see page 275).

How to step in and hold a boundary for your child

It's our responsibility to ensure our children's safety and well-being. Setting our children up for success helps us meet that goal even if it sometimes means saying 'no' or making choices our child will not like. When we see our child struggling in a situation they can't handle, rather than leaving them there (and blaming them when they fail), it's our job to step in to help them be successful.

Let's look at an example.

My children used to love going to indoor play areas. Their eyes would light up with excitement as they saw all the colourful slides, the toys and the other children playing.

I knew these places were often tricky for my daughter. It was stimulation overload! I would sit and keep a watchful eye on my children, but as time passed, I noticed that my daughter was getting more and more excited. In her rush to go up the big slide, she had started pushing other children out of the way.

I hurried over and used **SWYS**: *'It looks like you really want a turn on the slide.'*

I then added a **CAN DO** boundary: *'And pushing past them is not OK. Let's take a moment together and think of what you can do next time.'*

After a few minutes of downtime, I noticed that my daughter was still overstimulated and feeling overwhelmed by the noise and children. I realised that staying longer was setting my daughter up to fail, so I decided to leave early, not as punishment but in support of my daughter.

I called my son over, told him we were leaving and would come back another day. Then I picked my daughter up and said, *'It's time to go home now, sweetheart. It looks like it's too busy and too much for you today.'*

As we left the play centre, I hugged my unhappy daughter tightly. I reminded her that I loved her no matter what and said, *'It's OK to feel overwhelmed sometimes. Let's try again another day.'*

The message that my daughter received about herself was drastically different from what it would have been if her actions had been met with punishments or telling off. Despite struggling, she knew that I believed in her, supported her and had her back no matter what. The unwavering support and trust I have for my daughter continues to help her see the best in herself today.

WHAT HOLDING HEALTHY BOUNDARIES SOUNDS LIKE

- 'That's not OK with me.'
- 'I don't like that.'
- 'People aren't for hitting.'
- 'People aren't for shouting at.'
- 'I don't like being spoken to like that.'
- 'That's not going to work for me.'

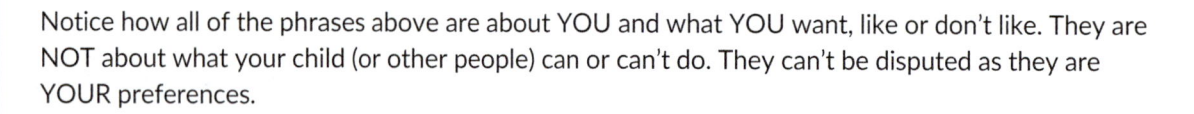

Notice how all of the phrases above are about YOU and what YOU want, like or don't like. They are NOT about what your child (or other people) can or can't do. They can't be disputed as they are YOUR preferences.

Let's look a couple of examples that may sound like boundaries but aren't.

✗ **'That's not kind. Don't you dare speak to me like that.'**

Notice how that sentence is all about the child and what they can't do. It actually puts the child in charge of holding your boundary and you in charge of controlling their speech. Completely backwards!

Can you also see how it uses shame and judgement to try to change your child's behaviour? We know that shame is an ineffective strategy. It affects your child's self-esteem and self-worth, and it hurts your relationship with them.

There's also an expectation that the child could have chosen to speak differently in the moment. Remember, the way you think about your child's behaviour affects how you respond. Thinking that they wanted to speak to you like this and that they're unkind doesn't leave you in a position to offer loving guidance and hold firm and kind boundaries.

Instead, when you say, *'I don't like being spoken to like that. That's not OK with me,'* that is a clear boundary. It puts you in charge of what you will do next, regardless of what your child does. It also models for your child what holding a healthy boundary sounds like so they will be able to do that themselves.

Here's another example of an ineffective boundary.

> ✗ **'Don't hit me. That makes me sad.'**

What that statement really conveys is: *'If you knew it made me sad, then you wouldn't hit me.'* It's giving the child information along with a dose of shame to get them to change their behaviour. This not only puts your child in charge of holding your boundary, but it puts them in charge of how you feel!

When you're not clear on your boundaries, it's confusing for your child. They respond to your words with child logic and reasoning, so it's not uncommon for a child to reply, *'I'm not making you sad. You're making me sad!'*

Instead, when you reply with, *'I'm not for hitting. That's not OK with me,'* it can't be disputed. It's not OK with you; you don't like it. And rather than trying to control your child, you're now on your child's side, coaching your child to find a healthy way to meet their needs without hitting you.

For example, they could get their frustrations out by stamping their feet or hitting a pillow. You can then finish by pointing out a STRENGTH when they find a solution that works for them.

'Look at you! You found a way to get your upset out! You got it out and calmed yourself down!'

Because children need repeated opportunities to see themselves as successful and to practise meeting their needs in healthy ways, finishing a tricky situation by pointing out a STRENGTH is the quickest and most lasting way to help your child change their behaviour. Their success gives them proof they can do it! (I'll teach you more about the STRENGTH tool in the third section of this workbook.)

I know how to get my mad out!

Don't look for **BLAME;** Look for **SOLUTIONS**

'Happiness is not the absence of problems; it's the ability to deal with them.' – Steve Maraboli

This quote really resonates with me. It comes to mind when I think of the purpose of **CAN DOs**.

When we coach our children to look for solutions, they start thinking, *'There must be a way.'* It actually programs their brain to look for possibilities in life. Because they've grown up knowing that solutions are possible and that they're problem-solvers who can figure things out, they are able to go after what they want in life. They automatically respond to tricky situations by finding solutions.

When we focus on finding solutions, it keeps us and our children moving forward.

By contrast, blame focuses our attention on finding fault. For example, saying or thinking things about your child, such as: *'Trust you to ruin the day! why can't you just be happy?'* or *'You're so lazy. You never clean up after yourself,'* leads to defensiveness, judgement and shame, which leaves us spinning in circles. No wonder it can feel like we're living in the movie *Groundhog Day*.

As it turns out, shame is not a good motivator. It leads to a sense of unworthiness and feelings of hopelessness. A human who grows up believing that nothing they do will make things better, grows up not seeing the possibilities in life. That shows up in all sorts of emotional and behavioural issues later in life.

Let's look at an example.

When my children were younger, they used to fight over whose turn it was to sit in the front seat of the car. Every. Single. Day. It would always end with them in tears and me wanting to scream.

Before I learnt how to coach them, I'm sure I did the usual things: told them off, shouted at them, banned anyone from sitting in the front seat of the car, threatened no screen time if they argued etc. Once, I remember making them walk home from school with me because the fighting had got too much. (True story!) I left the car outside the school gates and came back later in the day to drive it home.

But none of that helped us find solutions. Resentment grew, and if I hadn't changed my reactions, I bet I would still be dealing with the same issue to this day.

Here's what I finally said:

SWYS: *'You both want to sit in the front seat of the car.'*
CAN DO: *'I've noticed it's tricky when we don't have a plan for who's turn it is to sit up front. I wonder what we can do to make it more peaceful. Have a think about it, and we can discuss a plan this evening.'*

That evening, they devised a complicated rule: take turns in the front seat, but if a friend joined, their turn would be forfeited so they could sit with their friend in the back. If a journey included a motorway, they would swap seats midway or when we made a stop. Initially, they used a rota pinned to the fridge, but it soon became unnecessary.

To this day, nearly 10 years later, there has not been one argument over who sits where. And the beauty of this approach is that I didn't have to come up with a solution. They came up with a way that worked for them. By turning over the problem-solving to my children, they were more invested in the outcome and, as a result, more able to deal with future problems.

These real-life experiences bring out your child's **STRENGTHs** – turn-taking, being a team player, able to handle frustration and disappointment, adaptability, negotiation and problem-solving skills etc – abilities and skills they can use for life.

Changing the dynamic from blaming to finding solutions is how you create life long problem-solvers. It helps you work together as a team to find real solutions to tricky situations.

YOUR TURN:

Think of times in your daily life that feel a bit tricky.

It could be you've noticed that the morning is getting a bit tricky when trying to leave the house on time. It could be that bedtime is getting a bit dragged out. Or it could be bath, teeth-brushing, homework or screen time.

Instead of using threats, blame or shame to try to change your children's behaviour, use **CAN DOs** to invite them to find solutions to these tricky situations.

If your children are new to this, you may have to give them time to think of solutions. That's OK. You can tell them you'll be coming back to the conversation later in the day, just like I did above. Or if they are still toddlers, you can suggest some **CAN DOs** they can choose from.

At this stage, it's important to keep the conversations about finding solutions. If you find it slipping back into rehashing the past of 'who did what' or 'who said what', STOP and refocus on finding solutions.

Remember that every idea your child comes up with is a good idea. The question is just whether or not you like it since it has to work for you too.

Once when I said to my 8-year-old son, *'Bedtime is getting a bit tricky. I'm wondering what we can do about it,'* he replied, *'Stay up till 11pm!'* Well, clearly that wasn't a solution that worked for me. So I replied, *'You'd like that! However, that's not going to work for me,'* and we carried on brainstorming solutions that worked for him and were still within my boundary.

Your children might come up with a solution, and you're not sure whether it will work or not. Give it a try! Nothing is set in stone.

A client of mine told her son, *'I've noticed when the PlayStation is on in the morning, getting ready for school gets a bit tricky. I'm wondering what we can do about it.'* He thought of a solution – sleeping in his school clothes so he had one less thing to do in the morning! Well, this mum thought it was a funny idea and told her son, *'Let's try it!'*

It worked briefly, but he soon realised he preferred pyjamas and decided to keep the PlayStation off in the morning instead.

It's a good reminder that whatever idea your child comes up with, all you have to ask yourself is: *'Do I like it? Am I willing to give it a try?'* If not, keep coming up with other possibilities together.

Use this space to to think of solutions to your tricky situations.
Start with: *'I've noticed that ___ is a bit tricky. I'm wondering what we can do about it.'*

BOUNDARIES AND RULES

What is the difference, you may ask?

In Language of Listening terms, your boundaries are your preferences – what you like or want and what you don't like or don't want – and your rules are the things your child can do to stay inside your boundaries. Rules are there to help you hold your boundaries and help your child succeed.

Rules are NOT there to punish or control your kids.

In fact, when you have strong boundaries, you often don't need to make separate rules at all. When you've stepped into a coaching mindset and have experienced getting on your child's side enough, your perception shifts. Your boundaries become solid and children accept them 'as is'.

Here's a great illustration of how children accept things 'as is' when we do things consistently as part of our family life.

A little boy was walking home from school with his friend for his first ever play date. His mother overheard him tell his friend, *'In our home, we have a rule. We take our shoes off when we come inside.'* This mother told me that she has never mentioned this as a rule; it's just something they do in their family. This little boy was so used to taking his shoes off at the front door that, in his mind, it became a rule.

While doing things consistently can communicate some of your rules, sometimes rules need to be spoken to help children succeed. Rules tell them what is expected so they can manage their own behaviour and stay within the boundary the rule represents.

Think of rules as scaffolding support – the older your child becomes, the less scaffolding your child needs.

A rule is one way your child can stay within your boundary.

For example, if you want your child to stay safe, that's your boundary. So one rule you could set for your child when they are little might be holding your hand while crossing the road. When they get older and know how to stay safe crossing the road, you would change the rule to allow them to cross on their own. Same boundary, different rules.

CAN DOs are similar – for any boundary, there are many ways your child can stay inside it. The difference is that with rules, you usually decide; with **CAN DOs**, your child gets to decide which way to stay within your boundary. That's why the **CAN DO** tool is so powerful. You're helping your child decide how to meet their needs AND stay within your boundaries. That's problem-solving. This is the true win-win of coaching.

Along with problem-solving, you can coach your child to bring out their self-control and emotional self-regulation to help them stay within your boundaries. I'll teach you more about that in the **STRENGTHs** section of this workbook.

EXAMPLE

BOUNDARY	POSSIBLE RULES*
I want to leave the house on time in the morning. It's non-negotiable. My first questions are: 'How can I set us up for success? How can I manage the environment instead of my children?' Then I remind myself: 'How everyone gets ready is up to them. Younger children might need more of my support, but as long as everyone is ready to leave on time (my actual goal), that's OK with me.'	Clothes are put out the night before. School bags are packed and ready the night before. School shoes and sports bags are in the hall the night before. You can watch TV once you're dressed. You can play after breakfast. You sit in the kitchen for breakfast. (These were the rules when my children were little and needed more of my support to stay on task. Now that my children are teenagers, I don't need all of these rules. School bags packed and sports bags ready have just become 'how it is' in our home.)
Peaceful PlayStation playing	We take it in turns who plays first and have a rota to remind us whose turn it is. When your time is nearly up, check to see if you have enough time to finish a new level before starting one. When it's your turn, tell the person playing. You are not allowed to turn off someone else game even if it's your turn.

*These are a few rules that worked for me and my family. That doesn't mean they are 'right' for you. Rules are personal to you and your family. They need to support your child and work for your family.

YOUR TURN:

BOUNDARY	POSSIBLE RULES

From WANTS to possibilities

Whenever you feel stuck and things don't seem to be going to plan, use this chart to get back on track.

The first step to change is awareness. Become clear on what exactly you don't like about the situation. Is it that dinner time is getting a bit stressful? Kids arguing more than usual? Bedtime is a disaster? Whatever it is, fill in the first box.

Then fill in the boxes below for what you **DO LIKE** and **WANT**. Brainstorm possible solutions to get you what you want. Use all the tools you learnt in this workbook to help you find solutions.

Here's an example.

(Remember, this is an example, not advice for what you should do. Awareness is all about what works for you and your family. It's all about focusing your attention on finding possibilities and solutions.)

What you don't like	I don't like dinner time battles – kids bickering, youngest child getting up constantly, talking over one another.
What you do like	I like it when we can sit together, share stories and have fun as a family.
What you want	I want all the family to sit at the table together having pleasant, supportive conversations and getting a chance to share their stories with others listening.
Possible CAN DOs & Rules	**CAN DOs**: Ask kids for ways to help everyone share conversations without talking at the same time. Have TV dinner when everyone is tired. Point out STRENGTHs like 'waiting your turn' instead of 'not interrupting', and notice small steps in the right direction. **Rules:** Eat at the table or not at all. Sit during the meal. Clean up together before eating dessert. Use a talking stick to promote patience in waiting your turn to talk.
Solutions/Wishes	The kids solution was taking turns talking first at dinner, and they made a rota! The rule of cleaning up before dessert is helping us sit together longer at the table. Now, I wish everyone's table manners were better. (Start chart again to clarify what you want and find possible solutions.)

Your turn: From WANTS to possibilities

What you don't like

What you do like

What you want

Possible CAN DOs & Rules

Solutions/Wishes

Why We Slip Up When Holding Boundaries

HOW BOUNDARIES ARE FORMED

Children learn by observing and imitating the behaviours of parents and caregivers. They internalise these behaviours and use them to develop their own understanding of boundaries.

If your parents held boundaries by punishing and controlling you, you most likely learnt that boundaries are mean, controlling and all about getting other people to do things they don't want to do.

Or maybe you were raised to be a 'good' child and were taught either explicitly or implicitly that your own boundaries were selfish, and you weren't kind if you held them.

No wonder it's so hard for so many of us to hold boundaries calmly and confidently. But without healthy boundaries, resentment and anger grow, and we don't feel secure and safe in our relationships.

Understanding how you currently see boundaries opens up different possibilities.

What comes to your mind when you read the word boundaries?

How did your parents or caregivers typically hold boundaries with you?

Did your parents honour your boundaries growing up?

Were you allowed to say 'no'?

Were you allowed to have a different preference from your parents?

How do you feel when you hold a boundary with your child?

Do you feel differently when you hold a boundary with another adult compared to when you hold a boundary with your child?

Boundaries are your preferences and values – what you like or don't like. They are not judgements of right or wrong.

As I mentioned before, authentic boundaries are not a means of judging or controlling others. Stating them communicates what you are comfortable with or not comfortable with in a relationship so others don't have to guess.

It's easier for others to interact respectfully with you when they know what is OK with you and what is not.

By thinking of boundaries as personal preferences rather than moral judgements, you can approach them in a more positive and open-minded way. All members of your family can have different boundaries.

Let's look at some examples.

> **Here's a small list of some of my boundaries. They are all about what I LIKE or DON'T LIKE:**
> - I don't like my dog sleeping on my bed. My sister likes her dog sleeping on her bed.
> - I like my kids making a camp with the sofa cushions. My friend likes the sofa cushions staying on the sofa.
> - I like people taking their shoes off when they come into my house. I've many friends who don't mind if people leave their shoes on.
> - I don't like loud music on all day at home. I like quiet or my head feels like it's about to explode. My daughter loves music all day. Not right or wrong, just our preferences. (She now has headphones!)
> - I like my family sitting at the table for dinner. My friend likes to eat with her husband and have the kids eat earlier in the sitting room.
> - I like having my children's friends over for play dates during the week. My friend only likes play dates on the weekends.
> - I don't like scary movies. My children and husband love them. They watch them together, and I don't.
> - I like going for long walks. My family doesn't. I usually take walks by myself or with friends.

Notice that my boundaries are the core of who I am. They are what I care about, drive my decisions, and help me formulate rules to protect and honour myself.

By honouring my own boundaries, I am modelling self-respect for my children.

The starting point for holding authentic boundaries is becoming clear about what you LIKE and DON'T LIKE.

Write your list below:

Why is it so important to know what you like and don't like?

What we like and want in life is the essence of who we are. It's how we know our authentic self and what makes each one of us unique.

Boundaries inform what is or isn't OK with you in any given moment, how you want to be treated by others, how you want your belongings to be used, what you want to spend your time doing etc.

> - Holding boundaries that are authentically yours isn't selfish. It allows you to show up in the world as the most loving, kind and genuine version of yourself.
> - When you learn to hold authentic boundaries, you lead by example, allowing your child to be their authentic self too.
> - If we're not honest with each other and don't share our true preferences in life with others, then we never truly know each other.

Think about it: If you pretend to like or do things to avoid upsetting others, keep from being judged or gain acceptance, you're hiding your true self, and the other person never really knows you.

It's the same for your children too.

If you dismiss their likes and wants, don't let them hold healthy boundaries, don't respect their choices, call them silly, or tell them off when they share their preferences with you, then they will stop sharing their true self with you.

They're likely thinking: *'Why bother sharing with mummy or daddy? I'll just be told I'm wrong for wanting or liking something.'* In reality, you can't stop their wants; you just stop knowing what their wants are.

Sometimes, parents can become so focused on raising 'good' children that they forget to accept their children for who they are.

I've had many clients over the years share with me that their parents don't truly know them. They were so used to being told off for having a difference of opinion or trying to hold a personal boundary that they stopped sharing their true self with their parents. One client told me it was like she had two lives. She learnt to change her true identity when she was around her mother.

SUPER-STAR STARTERS

Using these phrases strengthens your child's inner guidance system. They program your child's inner voice so they grow up knowing what they like and want in life. They know their preferences matter and can trust themselves.

You noticed...

You're feeling...

You LIKE / DON'T LIKE...

You WANT / DON'T WANT...

You WISH...

It is important to you that...

You knew...

You figured out...

You decided...

You remembered...

Where can you use these phrases with your child?

You can use these phrases with yourself too!

Validate yourself and your preferences.

HOW TO STOP MOST OF YOUR FAMILY ARGUMENTS

Do you know what one definition of an argument is? It's two people each trying to convince the other person that they're wrong!

That's why arguing is so tiring. You have to explain AND defend your way of thinking at the same time.

Think about the last argument you had with your child. I bet you were trying to convince them to see things your way or trying to change their opinion or their 'want'. And the funny thing is, they were probably doing the exact same thing, trying to convince you to change your opinion or your 'want'.

So there it was – two people each trying to convince the other that they're wrong.

Instead of trying to use logic and reasons to get your child (or anyone) to change their mind, what if you are simply right for wanting what you want and your child is right for wanting what they want too?

Now, before you go thinking this means giving in to your child's wants, let me clarify. While your child is 'RIGHT' for liking and wanting what they want, it doesn't mean you have to give it to them. In fact, more than anything, your child just wants to know that what they want matters to you, regardless of whether or not they can have it. Deciding if they can have it remains up to you. The reason why is maturity.

As we discussed earlier, children think differently than we do. Because they live in the present, their wants will be right for the short term (instant gratification etc). But as an adult with access to long- term thinking, yours have the potential to be right for the short term AND the long term for both you and your child. That means decisions about what is best for your child should be made by you until your child gains the judgement, experience and long-term thinking they need to decide for themselves… which is what turning over problem-solving to them with **CAN DOs** inside your boundaries helps them do.

Understanding this healthy balance, you can comfortably say to yourself, *'Of course my child wants to play more on the PlayStation, and I'm correct for saying "no more screen time today".'*

You don't need to spend time convincing your child or over-teaching them all the reasons why too much screen time isn't good (they already know!) or trying to guilt trip them into seeing things your way.

When you're not trying to convince your child they're wrong for wanting what they want, you have the space to be on their side, help them deal with disappointment and frustration, and coach them to find ways to meet their needs and get what they want WITHIN your boundary.

Boundaries get simpler when you realise that you don't need to convince, fix, or use logic or reasons to get your child to see things your way.

Your child doesn't have to like or want the same things as you. They might have to change what they do, but they don't have to change what they think, feel or want.

Believe me, it's so much easier when you stop trying to get your child to agree and, instead, simply say, '*Of course you want to play more on the PlayStation, and no more screen time today.*'

Because they are allowed to think, feel and want what they want, and they feel understood and valued, they can be far more cooperative.

YOU ARE BOTH 'RIGHT'

Instead of thinking in terms of right or wrong, it's better to approach boundaries as individual preferences and perspectives.

Your child's likes and wants feel just as right to them as yours do to you. Your likes and wants and your child's are equal in importance to each of you; they both matter.

That's why I like looking at your likes and wants and theirs as balancing on the kitchen scales.

Read over the statements below, and notice what happens when you see what's perfect about each want. Instead of focusing on what is wrong or different, seeing the positive aspects of each want helps shift your perspective from confrontational to cooperative. This helps reduce the tension and stress in a situation, leading to more positive outcomes for all parties involved.

- Of course my child wants to run off down the road. They're exploring and don't yet recognise the danger, and I'm correct for keeping them safe.
- Of course my child wants to dash around the house like a lion before getting dressed, and I'm correct for saying, *'It's time to get ready for school.'*
- Of course my child wants more ice cream, and I'm correct for saying no to more ice cream.
- Of course my teen wants to borrow my car to go on a date, and I'm correct for saying, *'No night driving yet.'*

YOUR TURN:

How are you both right?

Example of holding a boundary with my teenagers:

'It's soooooo boring, I don't want to go.' Both my kids moaned, *'I'm not going. Walking round a stupid house looking at pictures, it's stupid!'* My teens were letting me know just how they felt about going on a family outing to a historic country house.

My husband and I wanted a day out with the kids that didn't include a trip to the movies or traipsing round shops. I had a brief feeling that this discussion might end in a flat-out refusal.

In the past, I would have tried to get them to want to go. I would have tried to convince and persuade them it was fun and that they would like it, saying something like: *'It IS fun. You might even learn something! You liked going to the last place we visited. You're just being difficult.'* Or I would have used shame and guilt to get them to comply, saying something like: *'After all I do for you, all you do is complain! Stop being so ungrateful.'*

But I knew those words would just lead to an almighty argument, causing more resistance. I reminded myself that my kids didn't have to like where we were going. How they felt about it was up to them. I didn't have to fix it for them.

So how did I respond this time?

'You find it boring! It's the last place you'd have chosen to go. And we're leaving at 10am.'

'Can we get a hot chocolate when we're out?' they asked.

'Of course!' I replied. *'That would be fun!'*

Fast forward a few hours... I watched my children walk together around the country house, pausing to look at the paintings and displays, smiling and having fun.

This is because when we try to change our child's opinion or try to make them like something they're sure they don't like, it often backfires, causing them to dig in their heels to prove their point. Granting them the space to form their own opinions shows respect and creates an environment where they feel understood.

And you'll have a much calmer and simpler time by holding your boundaries than by trying to control how your kids feel about things.

I can't begin to tell you how utterly freeing this is!

Where can you shift your boundary communication with your children? Where can you swap reacting to their words with letting them be, knowing they already have the ability within themselves to do just what they need to do to adapt?

Check in with yourself when setting a boundary.

Sometimes, you can get too used to saying 'no' and not realise how often it's your default response.

Pause before you respond to your child's next request, and ask yourself, *'Is "no" necessary?'* Is what your child wants to do actually OK with you or not?

Because boundaries are preferences, your boundary is 'just how it is' at any moment.

The good thing about authentic boundaries is that you are allowed to change your mind. They are flexible. And when things aren't working for you, you always have permission to do exactly that – change your mind.

> *'I've changed my mind. I've thought about it some more, and today it's OK with me.'*
>
> A 'yes' keeps you in charge of your boundary because you've granted permission.

It's OK for your children to be upset and not like your boundary.

Your child (or partner!) does not have to like or agree with your boundary. You are in charge of your boundary, and your child is in charge of finding a solution within your boundary.

Allowing your children to be upset and not like your boundary can be the hardest thing in the world. But you do your children no favours if you rescue them from their feelings. That sends the message that there's something wrong with feeling upset and that you don't have faith in their ability to handle disappointment or find solutions.

So when your children are screaming or sulking, remind yourself that you have the power to encourage and coach them to work through their frustrations, find solutions, persevere and adapt.

Practising and coaching your children to bring out their STRENGTHs helps you stay on your child's side and facilitate their growth.

It's very hard to hold boundaries if, when you hear other people's emotions or wants, you think you're responsible or need to fix things for them.

WHAT STOPS YOU HOLDING HEALTHY BOUNDARIES?

Establishing and upholding personal boundaries can be challenging if negative consequences were tied to them during childhood. This could involve having been shouted at or belittled, or having had your boundaries completely ignored.

On the other hand, if your parents lacked healthy boundaries, it might feel unfamiliar or uncomfortable to establish your own. Additionally, if you were expected to conform to your parents' thoughts, emotions and actions, you may now struggle with identifying and expressing your own feelings, desires and boundaries.

1 You don't hold your boundaries because you're worried about other people's reactions. You think you're responsible for or the cause of other people's upsets.

2 You think your boundaries are for controlling the outside world or stopping others from behaving in a way that makes you uncomfortable. It feels like situations or other people are responsible for or the cause of your feelings.

3 You think holding boundaries is mean and controlling and makes people do things they don't want to do.

4 When people don't agree with your boundary, you doubt yourself. You're unsure of what you want and may give in to other people's wants or try to get their approval.

5 When asked how you feel or what you want, you think there's a right way to respond. You tell others what you think you should feel or want, or simply go blank.

Do any of the reasons on the previous page resonate with you? Circle the ones that do.

Can you pinpoint a particular memory from your childhood?
Start to reflect on who gave you these messages about boundaries growing up, when or where.

How other people choose to respond when you hold a boundary is **their** responsibility, not **yours**.

We simply can't control other people, no matter how much we want to or how hard we try. The only person you have control over is yourself. You can control the choices you make and how you engage with others.

Letting go of the idea that boundaries control others is freeing and makes parenting easier. It gives you energy to focus on the control you do have and reduces the stress of constantly trying to fix others.

How to hold a boundary while coaching your upset child

1 Make your child 'right' for wanting things even if they can't have what they want.

2 Make it OK for them to feel disappointed.

3 Calmly set your boundary as 'just how it is' based on your preferences and judgement.

4 Do not get dragged into a discussion; you don't need to justify your boundary.

Your goal isn't to get your child to not be upset; it's to hold your boundary and support your child through their upset.

Remember, they are responsible for their own emotions and reactions, not you.

Here's an example of holding a boundary in public when your child is about to have a huge meltdown.

When you're concerned about others' opinions, it can be challenging to remain calm and validate your child during a public meltdown. Your first instinct may be to gain control over the situation.

Sometimes, it will feel as if you're holding off a huge meltdown by the skin of your teeth. It can be a struggle to keep validating your child when your buttons are being pushed. This can leave you feeling anxious or worried that you won't be able to control the outcome.

Remember to go easy on yourself and look for small moments of success.

If you have a child who acts 'strong-willed', I think this story will resonate with you and give you some ideas for how to bring everything back to calm quickly.

One day, I had to pop into the supermarket to grab something for dinner. We were rushed as my 8-year-old daughter's dance class was starting in 20 minutes. As I was walking down an aisle, my daughter ran off and quickly returned with an armful of sweets that she 'had to have right now!'

When I said, *'Not today.'* She began to get louder and more demanding. I paused and used a **SAY WHAT YOU SEE** response: *'You have your favourite sweets.'*

'Yes, I neeeeeeeed them,' she told me.

'You really want them. They're so yummy,' I replied. Holding my boundary, I said, *'We're running late, and we have snacks in the car.'*

She was getting more upset and said something like, *'It's not fair. I never get to buy sweets!'*

I knew this wasn't true but stayed calm by reminding myself not to get into an argument. I wasn't responsible for her happiness; I didn't need to feel guilty; and I knew she could calm herself down.

With as much sympathy as I could muster, I simply replied, *'Oh, girly!'* I was trying to remain calm at this stage but could feel myself getting annoyed. She was getting flustered.

So I simply said, *'Not today.'* I kept it really short and avoided diving into reasons. I knew she wouldn't hear my reasons anyway, and it would just invite her to tell me hers.

I bought our dinner, and we walked out to the car. I stayed with her in the car, listening and validating her even though what she was saying was illogical! She put the radio on, was grumpy for a minute, and then became calm again.

Drama over. The snacks in the car were fine.

NOTES

PEOPLE PLEASING

HOW PEOPLE PLEASING IS BORN

If you struggle to hold boundaries or to watch your child become upset when you hold one, you are not alone. Many parents struggle with this.

Do you ever feel like whatever you do, your child still isn't happy? …that if your child is upset, it's your fault? Maybe you spent years feeling guilty about causing other people's emotions, trying to please others and make everyone happy.

If this resonates, it's not your fault. You've been fed a lie! The belief that you cause other people's emotions and that they cause yours is mistaken. Isn't this what most of us have been led to believe?

It's even modelled in daily interactions and how people talk to each other.

> **How often have you heard people say things like this:**
> - ✗ '**You're making** mummy sad.'
> - ✗ '**You're making** me really mad right now!'
> - ✗ 'You're such a good girl/boy. **You're making** me so happy.'
> - ✗ '**You're making** Tilly sad. Share your toy with her.'

All these types of comments assume that we are the cause of others' reactions and emotions. It's this perception that keeps us stuck. If we feel like we're responsible for our child's happiness, or our child is responsible for ours, we learn to self-abandon, meaning that we deny our own emotions to please others in order to feel loved or worthy.

This is how people pleasing is born. We try to control another person's perception of us in the mistaken belief that that will make them love and accept us.

There is nothing the matter with you if you can't 'make' your child happy.

When your child isn't happy, they just aren't. Happiness is their responsibility. It's not your responsibility to change how your child thinks or feels. When you understand this, it enables you to see relationships in such a different light.

Let's look at an example:

> Suppose you organise a surprise party for a friend's birthday. They might react with excitement and joy or feel uncomfortable and overwhelmed. The way people respond to the same situation varies widely. How they react is entirely up to them.
>
> Instead of cause and effect, you can think of it as two things happening at the same time: you do something, **AND** the other person reacts to it in their own way. So if your friend likes their party, instead of thinking, '*I **made** them happy*,' think, '*I threw a party, **AND** they were happy*.' Happy or uncomfortable was up to them, not you.

We're not all tangled up with each other's emotions. How freeing is that?

And believe it or not, your child will thank you for it. They'll get to feel how they feel and work through it without the added burden of thinking they are making you feel a certain way.

It doesn't mean that you aren't a responsible parent, that you are trying to make your child's life difficult or that you don't care for their well-being. It simply means you are not responsible for their emotions and reactions. Theirs are not yours to fix.

ARE YOU A PEOPLE PLEASER?

The tendency to please others often originates in childhood. You may have had experiences that made it look like the only way to gain acceptance and validation was prioritising other people's needs and desires. Or you may have taken on the role of the family's peacemaker, doing whatever was necessary to avoid conflict. From experiences like those, you may have internalised the belief that you must earn love and approval, leading you to constantly put your own needs and wants aside.

Although people-pleasing behaviour may seem selfless and kind, it is often motivated by fear and a desire to control how others perceive and respond to you so you can feel safe. The misguided belief that it's selfless (and that selfless is a good thing) can lead you to neglect your own needs and boundaries.

As a result, people pleasing can leave you feeling physically and emotionally exhausted, unable to prioritise your own needs and take care of yourself or unable to hold healthy boundaries that you know would benefit your child.

If you don't model healthy boundaries for your child, they may learn to imitate the unhealthy patterns that you learnt in your own childhood and continue the cycle. However, by establishing and holding healthy boundaries yourself, you can break this cycle and enable your child to see what healthy boundaries look like so they can grow up to hold their own.

Let's look at a couple of examples:

1. Max knew the benefit of a good night's sleep for his children, but his children were always pushing back against his boundaries, especially when it came to staying up late to play video games. Max had always struggled with asserting himself and expressing his own opinions. More often than not, he found himself giving in to their demands, just to avoid conflict. He was worried that his children wouldn't like him if he held firm boundaries.

    Max realised that he had been doing his children a disservice. When he started thinking of his boundaries as a way to show them that he was a loving father who cared for their well-being, he was able to hold his boundaries more firmly and his children cooperated more easily.

2. Maggie struggled with setting boundaries with her family, fearing that she would be viewed as a failure if she did not meet their expectations. This belief had been ingrained in her during her early years. She had been brought up to be a 'good girl', and it had become an integral part of her identity.

    Maggie finally reached her breaking point. She was exhausted and stressed out. She knew something had to change. She learnt to set healthy boundaries with her family, started saying 'no' when she needed to, and made time for herself. She recognised that always doing everything for her kids had resulted in children who felt entitled and lacked confidence in their own abilities. She wanted to empower them to be more self-sufficient and to believe in themselves. Through her journey, she learnt that her family loved and respected her, no matter what.

People pleasers often have certain thoughts that drive their behaviour.

Here are some common behaviours that people pleasers may exhibit:

Put a tick next to the ones that stand out for you:

- ☐ You worry about what other people think of you.
- ☐ You agree with others in order to 'fit in' and be liked.
- ☐ You look for constant approval.
- ☐ You want to be accepted and liked by everyone.
- ☐ You fear others won't like you.
- ☐ You often feel responsible for others' happiness and well-being.
- ☐ You feel guilty setting boundaries.
- ☐ You fear that people not liking your boundary confirms that what you want doesn't matter.
- ☐ You feel judged by others.
- ☐ You tend to apologise excessively, even for things that are not your fault.
- ☐ You have difficulty asserting yourself and expressing your own opinions.
- ☐ You give and give and feel resentful that you don't get anything back in return.
- ☐ You have difficulty saying 'no' to others and feel guilty when you do.
- ☐ You never seem to have 'you' time.

Here are some common thoughts:

> It's OK if you don't relate to the thoughts in this list. You might not have them or you might revisit this page with fresh insights later.

Put a tick next to the ones that stand out for you:

- ☐ You think your own needs and wants are not as important as the needs and wants of others.
- ☐ You think you should always put others first even if it means sacrificing your own happiness.
- ☐ You think you have to earn love and acceptance from others by doing things for them.
- ☐ You think you should avoid conflict and keep everyone happy at all times.
- ☐ You think that your worth is tied to the approval of others, and you fear rejection.

BREAKING THE PATTERN OF PEOPLE PLEASING

Becoming aware and showing self-compassion are the first steps towards making lasting change. Although people pleasing might have been a useful coping mechanism for you in childhood to keep you safe and gain your parents' approval, it's no longer needed or helpful.

1 Start by recognising when you put others' needs before your own or when you agree to do things you don't want to do. Do this without any self-judgement. Use **SAY WHAT YOU SEE** for yourself to validate your own feelings, thoughts and experiences.

2 Become aware of why you're people pleasing. Is it to gain approval or avoid conflict? Use the list on the previous page. Once you identify the root cause, it will be easier to address.

3 Challenge the truthfulness of the beliefs behind your behaviour. Reflect on where you learnt these messages whether it was from family, culture or past experiences.

4 Practise setting boundaries and saying 'no' to others. Gain confidence setting boundaries by starting small and gradually working your way up to more significant challenges. Use the **STRENGTH** tool that I will teach you in the third section of this workbook to gather proof of your successes.

5 It will become easier for you to set your own healthy boundaries when you use **CAN DOs** that provide win-win solutions. You will come to recognise that you are not stopping others from achieving their desires but, instead, respecting your own needs. Holding healthy boundaries is a good thing! You'll be bringing out your child's **STRENGTHs** and abilities.

6 Taking care of yourself is so essential! Focus on doing things that bring you happiness and joy. When you prioritise your well-being, you'll feel more self-confident and less reliant on external approval. As a result, you will find it easier to give to others without sacrificing your own needs. That's the win-win!

EMOTIONS AND BEHAVIOUR

Our outward behaviour reflects our inner emotions.

When you're happy, content or self-assured, you'll act completely differently from how you would act if you felt ashamed, unlovable or angry.

As parents, we have been told far too often to focus on surface the behaviour and try to put a stop to it by telling our child off, punishing them or pushing them away. Oftentimes, we nag, criticise, shout, and threaten in the mistaken belief that this will put a stop to unwanted behaviour.

However, focusing on correcting our child's behaviour without first addressing the underlying cause will always backfire (see Behaviour Iceberg, page 40). When you coach your child to understand, accept and communicate their feelings and needs, their behaviour naturally changes for the better.

A lot of unwanted behaviour evolves from one thing: feeling powerless.

Misbehaviour from feeling powerless regularly shows up when children feel like they have very little control over what is happening, when they feel controlled or when they feel like their loved ones don't see the best in them.

To make up for feeling powerless, children demand, control, tantrum, refuse to comply etc.

If we react to their behaviour with threats and punishments, as we have been told to do, we end up adding to our child's feelings of powerlessness, so we get more of the behaviour we don't want.

Recognising the role we play in escalating these interactions allows us to take a different approach. Instead of 'adding fuel to the fire', we can use emotion coaching to de-escalate challenging situations with our child.

EMOTION COACHING

When you are an emotion coach, you:

- Nurture emotional intelligence
- Bring out your child's self-esteem
- Develop deep connections
- Understand your child's emotions so your child learns to understand their own and others'
- Validate their emotions so your child feels understood and respected
- Coach your child to regulate their emotions and bring out self-control to meet their needs in healthy ways

Emotion coaching Language of Listening style, allows your child's best self to shine through. It naturally enables your child to behave well, gain decision-making and problem-solving skills, and move on to find their own solutions within your boundaries.

The coaching skill of validating with SAY WHAT YOU SEE (SWYS) helps you connect with your child and respond calmly to their emotions. Allowing your child to feel what they feel removes their need to escalate to prove their feelings are valid.

The coaching skill of offering CAN DOs helps your child meet their needs within your boundaries. Meeting their needs helps your child move through big emotions and return to their naturally calm state.

The coaching skill of pointing out STRENGTHs proves to your child they can calm themselves down and manage their own emotions. They naturally change their own behaviour to reflect it.

Why your validation is so important.

- Accepting and validating your child's feelings confirms that it really is OK to have any kind of feeling. Feelings are nothing to fear.

- Validation assures your child that not only can they handle any emotion, but they can trust their feelings to automatically help them meet their needs. (I'll discuss this more on the following pages.)

- It helps your child feel safe and capable, which builds self-confidence.

- It allows your child feel their feelings fully so they can move on.

RANGE OF FEELINGS LIST

This chart is a Language of Listening® tool.
It shows the relationship between feelings and needs.

	Feelings You Like (connected & powerful)
★ SAY WHAT YOU SEE	amazed, appreciative, aware, brilliant, compassionate, competent, confident, connected, delighted, elated, empathic, empowered, free, fulfilled, grateful, great, in awe, inspired, invigorated, joyful, lovable, loving, moved, passionate, peaceful, powerful, present, proud, self-assured, serene, thrilled, valuable
⇧ SAY WHAT YOU SEE	adventurous, affectionate, bold, brave, capable, certain, cheerful, clever, creative, decisive, eager, enthusiastic, excited, expectant, focused, generous, glad, happy, independent, likable, outgoing, resolute, strong, surprised, thankful, trusting, undaunted, valued, welcoming
⇧ SAY WHAT YOU SEE	alert, able, acceptable, amused, appreciated, attentive, clear-headed, curious, determined, engaged, friendly, good, helpful, hopeful, interested, intrigued, kind, lighthearted, motivated, optimistic, persistent, playful, pleased, ready, sociable, upbeat
⇧ SAY WHAT YOU SEE	accepting, adaptable, adequate, agreeable, at ease, calm, comfortable, contemplative, content, cool, dependable, easygoing, introspective, okay, patient, pleasant, quiet, relaxed, relieved, reserved, rested, safe, satisfied, secure, serious, wishful
⇧ SAY WHAT YOU SEE	alone, annoyed, apologetic, awkward, bored, bothered, cautious, disengaged, disinterested, dissatisfied, distracted, frustrated, hesitant, impatient, insecure, irritated, judgmental, not okay, out of sorts, overwhelmed, pessimistic, regretful, self-conscious, shy, uncomfortable, uneasy, unhappy, unsure
⇧ SAY WHAT YOU SEE	agitated, anxious, apprehensive, bad, bashful, concerned, confused, defeated, defensive, disappointed, discouraged, doubtful, envious, inadequate, incapable, lonely, nervous, nostalgic, remorseful, resentful, sad, startled, tense, timid, unacceptable, upset, vulnerable, wistful, worried
⇧ SAY WHAT YOU SEE	alarmed, angry, awful, baffled, bewildered, culpable, desperate, disgusted, disoriented, distressed, embarrassed, enraged, exhausted, furious, hate, hated, hurt, ineffective, inferior, irate, jealous, lonesome, mad, outraged, rejected, sorrowful, threatened, unsafe, vengeful, weak
⇧ SAY WHAT YOU SEE	apathetic, afraid, ashamed, blank, dejected, depressed, desolate, devastated, grief-stricken, guilt-ridden, helpless, hopeless, horrible, in despair, isolated, lethargic, lost, miserable, numb, panicked, petrified, powerless, scared, terrible, trapped, unlovable, useless, worthless, wretched
	Feelings You Don't Like (disconnected & powerless)

© 2023 Language of Listening®. Reprinted by Camilla Miller with permission.

How to use the Language of Listening® Range of Feelings List

Vocabulary-building Tool: Look over the Range of Feelings List and select a few that you would like to add to your vocabulary and your child's. Words are arranged alphabetically in rows.

Coaching Tool: The left column shows the uplifting nature of SAY WHAT YOU SEE. Allowing your child to feel what they feel helps them meet their needs (experience, connection, power), which facilitates movement away from feelings they don't like at the bottom of the chart towards feelings they (and you) like better at the top. With validation, the general movement is from inward/fearful to outward/joyful.

Personalisation: While our deeper emotions are thought to be consistent from person to person, the feelings we are conscious of and how we experience them vary widely. To accommodate your experience, a wide variety of feeling words and words closely associated with feelings are included in the list. Extra space is provided so you can add more words or move any that feel out of place to you.

Practise using the Range of Feelings List.

A quick way to get familiar with the list is to look through it and select a few new feeling words to add to your vocabulary and your child's. Naming feelings when you validate them with SWYS can help your child connect with the thinking part of their brain and, in the case of big upsets, improve their ability to calm themselves down.

My new feeling words:

Your Preferences Matter

The feelings in this list may be arranged in a way that's new to you. Like most of us, you may have been taught to see feelings as positive or negative or good or bad. Those categories are loaded with judgement, which makes it extra hard to accept and validate all feelings. Instead, this list is organised according to your preferences, what you like and don't like, which takes the judgement out.

Look through the list again and see how the feeling words align with your personal preferences. Per the personalisation note on the previous page, if you see some that feel out of place to you, cross them out and move them up or down to a level that feels right to you.

When you've done that, notice how the feelings towards the top of the list, those that you like, naturally arise when your needs are met. When you feel connected and powerful, you're aligned with your true self. You feel confident and safe to reach out to others and explore the world outside of yourself.

The feelings towards the bottom of the list are the opposite. They arise when your needs are unmet. When you feel disconnected and powerlessness, you feel unacceptable and unsafe, so you shut down and turn inward to minimise external threats and maximise self-protection.

The connection between your preferences, feelings and needs is very real – you like how you feel when your needs are met and you don't when they are not. That's why you automatically begin to take actions to meet your needs. At every level, you are subconsciously motivated by your feelings to take actions that help you return to your natural state of joy and aliveness – the level you were born to like!

Maybe now it's easier to see why trying to stop or stuff your feelings is ultimately self-defeating. It works against your nature, while acceptance helps you follow your natural flow. To see what I mean, the next time you have a feeling you don't like, try to validate it, and then try to feel it more on purpose. It's hard to stay in a feeling you don't like without taking action to improve it. The same is true for your child.

SAYing WHAT YOU SEE
your child FEELING

SWYS is the quickest way to help your child understand just how right their emotional reaction is.

When we minimise our child's emotions, it's often in the effort to stop them from being upset. But it doesn't work. We can't stop emotions; they just build up and up and then explode or implode.

Let's say your child is feeling disappointed over not being invited to a friend's party. If you're scared of them feeling upset, you may try to dismiss their feelings: *'Oh, don't worry. Don't be upset. I'll take you out, and we'll have a great time'*, implying they shouldn't feel upset, and you're going to fix it for them.

Or you say something like, *'Don't be such a baby! You can't be invited to every party. You sound spoilt'*, sending the message that it's wrong for them to feel how they feel and people will judge them when they have big emotions.

When we meet their big emotions with validation, we help them develop systems to recognise and defuse their emotions so they no longer build up. You can reply, *'No wonder you feel disappointed. You really wanted to go!'*

When your child no longer has to prove that they're right to feel what they feel, they start to return to their normal state of calm.

Look back at the Range of Feelings List (see page 228). Validation and acceptance remove the weight of judgement so your child's feelings can naturally rise.

No matter where your child starts – anxious, angry, disappointed, sad, mad, embarrassed – **SWYS** facilitates the process of moving towards calm. You can then help them move on towards feelings of happiness and joy with **CAN DOs**, starting with a simple statement like, *'Must be something you can do to get through it!'*

Start by SAYing WHAT YOU SEE your child FEELING.

Let your child vent their emotions without fixing, offering advice or trying to change their viewpoint. Hold space to let them feel their feelings.

SAY WHAT YOU SEE your child FEELING - Younger children

'You're so frustrated, and you just want to do your own thing.'

'You feel impatient. You need me to listen to you first!'

'You look angry. You hate being interrupted.'

'You're just so bored! There is NOTHING to do in here!'

'You're feeling nervous that you won't be able to find your friends when we get there.'

'You're just so excited! You want to be there already!'

'You're afraid of the big trucks whizzing by.'

Use this space to practise:

SAY WHAT YOU SEE your child FEELING - Older children and teens

Older children don't always like their feelings being named. Move straight to validating their experience and why they're right to feel like they feel.

'That's so annoying, frustrating, awful...'

'You hate that!'

'You love that!'

'That's not what you wanted...'

'That felt unfair...'

'No wonder you feel so upset...'

'You wish you could...'

Use this space to practise:

Emotion Coaching in Action

Validating your child's emotions allows your child to feel what they feel and move on.

When my daughter was a toddler, she received a teddy bear that quickly became her favourite toy. One day when she was 6, she asked me to clean it as it had become dirty and smelly.

Before putting the bear in the washing machine, I double-checked with her to make certain she was sure about it. However, when the bear came out of the wash, we noticed that a part of its brown felt nose was hanging off. My daughter started crying.

I offered to sew the nose back on for her, but even after I did, the bear didn't look the same. My daughter was still upset and miserable.

I gave her a hug and validated her with SWYS: *'It's not what you wanted. You wanted her clean, and now you're sad. You wish you hadn't made that choice. You want her to look the same. You hate how her nose has changed.'*

Notice how I not only stated her emotion but went deeper. I expressed what my daughter wanted, what she wished was different and why she was correct to feel what she felt.

She was sobbing and moaning. *'Oh sweetie!'* I said and left the room. I didn't want to listen to the moaning.

Notice how I didn't try to talk her out of her upset or try to fix the situation by telling her I'd buy her a new bear. I also didn't try to remind her that she made the choice to wash her bear, tell her she was being silly, or say, *'That's what happens when bears go in the wash.'* None of that.

I validated her and trusted that she would know how to resolve her own upset. And she did! Without needing to defend herself, she was able to feel her feelings fully and move on. And in minutes, she was hugging her bear and feeling calm.

This whole experience helped her trust her feelings, gain confidence, and feel safe and capable.

Now, I'm not going to pretend emotion coaching is always going to be smooth sailing. I don't know where your child is on their journey of emotional regulation. If your child does have an epic meltdown, that's OK too. They will be gathering proof that ultimately they CAN calm down. We will be covering STRENGTHs in the next section which will greatly help you and your child.

Keep going. Keep trusting that, with your coaching, your child will learn to process their emotions, calm themselves down and move on.

When we feel threatened or powerless, there are three things we can control. All meet our need for power:

CONTROL THE THREAT

FIGHT (external control)

CONTROL OUR ENVIRONMENT

FLIGHT

CONTROL OURSELVES

FREEZE (internal control)

How our feelings help us meet our NEEDS

Our human instincts are truly incredible. Emotions play a crucial role in our decision-making and behaviour. They help us understand what is important to us or causing us stress or discomfort. They also motivate us to take action to meet our needs.

Let's look at how some common feelings help us meet our NEEDS.

Anger

Anger is a buildup of energy. It's a message that helps us recognise when our boundaries have been crossed. It's a take-action kind of emotion that's often the result of feeling attacked, invalidated or unfairly treated. It motivates us to make changes and helps us defend and protect ourselves.

When you're angry, YOUR actions and YOUR child's meet your needs for POWER.

1. FIGHT

Control the threat by fighting back (external control)

You can see this in your child when they yell, hit, kick, throw things, stamp their feet or speak rudely. They can become demanding and controlling of things and people.

You might see this in yourself when you shout, threaten or punish. You, too, become demanding and controlling of things and people.

2. FLIGHT

Control the environment by leaving to reduce the threat

You can see this in your child when they storm off and slam a door, hide in their room or run off.

You might see this in yourself when you storm off or want to run away and hide in the bathroom, hide in the garden or sit alone in your car in the driveway.

3. FREEZE

Control yourself by not moving at all, taking no action (internal control)

You can see this in your child when they freeze, refuse to do something, or cross their arms and won't budge or speak.

You might see this in yourself when you don't want to fight but can't just leave, so you stand there frozen and speechless, taking no action.

Fear

Fear comes from a real or imagined threat of harm. It plays an important role in keeping us safe as it kicks us into action to protect ourselves from danger.

When we feel able to protect ourselves from danger, our fear naturally decreases. On the other hand, when we feel helpless to protect ourselves from a threat, our fear increases.

When you experience fear, your actions meet your needs for CONNECTION and POWER.

1. FIGHT

Control the threat by fighting back, getting help to fight (external control)

You can see this in your child when they attack or try to control others they perceive as a threat. They may become louder and explosive, act out in a hyper way to scare off the threat, or try to recruit others to help overpower it.

You may see this in yourself when you try to control your child and their actions either to rescue them from a perceived threat or to save yourself from their actions if you perceive them to be a threat to your safety or emotional stability.

2. FLIGHT

Control the environment, change the situation to reduce the threat

You can see this in your child when they run away or hide behind you and refuse to go somewhere alone, participate in an activity or face a situation they are anxious about.

You may see this in yourself when you flee from a threat or when you back down or change your boundaries in order reduce a threat to your safety or emotional stability.

3. FREEZE

Control yourself by not moving at all, taking no action (internal control)

You can see this in your child when they cling to you, freeze up or numb out to dissociate from the situation.

You might see this in yourself when you freeze and go blank. It gives you a minute to reconnect with yourself, think and reassure yourself before taking action. It also allows you to observe and assess if a threat is real or not when you're having a panic attack or feeling anxious.

Rejection

We naturally desire acceptance, which makes rejection painful and challenging to overcome. Rejection can have a significant impact on the body. The brain regions that are triggered during rejection are the same as those activated during physical pain. Feeling rejected can manifest as a range of emotions such as fear, sadness and anger.

When you experience rejection, your actions meet your need for CONNECTION and POWER.

1. FIGHT

Control the threat by fighting back, getting help to fight (external control)

You can see in your child when they become defensive, angry and uncooperative or controlling of others. To empower themselves, they may launch a counter-attack on their own or with others to reject those who rejected them.

You may see this in yourself when you feel defensive or angry and, with others or on your own, try to put down or otherwise get back at the person or group who rejected you.

2. FLIGHT

Control the environment, change the situation to reduce the threat

You can see this in your child when they hide in their room or isolate themselves from others to reduce the threat of rejection. Or they may run to their friends or family who accept them to help insulate themselves from the threat.

You might see this in yourself when you withdraw from social situations, avoid contact with others who might appear threatening, or surround yourself with more accepting friends and family as a way to protect yourself from further rejection. Reaching out to others you trust to share your thoughts and feelings meets your need for connection.

3. FREEZE

Control yourself by not moving at all, taking no action (internal control)

You can see this in a child who freezes or stops trying to engage in order to avoid any missteps that could cause additional rejection. They may change their goals, try to change their desires to please others in an effort to connect, or decide they don't care about others and turn inward to connect with themselves first.

You might see this in yourself when you freeze and go blank, try to change yourself to please others, go into denial and refuse to accept that you have been rejected, or tell yourself that you don't care and turn inward to connect with yourself first.

Frustration

Frustration is a feeling of dissatisfaction that arises when we encounter obstacles or challenges that interfere with our ability to achieve our goals or desires. It can arise from a variety of factors such as external circumstances, our own limitations or mistakes, or the actions of others. Frustration can manifest as a range of emotions such as anger, irritation, impatience and anxiety.

But the most important thing to remember about frustration is that it contains a hidden STRENGTH – the feeling of frustration tells you that you haven't given up! You can tell because giving up would tip it over into disappointment, discouragement etc.

Frustration is a normal part of life that can motivate us to try harder or find alternative solutions to the problems we face. Therefore, it's important to develop healthy strategies for managing frustration and finding ways to work through or overcome the obstacles that are causing it.

When you experience frustration, your actions meet your need for POWER.

1. FIGHT

Control the threat by fighting back (external control)

You can see in your child when they whine, fuss, have tantrums, meltdowns and big physical reactions fighting against people or things that interfere with their goals. They're not giving up!

You may see this in yourself if you lose your temper, shout, or become physically aggressive towards others or external things that are in your way. You're not giving up!

2. FLIGHT

Control the environment

You can see this in your child when they run away or take a break from a challenge to do something else to build their confidence first (see The Running Leap, page 282).

You might see this in yourself when you drop a frustrating project, throw up your hands and walk away from a frustrating situation, or try to fix or change things right where you are.

3. FREEZE

Control yourself by not moving at all, taking no action (internal control)

You can see this in your child when they freeze, sit and stare at a frustrating problem unable to think, clench their fists or grab a fidget toy to distract themselves until they can relax.

You might see this in yourself when you freeze and clench your jaw or fists when you can't figure out what to do but haven't given up. If you blame yourself, you may keep going over the situation in your mind or try to distract yourself with healthy or unhealthy behaviours such as substance abuse, overeating, or excessive screen time in an effort to relax and gain perspective.

Sadness

Sadness is a normal human reaction to loss or disappointment. We feel sadness when we lose someone close to us, hear bad news, experience a big disappointment or think we can't cope.

Sadness is a cue to others that we need comfort, consolation and closeness. It's also a cue to ourselves that we need time to adapt and recoup. Tears help us adapt.

When you're sad, your actions meet your need for CONNECTION.

> You can see this in your child when they cry or come running to you for safety or comfort. Crying is their body's way of letting go of upsets, worries, uneasiness and a whole host of emotions. Releasing emotions and feeling validated by a loved one helps your child adapt when things don't go their way.
>
> You may see this in yourself when you're sad and want to connect with a good friend, find a place to vent your upsets and feel validated. Tears help you release emotions and adapt to things when they don't go your way.
>
> When you show empathy and validate your child's feelings, they learn to connect with others and themselves through empathy and validation.

Love

When you feel love, your actions meet your need for CONNECTION.

> You feel loved by others when you're truly accepted for who you are. A natural thing to do when you feel love for another is to reach out and physically connect with a touch or a hug. The actions you take and the acceptance that you receive in return confirm that you belong, which meets your need for connection at many levels. When you feel loveable, you're naturally more cooperative and considerate. Your child is the same.
>
> On the other hand, feeling unloveable is so painful that you go into action to protect yourself. You can see this in your child when they become aggressive, defiant or argumentative and keep others at arm's length. The pain of feeling unloveable is so real that they subconsciously put up a defensive wall to distance themselves from others and protect themselves from further pain.

Impatience

When you feel impatient, your actions meet need for EXPERIENCE and POWER.

> Impatience meets the need for POWER by motivating us to take action and go after our goals.
>
> You can see how impatience in your child helps them meet their need for EXPERIENCE. When they're impatient about something, they wriggle, fidget or go looking for a challenge, all of which help them wait until they can take the action they want.

Start spotting how your child's natural emotions push them to take action to meet their NEEDS.

Here are a few examples:

> 1. Albert was angry when he couldn't go to the park, so he met his need for power by throwing his toys. His mum didn't like that behaviour, so she helped him meet his need for power in a healthy way by allowing him to choose what activity they would do at home.
>
> 2. Sofia was frustrated when she had to stop playing on the PlayStation. She stormed off upstairs and slammed her bedroom door. Those actions helped her meet her need for power without hurting anybody or anything, and she calmed down quickly on her own.
>
> 3. Annie was disappointed and sad when she found out her friend wasn't going to be at nursery school today. She cried all the way to school and was validated by her mum, which helped her meet her need for connection. Crying helped her release her emotions and adapt, so she felt ready to go inside when they arrived.

Start to notice how, once your child's needs for connection and power have been met, they automatically return to their calmer, happier self.

> List a few examples of your own:

Here's an example of a tricky situation I had with my daughter to show you what it looks like to hold your boundaries WHILE spotting your child's NEED for power.

When your child feels big emotions, the actions they naturally take meet their needs. Your role is to SPOT the NEEDS their actions are meeting and coach your child to meet those NEEDS within your boundary.

As you read through this example, notice all the ways my daughter tries and meets her NEEDS and all the ways I hold my boundaries. Then notice what happens when I help her meet her NEEDS within my boundary.

No Playdate Today

I pick my 5-year-old daughter up from school, and she wants her best friend to come home with us. I say no to a playdate. I don't get dragged into a discussion about it. It just is 'no friends over today'.

We get home, and my daughter starts crying.

She tells me, *'It's so unfair! I never get friends to come over. You've made me so unhappy, and you've made my friend upset.'* I don't get into a debate or try to justify myself by giving her reasons. I know she's upset, so I remind myself that she must feel safe with me to tell me this and that her upset isn't a reflection on my boundary of no playdate today. It's her way to handle big feelings.

Her complaining goes on for while with big wailing and crying. She starts throwing things. **(Big physical actions meet her need for power although not in a way I like.)** I stop her by physically getting in her way. *'You can be upset, and you can't break my things,'* I tell her firmly.

I switch to SWYS: *'You're so mad at me! You wanted a friend to come round, and I said "no".'* **(My validation helps her meet her need for connection.)** At this stage, I leave her so I don't get dragged into her upset.

She follows me, *'I'm going to play on the computer all day, and you can't stop me!! I'm not going for a walk with you even if you want me to.'* **(Demands are another way she meets her need for power although, again, not in a way I like.)**

I respond calmly, *'You don't have to come for a walk with me. You can be mad.'* **(Allowing her to decide and feel the way she feels helps her meet her need for power and connection and de-escalates the power struggle slightly.)**

She decides and continues, *'Well, if I'm not going for a walk, then I'm getting a can of Coke!'* I smile to myself as she knows she's not allowed to drink Coke unless it's a very special occasion. **(This is a smaller demand than her first one of playing on the computer all day, which tells me her need for power is already reduced.)**

Now, it's a mad dash to the fridge as she tries to get a can of Coke. I block the fridge door and calmly hold my boundary, so she falls to the ground crying **(a call for connection)**. I lie down next to her and say, '*Oh girly, you're so mad and upset!*' She lets me lie next to her, and we have a rough play cuddle. **(Joining her on the floor with validation and understanding helps her meet her need for connection.)**

'*I'm thirsty!*" she shouts at me. '*Get me water!!*' **(Since this is an even smaller demand, it tells me her need for power is almost met.)**

Although she sounds SO demanding, and that isn't OK with me, I recognise that what she's asking for IS OK with me – water! And I know that giving her what she wants now, even though it isn't the main thing she wants, will help her meet her remaining need for power and connection.

So I tell her, '*You know! This time, I would love to get you a glass of water.*'

I get her glass willingly, and amazingly, it's like a switch goes off. Just like that, it's all over. We go for a walk and have a lovely time together. **(Her need for power and connection are met.)**

These are the main points:

1. I didn't get dragged into a discussion about the boundary.
2. I used validation and let her have her upset.
3. I gave her space.
4. I helped her meet her NEED for POWER and CONNECTION.
5. She moved on.

Looking at behaviour in this way takes time. Since we're so used to judging behaviour as good or bad and trying to control it by punishing our child, we actually need to rewire our brains to stay out of judgement. Rewiring requires practice.

When you learn to see your child's behaviour through the lens of unmet needs, it allows you to laugh at tricky situations and recognise how creative your child is at meeting their NEEDS. And when you see that, it's easier to hold your boundaries calmly and watch as your child adjusts their own behaviour to fit inside your boundaries.

Considering your OWN emotions, complete the NEEDS exercise below.

EMOTION	What actions do you typically take?	What need(s) do those actions meet?	What helps you move towards calm?	What doesn't help?
Angry				
Afraid				
Rejected				
Frustrated				
Sad				
Impatient				

Considering your CHILD's emotions, complete the NEEDS exercise below.

EMOTION	What actions does your child typically take?	What need(s) do those actions meet?	What helps them move towards calm?	What doesn't help?
Angry				
Afraid				
Rejected				
Frustrated				
Sad				
Impatient				

Notice and recognise emotions by feeling them in your body.

Often, we override our body's warning systems and ignore what our body is trying to tell us. For many of us, we may not have been taught to handle our emotions. Instead, we were taught to suppress our emotions for fear of being rejected or were told that big emotions were bad.

Emotions are a form of communication. To feel connected to ourselves and others, our emotional messages need to be heard. Suppressing our emotions to protect ourselves from rejection or judgement and gain acceptance conflicts with our need to be heard. This internal struggle drains our energy and builds up stress, which can lead to emotional explosions or implosions, burn out and physical illness.

Instead, try noticing what is happening in your body, accepting it and feeling it fully without judgement.

Identifying and naming your emotions and recognising their associated bodily sensations validates your emotions.

When you prove to yourself that your emotions are real and valid, you learn to trust your inner guidance system. Trusting your own emotions and knowing how to meet your needs in healthy ways are such a powerful gifts to give yourself.

When you are in touch with your emotions and have learnt to trust your inner guidance system, you are better equipped to respond to your child's needs with empathy and understanding. This can help you create a supportive and nurturing environment for your child, which can foster their own emotional development and wellbeing.

To get you started...

> I know I begin clenching my hands together and feel a tightness in my chest when I start becoming frustrated. What about you?
> *What body part do you feel frustration in? What does it feel like?*

Consider where in your body you feel different feelings. Use the body image on the next page to colour your emotions into those parts of the body.

You can use the Range of Feelings List to guide your colour choices or get creative (see page 228).

You might colour the head red or black to represent feeling scared, angry or powerless and colour the hands and legs yellow for impatience. You might colour orange across the chest or in the tummy to represent feeling anxious, defensive, or worried. Love and peaceful feelings might be coloured in the heart area as green, blue or purple or another color you find soothing.

Then, invite your family to colour their emotions into the additional body images on the following page.

It's a good way to get the whole family talking about their emotions. You can use the Range of Feelings List to reflect on the whole range of emotions and increase everyone's emotional vocabulary.

Often children are unaware that adults feel emotions in the same ways they do. Be sure to share with them how you feel and where you feel it in your body.

Where do you feel emotions in your body?

Colour in the body to represent your bodily sensations.

Where do your family members feel emotions in their bodies?

Start a daily practise of bringing awareness to your emotions.

By developing a greater awareness of your emotions, you'll begin to notice that you have more control over your reactions and are becoming more able to pause before you react.

Often, you'll start to notice the build-up of emotions in your body well before you get into the orange or red emotions on the Range of Feelings List. Being aware allows you to validate your own emotions or your child's before such big emotions take over.

When you are in touch with your emotions, it's easier to identify what triggers them and find healthier ways to cope with them.

Setting reminders on your phone can help you increase self-awareness by reflecting on your thoughts and emotions throughout the day. This can help you gain insight into your reactions to different situations and identify patterns in your behaviour.

Setting a reminder transformed my school pickup.

By reflecting on my thoughts and emotions, I noticed that picking up my kids from school often felt overwhelming. When the hustle and bustle of the day left me feeling stressed, it was challenging to fully engage and handle tricky situations the way I wanted to with patience and understanding.

So I decided to set an alarm on my phone a few minutes before I left for the school pickup. The purpose was to remind me to pause, take a deep breath and check in with my emotions. In those brief moments of self-reflection, I gained clarity about my emotional state. I reminded myself that whatever I was feeling was valid, and it was OK to have off days.

The purpose of this exercise was not to suppress my emotions but to understand them better. With a sense of calm and presence, I hopped into my car and headed to school ready to greet my kids.

This small ritual helped me to be present so I could show up for my kids in the best way possible.

Set an alarm on your phone to check in with yourself 3 times a day.

Ask yourself: 'What am I feeling?
What do I need in this moment to meet my needs?'

Use this space to track your emotions.

THE THIRD STEP IN YOUR COACHING MODEL:

THE STRENGTH TOOL

THE STRENGTH TOOL

When you start with SAY WHAT YOU SEE (SWYS) and see something your child does that you DO LIKE, you point out a STRENGTH to connect your child with their inner greatness.

Think of it as praise in a new way, one that actually works to help your child see their inner greatness. Using the coaching tool of adding STRENGTHs helps your child to connect and identify with who they really are.

It encourages them to rely on their inner guidance and positive inner voice. Your child knows who they are, can see it in themselves, and has confidence in their abilities.

This is how your child becomes able to control their own behaviour and actions. (Isn't that SO much easier than trying to control their behaviour for them?)

STRENGTH TOOL IN ACTION

By using the STRENGTH tool, I began noticing all the ways my 5-year-old daughter was helpful, thoughtful, patient, considerate, and kind.

I used SWYS and added a STRENGTH:

'You picked up your toys and put them away. That shows you're helpful.'

'You helped your brother find his book. That shows you're patient and thoughtful.'

'You noticed that your friend was feeling sad and gave her a hug. That shows you're kind.'

This powerful approach helped me focus on my daughter's positive qualities and encourage her to see the best in herself.

One day, she came to me bubbling with excitement. *'Mummy, look at me!'* she exclaimed. *'I laid the table for dinner all by myself. Aren't I helpful and kind?'*

My heart swelled with pride as I saw her beaming with confidence. She had carefully placed the plates, knives, forks and napkins in their proper places.

She had internalised the STRENGTHs I had pointed out to her and saw herself as someone who possessed those positive qualities. It was a beautiful moment because it meant that the tool had truly landed. She had embraced it as part of her identity.

I realised that she didn't lay the table to please me or out of fear of consequences.

No! She laid the table because that's what a kind and thoughtful person does. She had learnt to tap into her inherent goodness and express it in her actions.

That's the impact of the STRENGTH tool. It extends beyond mere behaviour modification. It goes deeper, transforming your child from the inside out.

List of STRENGTHs

Explore the list below.
Take a moment to appreciate the wonderful STRENGTHs your child already has.

Assets

Able, Adaptable, Adventurous, Ambitious, Coordinated, Creative, Daring, Eager, Energetic, Finder/Spotter, Flexible, Hard-working, Imaginative, Inspired, Musical, Resourceful, Spontaneous, Spunky

Emotions

Comfortable with your feelings, Enthusiastic, Expressive, Know how to calm yourself, Know how to get the mad out, Know how to help yourself feel better, Know how to show joy, Know how you feel, Love big feelings, Peaceful, Sensitive

Relating

Accepting, Attentive, Caring, Considerate, Fair, First-time listener, Generous, Includer/Inclusive, Kind, Know how to look out for other people, Know how to share, Know how to take turns, Listener, Loving, Loyal, Negotiator, Thoughtful, Welcoming

Responsibility

Dependable, Helper, Honest, Keep your things safe, Know the importance of ____, Leader, Money- saver, Organiser, Recycler, Reliable, Responsible, Thrifty, Trustworthy, Wise with money

Safety

Aware, Brave, Careful, Cautious, Danger-spotter, Keep yourself safe, Know the rules, Like to know the rules, Noticer, Rule-follower, Safety-minded

Self

Ask for what you want, Committed, Confident, Determined, Don't give up easily, Have self-control, Know exactly what you need, Know how to care for your body, Know how to entertain yourself, Know how to have fun, Know how to stop yourself, Know what is important to you, Know what works for you, Know what you like/want, Listen to your heart, Look after yourself, Patient, Persistent, Resilient, Self-assured, Self-aware

Self-direction

Capable, Conscientious, Efficient, Experimenter, Explorer, Have sound judgement, Judicious/Well-judged, Know what to do, Like to make the rules, Not afraid to try new things, Nonconformist, Self-directed, Self-motivated, Self-reliant, Sensible, Wise

Speaking

Assertive, Clear communicator, Connective, Emphatic, Expressive, Inspiring, Polite, Speak up for yourself, Stand up for yourself, Subtle, Well-spoken

Thinking

Curious, Decision maker, Decisive, First-time rememberer, Focused, Intellectual, Knowledgeable, Learner, Observant, Pay attention, Perceptive, Planner, Problem-solver, Quick decision-maker, Rememberer, Savvy, Studious

IN ORDER FOR YOUR CHILD TO SEE THEIR INNER **GREATNESS,** YOU HAVE TO SEE IT FIRST

We're often told to point out our child's flaws in the mistaken belief that it will change their behaviour.

We think

- Pointing out how our child is unkind is going to make them be MORE kind
- Pointing out how our child is irresponsible is going to make them be MORE responsible
- Pointing out how our child is aggressive or rude is going to make them calmer and MORE thoughtful

In fact, the opposite is true.

That's because when we tell them they're unkind, or irresponsible or aggressive... well, our kids believe us. It becomes who they believe they are. Our judgements and our opinions directly impact our child's experience of themselves and their beliefs about themselves, which in turn, influence their behaviour.

One of my clients thought her son was unkind because he often fought with his younger brother. She labeled his behaviour as unkind and repeatedly pointed it out. When she changed her focus, she saw that he actually wanted to play with his brother. His behaviour was a result of running out of options on how to respond when his brother refused to play. By pointing out his STRENGTHs of kindness, inclusiveness, and playfulness, she was able to coach him to bring out his self-control and ability to handle disappointment. His behaviour changed overnight!

When we learn to look behind the behaviour, we get to see our child's true self and coach them to manage their own behaviour.

THE IMPORTANCE OF THE STRENGTH TOOL

The Language of Listening premise behind STRENGTHs tells us:

> 'All children have every possible inner strength. Children act according to WHO they believe they are.'

Your child's behaviour is guided by their awareness of their inner STRENGTHs. This may sound far too simplistic, but the truth is, it really is that simple.

- *A child who believes they are kind will act kindly.*
- *A child who believes they are brave will act bravely.*
- *A child who believes they are capable, thoughtful, reliable etc will show you all the ways they are.*

When you prove to your child they have a STRENGTH, they naturally change their own behaviour to reflect it.

Your child needs to see their greatness and gain confidence in their abilities. When you point out your child's STRENGTHs, you're setting your child up for success. They get to have a positive inner voice, believe in themselves, and feel capable and secure in their self-worth and value.

You need to give your child real-life, physical proof and repeated opportunities to see and experience themselves in a positive way and gather proof of their abilities and value.

It starts with you seeing your child as the best version of themselves. When you choose and decide to see your child as their best self, they have much more of an opportunity to see themselves as their best self too.

see THE BEST IN them

The way you respond to your child shapes their view of themselves, others and the world around them.

As I explained earlier (see How Beliefs Are Formed, page 112), your child's everyday experiences and interactions are fundamental to their development. They determine their own identity from their interactions with others around them. When you demonstrate that you see them and love them for who they are, and show them through your words and actions that you see the best in them, they learn to see themselves in those ways too.

Likewise, if you tell them off, point out their faults, blame, shame or humiliate them, they learn to see that in themselves, and it shapes their view of themselves, others and the world around them.

It's easier to see your child as their best self when you know that all children have every possible inner STRENGTH already. Nothing is actually missing that you have to somehow teach them or impart to them from the outside. Your child is already kind, brave, thoughtful, responsible, knows what works for them, determined etc and has all the other STRENGTHs.

Their STRENGTHs are already wired into them. When you think your child is not displaying a particular STRENGTH, start looking for it, and you'll find evidence of it.

Spotting STRENGTHS builds trust.

When her little boy zoomed off on his scooter, one of my client's first reactions used to be to shout, *'Be careful!'* out of fear that he would get hurt. However, this only caused her boy to go even faster, which she responded to by telling him off for not listening.

After learning to see STRENGTHs and pausing to observe before reacting, this mum started seeing things that she had missed. She noticed her son would stop briefly, turn around to check that she was watching and then zoom off. That helped her realise that, in fact, he was going fast to prove to her he did have self-control and knew how to keep himself safe. She also noticed he would stop at the beginning of each driveway, look back and wait to make sure she was following before continuing on his way.

By looking for STRENGTHs, she noticed he already knew how to keep himself safe. He was self-aware and a danger-spotter. With greater trust in her son's abilities, she was able to allow him more freedom to explore and have fun on his scooter.

Here's an example of what can happen if, instead, we micromanage and overschedule.

Ella's parents wanted to ensure that she was successful and happy in every aspect of her life. They meticulously monitored Ella's activities, making sure she completed her homework and attended after school activities. From math tutoring to piano lessons, drama club and football practice, Ella's schedule was packed to the brim. They were also overly concerned with her emotional state, her down time, what she ate… All driven by their deep love and desire to ensure her well-being.

While Ella's parents had good intentions, their micromanagement left her feeling anxious and disempowered. Their constant vigilance felt like judgement. It sent the message that they doubted her abilities and decision-making skills. This strained their relationship and affected Ella's self-esteem as she began to feel undervalued and untrusted.

Sometimes, as parents, we can become so focused on pushing our children towards success that we fail to recognise their STRENGTHs in the present moment. This narrow focus can leave our child feeling inadequate as though they will never be able to meet our expectations.

It is important for us to recognise our child's STRENGTHs and encourage them to make their own decisions while still providing guidance and support as needed. This helps build a stronger sense of trust and mutual respect between us and our child.

Start pointing out
your child's greatness and
see the best in them
so they learn to see
the best in themselves.

You'll be amazed at how quickly their behaviour changes for the better.

Always start with SAY WHAT YOU SEE, and then add a STRENGTH.

When you see a behaviour you like, starting with SAY WHAT YOU SEE gives your child undeniable, physical-world proof of what they did. What they did matters because...

Children decide who they are based on what they do.

When you name a STRENGTH after showing a child what they did, they identify with that STRENGTH as WHO they are. And because children act according to who they believe they are, their inner guidance does the rest.

This tangible connection with what they DO and WHO they are creates a genuine belief in their abilities that extends beyond external validation.

Remember: a child who believes they are responsible acts responsibly; a child who believes they have self-control controls themselves; a child who believes they are brave acts bravely...

When you show your child WHO they are, there is no need for you to reward or control their behaviour. Your child will naturally change their own behaviour to reflect how they see themselves.

Simple Starter Phrase

SAY WHAT YOU SEE + STRENGTH
'You (did) _____. + That shows _____.'

'You kept looking when you couldn't find your book. That shows you're persistent.'

'You got dressed all by yourself. That shows how independent you are.'

'You found a way to make that work. That shows you're a problem-solver.'

'You put your toys away. That shows you know the rules.'

'You waited to cross the road. That shows you know how to stay safe.'

'You were disappointed, and you calmed down. That shows you know what you need to feel better.'

'You pay attention to your surroundings. That shows you're self-aware.'

'You took your time and double-checked your work. That shows you're careful.'

'You made your bed and packed your bag for school. That shows you're self-reliant.'

'You made sure all your friends felt included. That shows you're caring and loving.'

'You waited until you felt ready to go down the big slide. That shows you trust your instincts.'

'You cleaned the kitchen after cooking. That shows you're responsible.'

'You listened to what your sister wanted too. That shows you're considerate.'

'You came off screens when agreed. That shows you keep to your word.'

'You sent me a message so I'd know you were running late. That shows you're dependable.'

'You spoke to me calmly when you were frustrated. That shows you have self-control.'

'You adapted to a last minute change of plans. That shows you're flexible and resilient.'

'You know what matters to you. That shows you're clear about what's important in your life.'

'You noticed that Grandma was feeling sad. That shows you're perceptive.'

'You found a way to make it work. That shows you're determined.'

'You always ask lots of questions. That shows you're curious.'

Add your own examples of
SAY WHAT YOU SEE + STRENGTHs

Here's an example of using the 3 steps of the coaching model and how differently the situation ends when you point out STRENGTHs.

I was having lunch at a local café. After a short while, my son, age 3, wanted to get up out of his seat. I leaned in close and offered a few calming words to try to get him to sit a bit longer. It didn't work. He screeched even louder.

My cheeks turned red as the other customers glared at this unfolding power struggle. When I realised my child wasn't listening, I remembered that I needed to listen first.

So I immediately switched to SWYS and validated what my son wanted: *'You want to walk around. You want to explore. You're done with sitting. You want to go to the playground now.'*

The great part here is that you know when your child feels heard because they stop and listen to you. The communication gap is closed, and you're ready to find solutions that work for you both.

Next, I coached my son to find solutions within my boundaries. I started by asking myself a few questions and becoming clear on what my boundary was for this situation.

- Is it OK for my son to be walking around our table?
- Is the café full?
- Will he be disrupting anyone?
- Is it age-appropriate behaviour?

What you want to happen is not right or wrong; we all have our own preferences. Being clear on your boundary and what you want helps you to see what solutions are possible.

The magic of connecting with your child and validating their wants first helps them be receptive to your guidance. So you now get to guide your child towards solutions that you DO like.

A CAN DO is literally what your child can do to meet their NEEDs within your boundary. Looking for CAN DOs helps you focus on finding solutions that work for everyone.

Here are a few examples:

- 'You want to get up out of your seat, AND it's a busy café. You can walk around our table just here. That's OK with me.'
- 'You've finished your biscuit, AND we're not all finished. Must be something you CAN DO to keep busy while we finish.'
- 'You want to move. You're done with sitting. You can come with me to pay the lady. Would you like to hold the receipt?'

CAN DOs acknowledge your child's needs while holding your boundaries. They are solutions that work for everyone.

Or you can turn the problem-solving over to your child.

'You're done sitting; you want to do something. We're leaving soon, and you need to stay close. Hmm, must be something you can do.'

Your child may come up with solutions that you wouldn't, such as building a napkin tent for an imaginary character on the table, imagining what it would be like to walk on the ceiling if the room were upside down, or staying close and helpful by picking up toys that the baby at the next table keeps dropping.

When a solution works, make sure to acknowledge your child for their success and name their STRENGTHs:

- *'You wanted to get up out of your seat, and you found something to do that helped you wait. That shows patience.'*
- *'You wanted to go to the playground but stayed close, walking round our table until it was time to go. That shows self-control!'*
- *'You came up with a solution that works for everyone! That shows you're a problem-solver.'*

When you finish your interactions by pointing out STRENGTHs, it allows your child to see their ability to do things like problem-solve and manage their own behaviour.

Why pointing out STRENGTHs works
(even after a tricky situation).

Children act according to who they believe they are, so the STRENGTHs you point out to them now will affect their behaviour in the future.

Named STRENGTHs become part of your child's assets that stay with them wherever they go. So how you respond on this café trip doesn't just impact your mutual enjoyment of this trip – it sets you and your child up for success on all your future outings too.

By contrast, pointing out your child's flaws sets you and your child up for future trouble. If the trip to the café ends with your child thinking of themselves as always spoiling things for others, never listening or always wanting their own way, that's how they will behave on future outings too.

Children who know their STRENGTHs get to have an inner voice that tells them, *'Oh, yes! It did take patience to wait while the others finished. I did find a solution. I'm a problem-solver, and I can do it again!'*

In any tricky situation, the three steps of the Language of Listening coaching model are the keys to gaining willing cooperation and bringing out your little one's inner STRENGTHs.

Start with SWYS to clarify what they want, offer CAN DOs to help them find their own solutions within your boundaries, and then point out their STRENGTHs so they can control their own behaviour in the future. Now that's what I call a win-win!

STRENGTHS AND PRAISE ARE NOT THE SAME

Typical praise can sound like:

- *'Good girl!' or 'Good boy!'*
- *'You make me so happy.'*
- *'I like the way you...'*
- *'Well done!' or 'Wonderful!' or 'Great job!'*
- *'You're super, clever, pretty...'*

Unfortunately these words, however well-intentioned, don't achieve the results we want for our child. Most of us have been taught the importance of praise. However, typical praise is actually very controlling. Praise has a hidden agenda. It's a verbal reward used to control our child's behaviour and get them to comply.

Many of us have been advised to follow the mantra *'Praise the good and ignore the bad'*. We're instructed to shower our children with praise when they behave and please us, and ignore them when they don't. However, this faulty logic implies that our children are only worthy of our love, connection and attention when they're compliant and easy to deal with. I know that's not our true intention, but that's the message our child hears. (It's often the same one we received in our own childhoods.)

I remember when my children were little, I used to give my easy going and compliant son a lot of 'Good boy' praise while my more lively and spirited daughter rarely received any. One day, she asked me, *'Mummy, why don't I get 'good girled' like my brother? Does it mean I'm bad?'* I was shocked! I didn't realise that praise could create feelings of judgement and comparison or that our kids might start to doubt their worth based on how often they receive it.

When you think about it, praise is all about the adult, their opinion and their judgements. It's not about the child or what the child thinks and feels. The problem with this is that it strengthens the child's reliance on other people's opinions, increases their concern about other people's judgements and often leads them to believe that their main STRENGTH is pleasing others.

When you stop praising, there's a subtle and profound difference. Instead of controlling your child, you will be using STRENGTHs to help your child connect to their inner greatness and change their own behaviour permanently.

Pointing out your child's STRENGTHs is much more powerful than praise. You'll see your child stand taller, their eyes shine brighter and their face beam with pride. Watch for it!

SWAP PRAISE FOR STRENGTHS

Think about the times you use praise with your own child, and list a few.
Practise swapping them for **STRENGTHs** in the space below.

PRAISE → STRENGTHs

Examples:

'Good boy!'

'You make me so happy!'

'Well done!'

Start with **SWYS** and then add a **STRENGTH**.

'You gave you friend a hug. You're thoughtful.'

'You found a way. You're a problem-solver.'

'You took your time. You don't give up easily.'

Your turn:

What STRENGTHs do you want to see in your child?

Recognising that your child already has every possible STRENGTH, even if it's not immediately apparent, helps you stay calm and focused on uncovering and bringing out their STRENGTHs. That's what coaching is all about.

Knowing it's already there is SO important because, for your child to see it in themselves, you must see it first.

> Write down a list of STRENGTHs you want to look for in your child. Then, in your daily use, swap praise for these STRENGTHs.

STRENGTH OF THE WEEK

It can feel overwhelming to look for all the STRENGTHs at the same time. Instead, you can pick a **'STRENGTH of the Week'** and have the whole family practise spotting it in each other. Or you can choose a STRENGTH that represents the whole family unit such as 'team' or 'respectful of each other' and gather proof of that.

This is not the same as a reward chart, it's not about controlling your child's behaviour. You're not making them earn something or receive anything in return for their behaviour.

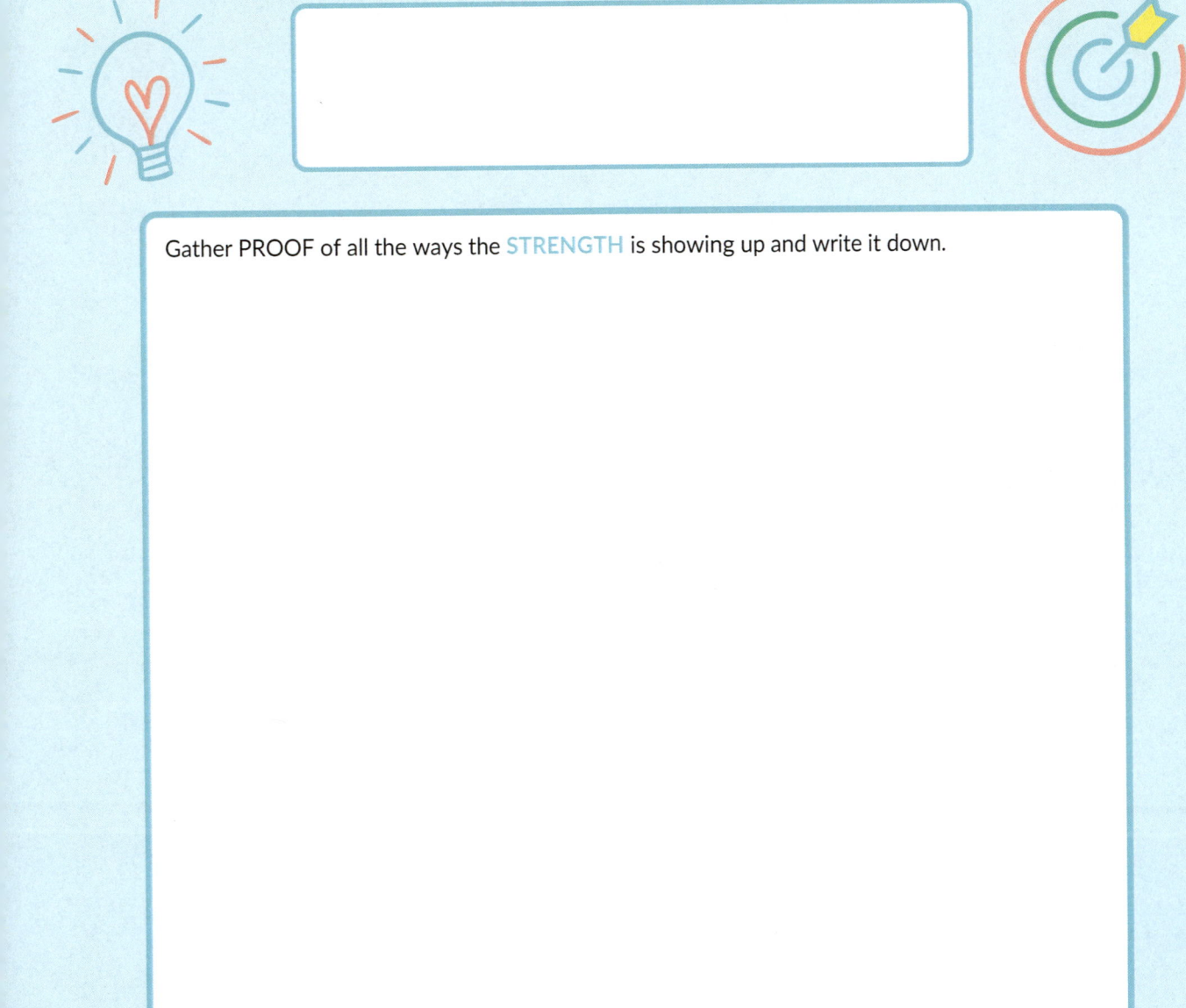

Gather PROOF of all the ways the STRENGTH is showing up and write it down.

Hidden STRENGTHs will help you dive deeper into finding your child's STRENGTHs.

Acknowledging a hidden STRENGTH changes how your child sees themselves and shifts their behaviour at the source because it changes who they believe they are.

HIDDEN STRENGTHS

Spotting STRENGTHs doesn't always come naturally. If your brain has been wired to find fault, it takes time to retrain it to spot STRENGTHs instead. Keep going. Even if you're sure you can't see any… they have to be there, so keep looking!

Looking for hidden STRENGTHs is a new way of looking at behaviour. Even if your child is doing something you don't like, stepping into their world and looking for a choice they made or their reasons for their actions will help you see beyond the surface behaviour.

By making your child right and validating their experience and perspective, you're on your way to finding their hidden STRENGTHs.

Changing how you see your child can really shift how your child sees themselves.

When you point out a hidden STRENGTH, it proves to your child that they're capable and that you see the best in them. That's why it's so powerful to point out the STRENGTH hidden in a behaviour you don't like before offering a CAN DO. It helps your child meet their NEEDS for connection and power, which makes it easier for your child to cooperate. Spotting hidden STRENGTHs puts you solidly on your child's side.

SPOTTING HIDDEN STRENGTHS

Let's look at an example of a child anxious about going to school.

If we think we have an anxious child, our typical response is to focus our attention on fixing their anxiety. We may try to convince them they have nothing to worry about: *'Oh! You're fine! Look at all your friends who want to play with you. You'll be OK once you're at school... You love it there. Your teacher thinks you're great!'*

Unfortunately, as our child doesn't have the same view as us, they aren't going to believe a single word we say, and it's not going to change their view of themselves.

Or alternatively, we may let them stay at home. However, that could backfire by sending the unintended message that we don't have faith in their abilities and add to their anxiety, not reduce it.

Instead, try looking for STRENGTHs and bringing them out.

Knowing every STRENGTH is already there, you'll be better able to stop fretting and worrying. (Not always easy, I know!) When you have faith that your child already has the inner STRENGTH they need, you get to see their behaviour in a whole new light.

Instead of worrying about how anxious your child is about going to school, how might things change if you knew to look for your child's hidden STRENGTHs?

Imagine looking for these in your anxious child:

- How brave they are
- How they can do hard things
- How adaptable they are
- How they can find solutions
- How they know what they like and don't like, and know what they need
- How they have self-control
- How they are appropriately cautious
- How they are reliable
- How they are resilient
- How they are self-motivated
- How they know what to do

Imagine your child seeing those STRENGTHs in themselves rather than believing they are anxious!

You have the power to define your child's experience and give them a new way to make sense of their reality. By changing the way you talk to and about them, you can help your child develop a positive self-image that will serve them well in their future endeavours.

Spotting hidden STRENGTHs is the first step in changing how your child views themselves and how they make sense of their experiences. Helping them change like this, from the inside out, builds their belief and confidence in their own abilities. It's the most permanent way to help them build self-esteem.

SEEING THE BEST INTENTIONS

Lena had got used to people giving her a hard time and judging her as defiant and aggressive. She felt frustrated a lot of the time like nobody really got where she was coming from. So, whenever she faced criticism or felt like she might be rejected, her go-to reaction was to become argumentative and defensive.

Sadly, her parents and teachers often misinterpreted this as naughty or defiant behaviour. And what did they do? Yep, they dished out more punishments and criticisms. Lena was no stranger to school detentions and having her phone taken away, which only made her feel worse.

Her parents didn't realise how tough it was for her. Instead of understanding, they pointed fingers and blamed her for her behaviour, further intensifying her defensiveness.

But here's the thing – Lena wasn't trying to be rude or aggressive on purpose. She was just trying to shield herself from more hurt. Her behaviour came from a place of fear and insecurity.

I see this behaviour all too often – children challenging authority, pushing back against rules, or engaging in other forms of rebellious behaviour. Society often tells us that these children need more punishments and telling off or that permissive parenting is the root cause of their behaviour.

However, the truth is quite different. We cannot overestimate the emotional pain that arises from feeling misunderstood. Regardless of our age, we all long to have our best intentions seen by our loved ones, to experience a sense of belonging, to know that we truly matter and to feel confident in our abilities.

Many times, we see children as being defiant when they are actually just trying to defend themselves from criticism, judgement or rejection in order to protect themselves from hurt.

When we understand our child's perspective and recognise their best intentions, we can truly connect with them. Remember, it's only when we establish a true connection that our child will be open to our guidance.

Get on your child's side by seeing their true intentions.

Lena's mum made a conscious effort to stop jumping to conclusions and labelling her daughter as defiant or aggressive. Instead, she chose to focus on Lena's intentions and respond with empathy, curiosity and support.

When Lena responded to a simple question with what appeared to be rudeness, her mum took a moment to pause and reflect. Instead of getting frustrated, she realised that Lena's behaviour was a way of expressing her feeling of being unheard and misunderstood. It didn't take long for her to understand that Lena's 'defiant' actions were actually in response to feeling controlled, threatened or vulnerable.

Lena wasn't trying to be defiant. She was just trying to stand up for herself the best way she knew how. She didn't want to be unfairly judged or criticised! She wanted a chance to share her perspective. What Lena truly needed was for her mum to be on her side and to see the best in her.

As time passed, Lena became confident that her mother would not judge her or assume the worst in her. She began to trust her mother more and open up to her guidance. As a result, her behaviour changed for the better. Knowing that her intentions would be understood helped Lena feel safe.

What about you? What hidden STRENGTHs can you see in your child's behaviour?

Remember! When you prove a STRENGTH, you change a behaviour.

Keep a record of the hidden STRENGTHs you've spotted in your child.

5 WAYS TO SPOT HIDDEN STRENGTHS

It starts with you seeing your child as the best version of themselves.

Hidden STRENGTHs provide a lens through which you can understand the motivations behind your child's behaviour. By recognising these STRENGTHs, you gain insight into the incredible person your child truly is and are able to reflect it back to your child so they see it too.

1. Look for the CHOICES your child is making.

Whatever action your child takes demonstrates their thought, judgement, self-control and STRENGTHs. So when your child does something you don't like, pause and look for a hidden STRENGTH.

A child who used to throw the TV controller out of frustration and now throws a pillow at you instead is making a choice. Pointing it out as a hidden STRENGTH helps them move forward.

SWYS + STRENGTH
'You threw a pillow at me. You thought about what to throw and threw something soft. That shows you have self-control even when you feel angry.'

Instead of focusing on the fact your child had a meltdown or telling them off, pause and point out their choice after everyone is calm.

'You got upset when there wasn't anything for breakfast that you wanted to eat. You grumbled but chose something from what we had. That shows you're flexible.'

SWYS + STRENGTH + CAN DO
'You were so angry when your brother knocked down your toys. You screamed but didn't hit him. That took a lot of self-control. Next time you can try growling or stomping your foot.'

'You hit my arm with an open hand, not your fist. You wanted me to know you were mad but were careful not to hurt me. Next time, you can try stopping your hand in the air and telling me how mad you are.'

2. Look for the ways your child SELF-CORRECTS their behaviour.

Instead of pointing out what went wrong or how your child messed up, PAUSE and give your child a chance to correct themselves. That gives you a chance to point out a hidden STRENGTH.

SWYS + STRENGTH
'You almost grabbed Helen's doll but stopped and asked her instead. You remembered the rules.'

'You got frustrated, walked away, and then came back and tried again. You found a way to make it work.'

'You ran down the road and knew just where to stop. You found a place to stop and wait for me safely.'

'You knew just what you needed to calm yourself. You… (tell them what they did to calm themselves).'

'You wanted to keep playing but stopped to come for a bath. That took self-control.'

'When you were angry at your brother, you started to scream and then growled and stomped your foot instead. You know how to get the mad out!'

'Instead of hitting me, you stopped your hand in the air and told me how mad you were. That's clear communication.'

3 Look for the best INTENTIONS in your child.

This is a big one for children who are usually told off or blamed. They need to know that you see their best intentions. You can help your child develop that kind of positive self-talk about themselves by pointing out their hidden STRENGTHs.

Helpful Phrases
'You didn't mean to do that.'
'You were trying to...'
'You meant to...'
'You wanted to...'

Examples
'You wanted to see if you could have a go. You were trying to get his attention.'

'You wanted to finish what you were saying. You hate it when people interrupt you.'

'You want that toy. You don't want to have to wait.'

'You were trying to get me to move. You know just how you want to walk down the road.'

> *'The world feels like a much safer place with someone who recognises your true intentions.'* – Sandy Blackard

4 Listen for the wants/wishes behind your child's COMPLAINTS.

Did you know a complaint is really a wish in disguise? Listen for your's and others' complaints. Can you notice the wish or want behind each complaint?

Flip a complaint around by connecting your child with the wish or want behind it.

Complaint: *'I hate this toy!'*
Wish/Want: *'You want a different toy!'*
STRENGTH: Child who knows what they want.

Complaint: *'I never get to choose what to do!'*
Wish/Want: *'You wish you could decide what to do!'*
STRENGTH: Child who likes making decisions.

Complaint: *'She's always taking my toys!'*
Wish/Want: *'You want her to respect your belongings!'*
STRENGTH: Child who appreciates respect.

Complaint: *'I'm bored!'*
Wish/Want: *'You wish things were more fun!'*
STRENGTH: Child who likes exciting things.

Complaint: *'I never get to have a playdate!'*
Wish/Want: *'You wish you could have friends round daily!'*
STRENGTH: Child who loves friends and entertaining.

5 Look for cooperation in a BOUNDARY STRETCH.

Ask yourself: *'How is my child still INSIDE my boundary?'* **Acknowledge any cooperation or recognition of your boundary, and then clarify your boundary. Or, if the stretch is OK with you, then grant permission.**

'You're right! You knew not to hit her, AND pushing is not OK either. Must be another way you can play that works for you both.'

'You came to the table for dinner with your firetruck, AND the dinner table's not for playing with toys. Must be something you can do to keep busy at the table.'
Or grant permission: *'Looks like you know not to play while eating. Keeping it close to you is fine with me.'*

'You're right! You know that screen time comes after homework, AND you like listening to music while you work.'
If that's OK with you, grant permission: *'It's OK if you use the iPad to listen to music. That works for me.'*

The Running Leap – a new way to see reluctance or setbacks

When your child appears reluctant to tackle a new challenge or has what looks like a setback, the fourth premise of Language of Listening gives you another way to understand what is actually happening and reveals more hidden STRENGTHs.

> 'All growth is through acceptance.
> Children set exactly the right level of challenge for growth.'

Think about a stream running through a wood. When you come up to it, you wouldn't just try and jump across it; you'd back up in order to gain momentum before running forward and leaping across. That's exactly what your child does.

When they come up to a challenge that feels too big, they don't back away, they BACK UP to meet their NEEDs first so they can succeed.

When your child hesitates or appears to avoid a challenge, rather than see their 'inaction' as reluctance, you can look for the Running Leap in the actions they ARE taking and recognising how those actions are meeting their NEEDs (see page 159). Then you can witness your child not as giving up or procrastinating, but as gathering momentum to take a Running Leap forward with confidence.

While the temptation to push your child to succeed is natural, it's crucial to recognise that they already possess an innate desire to succeed and excel in life. Your kids inherently want to do well. They strive to become the best version of themselves and are constantly setting challenges to help themselves grow. The Running Leap encourages you to trust their internal drive.

Consider your trust as allowing a stream to flow naturally; your child knows when to take a step back, gather proof of their capabilities, and then gracefully grow. By adopting this perspective, you can step back and observe your child's intuitive understanding of their own NEEDs, and provide them the space and support they need to thrive on their unique journey toward success.

Let's look at a couple of examples:

1. Suddenly, Mica began to lose interest in reading her schoolbooks, leaving her mother puzzled. Over time, she began to notice that Mica enjoyed reading her picture book collection instead. Rather than dismissing this as laziness or proof Mica wasn't academic, her mother looked for the Running Leap. What she saw astonished her. Mica wasn't retreating; she was building confidence by reading books she already knew. As her comfort grew, so did her enthusiasm for reading her schoolbooks, demonstrating that she knew what she needed to progress at her own pace. By pointing out that hidden STRENGTH, her mother helped Mica learn she could trust herself.

2. Bob's mother, keen on fostering his interest in sports, encountered resistance when suggesting he join a sports club. Bob didn't want to go. Instead of viewing Bob as simply shy, introverted, or withdrawn, his mother looked for the Running Leap. She observed that when Bob's friend or his younger brother went with him, he was less reluctant and had a great time once he was there. That told her Bob knew what he needed to increase his comfort level when navigating the unfamiliar; he just needed one person he knew. When she pointed that out, Bob's confidence expanded.

Recognising the Running Leap in a child's journey allows you step back and marvel at your child's innate wisdom while they gather momentum. In doing so, you can point out and celebrate their STRENGTHs – self-trust and knowing exactly what they need to move forward in life. It's this that builds resilience and provides a solid foundation for your child's future endeavours.

> Where can you spot your child backing up for a Running Leap in their growth?

Contrary to popular belief, letting children fail is not the best way for them to learn.

In fact, the most effective and empowering way for children to learn is through success, and even better, with your guidance and support.

Small Steps in the Right Direction

Pointing out STRENGTHs is teaching by success.

It's easy to focus on the end goal in parenting – so easy that we often miss the small steps and successes in the right direction. How rewarding for you and your child to notice, gather proof and rejoice in the small successes that lead to change.

What are some of the steps in the right direction?

Screaming → Stomping → Growling

- A child who shifts from screaming to stomping to growling is calming down.
- A child who used to hit and kick and is now stomping to calm down is showing self-control.
- A child who used to lie on the floor kicking and screaming and is now storming off and slamming his bedroom door is showing self-control.
- A child who used to demand, shout and call you names and is now muttering under her breath is showing self-control.

When looking back on the week, you'll want to remember what IS going well. Time goes so fast! Keeping track of the small steps in the right direction helps you stay present and enjoy the journey to success.

> What are some of your child's small steps in the right direction?
> *Keep track of the steps you see during the week by writing them down here.*

SPOTTING SELF-CONTROL

Brodie had been struggling with his son's behaviour for a while. His son, Stan, would often get angry and lash out during arguments, resorting to name-calling and swearing. Brodie had tried his best to teach Stan to manage his emotional outbursts, but it seemed like an uphill battle.

One day, after a particularly heated argument, Stan stormed out of the room and slammed the door shut. Brodie was ready to storm in after him and continue the argument, but something stopped him. As he stood there, he realised what a big surprise it was to see his son walking away without angry words!

He began to reflect on the situation and was overjoyed when he realised that his son had shown incredible self-control! Stan had managed to walk away and calm himself down with a door slam instead of the usual verbal outbursts. Brodie didn't like the door slam or the frustration behind it either, but still, he recognised walking away as a huge step forward!

Brodie walked over to Stan's room and knocked on the door. Stan opened it, looking sheepish and apologetic. In two short sentences, Brodie changed everything:

SWYS + STRENGTH: *'It wasn't easy to walk away like that, but you did it. You showed incredible self-control.'*

Stan's face lit up, and he hugged his dad tightly. It was a special moment. Brody knew that his son was on his way to managing his emotional expressions better. It was the first step in the right direction.

Brody had learnt that his son was capable of change, and it all started by spotting that one small act of self-control.

So, why is self-control so important to bring out in your child?

> Self-control is crucial for your child's development. It involves mastering their impulses, emotions, and reactions. Essentially, it's the foundation of personal power, and it equips them with the tools to master their own behaviour effectively.

Here are a few examples of spotting self-control.

- My child willingly shared their toys with a friend without any prompting.
- After a little wobble, my son willingly turned off the TV when asked.
- My daughter communicated her feelings calmly without resorting to tantrums.
- My son concentrated and completed a puzzle without getting frustrated.

YOUR TURN:

> Start noticing small steps towards self-control in your child, and make a note of them here.

Notice how your judgements and reactions change when you start seeing your child's behaviour through the lens of STRENGTHs.

Using STRENGTHs to help your child change their behaviour

Let's look at a couple of examples.

You know those moments when your kids just won't stop fighting? Or when they answer back and sound rude? It's frustrating, right? The usual tactics—telling them off, dishing out punishments, or even rewarding them for behaving well—seem to fall flat. If anything, it feels like more proof that they're stuck in this endless cycle of bickering or answering back.

But what if I told you there's a quicker and more effective way to change behaviour? Instead of focusing on what they're doing wrong, shift your focus and start looking for STRENGTHs.

In the heat of a challenging moment, of course you have to get through the situation and bring things back to calm. You can use SWYS + CAN DOs to do that.

However, for the long term change that you want to see in your child's behaviour, it's about helping your child see the STRENGTHs they already have within.

Look at the second column in the chart opposite. Notice what your child needs to know in order to stop bickering and fighting or answering back and sounding rude.

When you shine a big bright light on these STRENGTHs and point out all the ways they currently show up, you give your children repeated opportunities to see themselves as successful. This is when something magical happens, they gain confidence in their abilities and they naturally change their own behaviour to reflect it.

When we create an environment where kids can see themselves in a positive light, their behaviour naturally shifts. It's like watching a superhero discovering their powers - it's transformative and powerful.

What behaviour don't you like?

Think about all the STRENGTHs your child needs to see in themselves in order to behave in a way you do like.

Use this chart to identify what STRENGTH your child may not know they have yet. Then use your coaching skill of SWYS + STRENGTH to gather proof and reconnect them with who they really are.

What's the behaviour you don't like?	What STRENGTHs does your child need to know they have so they can manage their own behaviour?	Where can you currently see these STRENGTHs showing up? Look for them. They have to be there!
Children bickering and fighting	Accepting Caring Clear communicator (of their needs & wants) Considerate Generous Have self-control Inclusive Kind Know how to look out for other people Know how to share Know how to take turns Negotiator Problem-solver	*I saw him take turns with his sister, patiently waiting for her as she picked a game to play.* *I saw my children laughing and playing together for ages.* *My son offered to make me a sandwich for lunch.* *He included his cousin when she came to visit, inviting her to join in and making her feel welcomed.*
Child answering back and sounding rude	Clear communicator Connective Considerate Inspiring Kind Loving Polite Thoughtful Well-spoken	For practice, start here:

YOUR TURN:

Think about all the STRENGTHs your child needs to see in themselves in order to behave in a way you do like.

Use this chart to identify what STRENGTH your child may not know they have yet. Then use your coaching skill of SWYS + STRENGTH to gather proof and reconnect them with who they really are.

What's the behaviour you don't like?	What STRENGTHs does your child need to know they have so they can manage their own behaviour?	Where can you currently see these STRENGTHs showing up? Look for them. They have to be there!

NOTES

SUCCESS TRAINING

SUCCESS TRAINING

Success Training is teaching by success, which is how kids learn best.

Our children are learning. There are going to be times during their struggles when it may be too difficult for you to find a STRENGTH or a hidden STRENGTH.

Success training is an approach to guide and support your child through their challenges, helping them discover and then build on their STRENGTHs. When faced with persistent struggles, success training becomes a valuable tool.

Success Training is setting your child up for success. It's about being proactive and setting up situations that help your child do something that brings out a STRENGTH.

It's through success that your child gains skills and provides proof for themselves that they can do it.

Let's look at an example of success training in action.

Gabby, understood the effectiveness of Success Training in fostering responsibility in her daughter, Remi. Instead of resorting to constant reminders and nagging, Gabby chose a more empowering approach.

One morning, after Remi had left her towel on the bathroom floor, Gabby resisted the urge to correct her daughter. Instead, she tried a brief SWYS response, *'Towel,'* and waited.

Gabby knew that waiting created an opportunity for Remi to take the desired action on her own. As she watched, Remi glanced at the towel on the floor and picked it up! Gabby responded with a STRENGTH, *'You knew to pick it up.'*

This simple act of waiting conveyed a message of trust to Remi and allowed her to self-correct by picking up her own towel and hanging it where it belonged. Gabby seized the moment to go further and highlight Remi's hidden STRENGTH, saying, *'You know how to clean up after yourself,'* which was the exact opposite of the message she'd been inadvertently sending with her constant reminders and nagging!

By giving Remi the space to self-correct, Gabby not only avoided the usual friction of reminders but revealed Remi's hidden capability. This Success Training not only kept the bathroom tidy but also planted the seeds for Remi to take responsibility for herself and experience the satisfaction of self-correction.

SUCCESS TRAINING TOOLS

3 WAYS TO SET YOUR CHILD UP FOR SUCCESS

1 — WAIT, DON'T WARN

Just **SAY WHAT YOU SEE** and wait.

Waiting creates an opportunity for your child to take a desired action or self-correct (see Self-corrections in the 5 Ways to Spot Hidden Strengths chart, page 280).

Waiting sends a message of trust and gives your child the opportunity to initiate the action and make corrections themselves.

EXAMPLE

SWYS and wait:
'There's food on the floor.' (Wait.)
'Towel!' (Wait.)

When you give your child a chance to correct themselves, you give yourself a chance to point out a hidden **STRENGTH**:
'You knew to pick it up.'
'You know how to clean up after yourself.'

2 — SHOW ME

Use *'Show me...'* to find out what your child already knows before giving instruction.

'Show me...' assumes your child already has the **STRENGTH** you're trying to teach them and gives them the chance to find it in themselves.

Often when you use *'Show me...'* and point out your child's small successes, no instruction is needed.

'Show me...' can produce surprising results because it allows your child to take the lead and demonstrate their own **STRENGTHs**.

'Show me...' is also a great tool for reengaging a frustrated child when they think a task is too hard.

EXAMPLE

If your child starts running off down the road, instead of warning them to be careful, you can say, *'Show me where you can stop safely.'*

You'll probably get to add, *'You know where to stop and wait. You checked where I was. That's careful!'*

If your child says they can't do something, *'Show me the hard part,'* can help them focus on just one thing instead of feeling overwhelmed. When they reengage, point out any little thing they're doing right so they experience success along the way.

If they don't want to try anymore, *'Show me what you want me to do,'* will allow them to direct you. That can help them meet their need for power and participate at a safe distance without the risk of failure.

The goal of *'Show me...'* is not to force your child into a challenge they think is too hard; it's to help them experience success for as long as they are willing to stay engaged. They will know when to break away. That's a **STRENGTH** too!

3 | YET

Yet is a future statement of a STRENGTH. It tells your child they have a STRENGTH, and even though it's not fully accessible to them yet, it will be.

Yet is a statement of confidence without pressure that keeps the door open for your child to try again when they're ready.

It's a Success Training tool that sets your child up for success in the future.

EXAMPLE

'You're not ready to jump in the pool yet. You can try next time.'

'You're trying and trying, and no solution yet.'

'You haven't found a stopping place yet. You're thinking about it.'

'You don't want to join the other kids yet. You want to watch them for a while first. You'll know when you are ready.'

Small steps in the right direction

USING SUCCESS TRAINING TO STOP HITTING, BITING AND KICKING

Christina was at her wits' end with her toddler's behaviour. He would hit and bite her. She had tried everything from gentle touches to timeouts, but nothing seemed to work. Her son's behaviour only just kept getting worse. That was before she started using Success Training.

Christina learnt that understanding her son's true goal was key to helping him stop the hitting and biting. She realised that her son had a high need for power, and hitting and biting were meeting this need (although not in a way she liked). With this new understanding, Christina was able to get on her son's side and help him find alternatives that would meet his need for power in ways that worked for everyone.

Using Success Training, Christina learnt how to bring out her son's STRENGTHs and help him feel good about himself.

To acknowledge her son's true intention and validate him she started with SWYS:

SWYS: 'You're so mad! You want to hit.'
CAN DO: 'And I'm not for hitting. Must be something else you can hit! You can hit the sofa!'
Child: (hits the sofa.)
CAN DO: '**Show me** again.'
SWYS + STRENGTH: 'Wow! You hit it really hard that time! You know how to get your anger out!'
Child: (hits the sofa again then looks around.)
SWYS: 'Again... There! Now, you're looking for something else to hit.'
STRENGTH: 'Yes! You can hit the floor! You know what to hit!'

To be able to stop behaviour you don't like, children need other actions to replace it that actually work for them. If it doesn't work to meet their needs, they will return to the unwanted behaviour.

By helping her son find alternatives that met his need for power, Christina helped him replace his hitting and biting behaviour with new actions that worked for them both. Stopping himself and changing his own actions showed him that he had more self-control than he thought. This built his confidence and self-trust and helped him start managing his own behaviour.

With time and practice, her son learnt how to get what he wanted (his true goal) without resorting to hitting and biting. Christina was proud of the progress her son had made, and their relationship grew stronger because of it.

USING SUCCESS TRAINING TO END HOMEWORK BATTLES

Freddie's son, was sitting at the kitchen table, staring at his math homework with a frustrated expression. He had been working on the same problem for the last 20 minutes and was getting nowhere. He was ready to give up.

Child: *'I don't get it. It's too hard.'*
SWYS: *'You've been trying and trying, and don't get it yet. It just feels too hard.* **Show me the hard part**.*'*
Child: (points and starts making a weak effort)
SWYS: *'Ah! Something about that part doesn't look right to you. And you're right. There. You found the mistake and fixed it.'*
STRENGTH: *'Mistakes don't stop you. You just learn from them.'*
SWYS: *'And you got that part right. Now, you're focusing on the next step.'*
Child: (continues to work with support and encouragement)
STRENGTH: *'Look at that! You're getting the hang of it. You did it!'*
Child: (feels more confident and motivated to continue)
SWYS: *'You did that one too. You're making progress! It looks like you're finding it easier as you go.'*

Carry on recognising and acknowledging every small success your child achieves as they work towards finishing their homework, and verbalise what you observe using SWYS.

If your child missed or skipped a step, continue to objectively describe what happened without criticism or negative corrections.

You can encourage them further by letting them know how close they are to finishing with phrases like this:
SWYS: *'You've tackled most of it. Just one more step to go!'* or *'There's one sneaky one left.'*

By focusing on their successes and allowing them to problem-solve independently, you are empowering them to take ownership of the process. When kids feel empowered, they are naturally more open to asking for and accepting help when needed.

By practising Success Training, both you and your child can stay focused on their successes. The more success you see, the easier it will be for you to step back and let them take control of challenging tasks.

USING SUCCESS TRAINING TO BUILD FRIENDSHIPS

Asher had difficulty initiating play with other children, and this often led to conflicts. Rather than feeling frustrated and resorting to telling him to 'play nicely' or threatening him with no more playdates, his mother used the opportunity to practise Success Training.

As she observed Asher, she saw that he was attempting to play with his friend. She remembered **'Wait, don't warn'**, which allowed her to wait, focus on his successes and self-corrections, and point out his STRENGTHs.

For example, Asher almost pushed his friend. Instead of telling him, *'Be careful,'* his mum waited, saw him self-correct, and pointed it out:
SWYS: *'You almost pushed your friend, and you paused. You're taking turns playing with the ball.'*

And each time he waited his turn, she pointed that out:
SWYS + STRENGTH: *'You're waiting your turn. That takes patience. You're showing him that you are a good friend.'*

When a kerfuffle happened, she continued to use objective observations to describe what was happening without placing blame and then pointed out STRENGTHs when they showed up:
SWYS: *'You both wanted to play with the same toy, and you both got upset... You had different ideas about what game to play... Now, you're trying really hard to include your friend in the game.'*
SWYS + STRENGTH: *'You listened to your friend's ideas about what game to play. That shows you're considerate.'*

By using Success Training, this mum was able to observe and identify her son's STRENGTHs and successes, and he was able to gain confidence in his friend-making abilities. As a result, Asher started believing in himself too, and the confidence he gained was reflected in his actions.

When we focus on seeing and bringing out our child's STRENGTHs, it becomes easier to let go of our fears. This shift in perspective helps us notice even tiny successes as our child moves towards their goal. When we celebrate our child's success, they feel empowered and much more able to cooperate and manage their own behaviour.

Give it a try!

Start discovering your child's small successes in the right direction that you might have otherwise overlooked, and make a note of them here.

A quick recap – putting the 3 steps together

SAY WHAT YOU SEE

Using neutral observations, describe what your child is doing, saying, feeling or thinking. (Remember NO judgements, fixing, teaching or questions.)

1

Step into your child's world and describe what you SEE. Just **SWYS** your child Doing, Saying, Feeling or Thinking.

This step is so important because it gets you out of judgements and assumptions and onto the same side as your child. Focusing on what your child wants, helps you understand things from your child's perspective.

CAN DOs

Look for the NEED and offer CAN DOs to help gain willing cooperation and help your child gain problem-solving skills.

2

When your child does something you DON'T like, offer a **CAN DO**. Remember there is always something the child **CAN DO** in every situation.

In order to help kids cooperate, you need to stop thinking in terms of wining and losing and, instead, focus on what they **CAN DO** within your boundary. Offering a **CAN DO** helps your child meet their needs for connection, experience and power, even in tricky situations when emotions are high.

STRENGTHs

Point out your child's STRENGTHs to help them see their greatness and gain confidence in their abilities.

3

When your child does something you DO like, point out a **STRENGTH.**

Children act according to who they believe they are, so the more you point out the **STRENGTHs** you see in your child, the more they will believe that is who they are, and the more they will show you those **STRENGTHs**.

Your turn!

SAY WHAT YOU SEE

Using neutral observations, describe what your child is doing, saying, feeling or thinking. (Remember NO judgements, fixing, teaching or questions.)

1

CAN DOs

Look for the NEED and offer CAN DOs to help gain willing cooperation and help your child gain problem-solving skills.

2

STRENGTHs

Point out your child's STRENGTHs to help them see their greatness and gain confidence in their abilities.

3

GETTING YOUR FAMILY ON BOARD

WHEN YOU AND YOUR PARTNER ARE NOT ON THE SAME PARENTING PAGE

Throughout this workbook, I've talked about how the judgements and beliefs that we formed in our childhoods shape the way we parent now. No wonder two people raised in different families with different experiences, backgrounds and cultures would have different beliefs about parenting!

What actually brings you together is understanding that you share a common goal. In all the years of supporting families, I've never known a parent who doesn't want the best for their child. Each one just may go about it in a different way.

It's important to recognise that the same principles that work in building a positive relationship with your child can be applied to your partner as well. By listening, validating and truly hearing your partner's perspective, you can create a deeper sense of connection and understanding, which will aid your collaborative abilities as a parenting team.

Ultimately, the key is to approach parenting and your relationship with empathy, curiosity, and a willingness to learn and grow together. Trying to convince someone to change their beliefs or wants is rarely effective and can often lead to further conflict and resentment. Instead, by focusing on your shared goals and working together to find solutions that meet everyone's needs, you can create a more harmonious and supportive family dynamic.

A good place to start the process of getting on the same page is your past and your partner's. Understanding the experiences that shaped each of your beliefs and concerns about parenting will help you understand each other's perspective.

If your partner is willing, ask each other this question. (You can offer to listen first and use your coaching skills to model how to validate their experience and conclusions. Then ask them to do the same for you.)

> What experiences in your childhood, good or bad, have shaped your beliefs about parenting?

A Shared Vision

When you have a clearer understanding of each other's perspective on parenting and the childhood experiences that shaped it, you can move on to discuss your individual goals and desires for your family. They will help you find common ground on which to build a shared vision.

Here are some questions to ask of yourself and your partner and some sample responses to get you started:

> What is your main objective for raising your child(ren)?
>
> *To raise self-confident, independent, secure children in a happy family that shows respect and love towards each other, cares for each other*

> What family values are important to you?
>
> *Respect, unconditional love, seeing the best in each other*

> What are your STRENGTHs as a parent?
>
> *Patience, flexibility, empathy*

> How do you think your parenting styles complement or differ from each other?
>
> *I'm an early bird / you're a night owl! I have more patience / you express yourself more clearly*

> What are your non-negotiables?
>
> *Respect for others; a family environment where children feel comfortable expressing themselves without fear of judgement or punishment; lead by example where being kind, inclusive, truthful and acting with integrity are valued*

> What kind of atmosphere do you want to create in your home?
>
> *Loving, warm, welcoming*

Your Turn!

What is your main objective for raising your child(ren)?

What family values are important to you?

What are your STRENGTHs as a parent?

How do you think your parenting styles complement or differ from each other?

What are your non-negotiables?

What kind of atmosphere do you want to create in your home?

When other family members aren't on board with this way of parenting

Despite having the best of intentions, no matter how hard you try, you cannot force change on someone who does not want to change. Instead, you can control your own response and actions, and lead by example. By modelling healthy communication, setting boundaries and living according to your values, you can inspire others to follow suit.

It's also important to recognise that change is a gradual process. It may not happen overnight. It may take time for others to observe and learn from your example, and make their own choices about how they want to behave or communicate.

Ultimately, the best way to promote change in others is to focus on your own growth and development and create a positive and supportive environment that encourages others to do the same. By being the change you want to see, you can create a ripple effect that spreads to those around you.

For example, my mother-in-law couldn't understand 'my way of doing things'. She'd often tell me she couldn't see how it would get the results I said it would. My goal wasn't convincing her to see things my way, my goal was to listen to her and understand her concerns while being secure in why I'm doing things the way I do. Having witnessed the positive outcomes, my mother-in-law now understands and appreciates my approach.

People are often resistant to change and may feel defensive if they perceive that their beliefs or values are being challenged. In fact, research has shown that when people feel threatened, they are more likely to double down on their existing beliefs, becoming even more resistant to change.

How to coach your child to respond when others react to them differently.

When you teach your child that people often have different ways of doing things and follow different rules, you can help them recognise and understand differences in the actions and behaviours of others.

For example, by explaining to your children that Grandma grew up in a different time and with different cultural norms, you are helping them understand and accept those differences. It's also important to emphasise to your children that, just because someone grew up differently, it doesn't mean that their actions or beliefs are always right or appropriate.

Encourage your children to ask questions and think critically about the messages they receive, even from family members. As your children develop their own relationships with other relatives, maintaining a strong connection with your children and keeping lines of communication open will enable you to assist them in navigating uncomfortable or confusing situations with others in ways that feel respectful to all involved.

Preparing your child for the real world

I'm often confronted with others' concerns about whether our approach prepares children for the real world, with the argument that not everyone will support or understand them, so we should toughen them up. I strongly disagree.

I respond by emphasising that firstly, our children are already living in the real world; they are not growing up in some alternate universe. And secondly, the argument itself is flawed. It's like suggesting that someone should get used to a cracked screen on their phone just because it might break in the future. As if they should just accept and tolerate negative experiences because they might encounter them some day. And thirdly, why should we prepare our children for a life dictated by the behaviour of others that they don't like or agree with?

By encouraging them to expect respectful treatment from others, we help them develop the skills and abilities to reciprocate that respect towards others as well.

As parents, we play a crucial role in shaping our child's understanding of the real world. When we provide our child with a foundation of love and respect, we model healthy relationships, and our child learns that they are deserving of love and respect from others. It enables them to choose their friends wisely and discern who deserves a place in their lives.

On the contrary, when we resort to tactics like shouting, controlling and manipulating, our child may grow up normalising these behaviours, which could make it difficult for them to recognise unhealthy patterns in their future relationships.

As parents, we have the valuable opportunity to guide and coach our children as they navigate the world. When you spend time coaching your child, you nurture their sense of self, emotional intelligence, resilience and interpersonal skills, all of which will help them build healthy relationships.

Coaching helps prepare your child for success in the real world as it is now and will help them reshape the parts they don't like to create a better world in the future.

Parenting is
MESSY

Don't base your idea of parenting success on not having a tricky situation. Base it on how you got through a tricky situation. Track your successes.

Success Tracker

At the end of each day, review the small shifts and changes YOU are making. Look for evidence that you're making progress and heading in the right direction.

Remember, when you point out your child's **STRENGTHs**, you are teaching by success.

Changing your reactions happens in a series of small steps and choices. It may feel tricky at first. You may miss things or feel like the negatives outweigh the positives. But with practice, you'll start to notice more and more improvement and gather more proof of your success and your child's.

On the following pages, write down any small steps you or your child take in the right direction. It could be a shift from a tantrum lasting 20 minutes to now lasting only 10 minutes, or a shift from you yelling to **SAYing WHAT YOU SEE** through gritted teeth. Moving in the right direction is success!

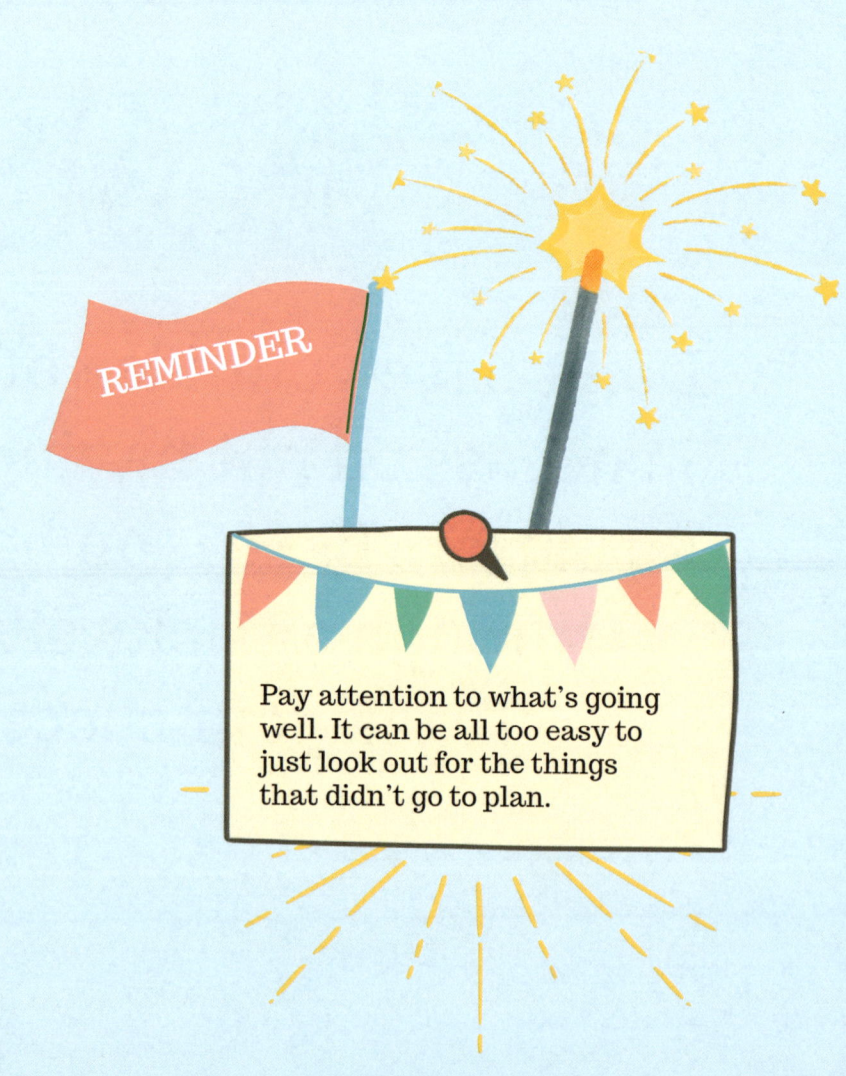

REMINDER

Pay attention to what's going well. It can be all too easy to just look out for the things that didn't go to plan.

WEEK OF...

Success Tracker

Mon

Tues

Wed

Thurs

Fri

Sat

Sun

Mon

Tues

Wed

Thurs

Fri

Sat

Sun

WEEK OF...

Success Tracker

Mon

Tues

Wed

Thurs

Fri

Sat

Sun

Mon

Tues

Wed

Thurs

Fri

Sat

Sun

WEEK OF...

Success Tracker

Mon

Tues

Wed

Thurs

Fri

Sat

Sun

Mon

Tues

Wed

Thurs

Fri

Sat

Sun

YOU DID IT!

You've made it through the workbook! I bet your head is swimming with all sorts of thoughts, ideas and excitement. There are so many possibilities for integrating the tools and techniques into your daily family life.

Maybe things are going smoothly, and you're already seeing the changes you want. Or maybe you've got more questions, and things still feel a bit tricky. That's OK too.

Language of Listening is called that because it really is a new language! It takes practice and daily use to become fluent. This workbook is not meant as a rigid instructional manual but more like your ongoing guidebook to how humans 'work'.

This is only the start.

Keep implementing all you've learnt in this workbook and you'll see just how much simpler, easier and enjoyable your life with your child can be when you use the three-step coaching model. I'm sure you're asking the same question I did all those years ago: '*Why did no one tell me this before?!!*'

Keep going. Keep making progress and building upon your successes and those of your child.

And remember, this is only the introduction to the Language of Listening tools. There's so much more to learn and discover. I share more in depth work in my coaching practice and courses.

If you and your family have benefitted from using this workbook, I would love to hear from you. Maybe you'd like to share your successes with me or maybe you have more questions you'd like answered. Or if you are interested in exploring personalised guidance, please don't hesitate to reach out to me. I offer one-on-one sessions that cater to your specific needs and challenges – I'm here for you.

Please reach out and email me: **camilla@keepingyourcoolparenting.com**

Thank you for taking this parenting journey with me.

ABOUT THE AUTHOR

Camilla Miller is the mum of two teenagers living in the U.K. She knew there had to be a way to raise kids that didn't include constant struggles, naughty steps or reward charts, and she was right. When she discovered Language of Listening, her first thought was, 'Why did no one tell me this before?!!'

Camilla's two years of intensive training and outstanding achievements as a professional parent coach have earned her the title Authorised Master Language of Listening Coach. In addition to this workbook, Camilla has coauthored a set of three *Language of Listening Phrase Books* with hundreds of practical examples of how to SAY WHAT YOU SEE and add CAN DOs and STRENGTHs in everyday life with children.

Camilla's passion is to support parents to really understand their children, especially the more challenging reactive kids, and give parents the tools they need to transform family life. She coaches parents privately and through her courses and workshops. You can find out more at her website: keepingyourcoolparenting.com

RE - #0003 - 080324 - C334 - 254/203/19 - PB - 9781399967501 - Matt Lamination